Self-Regulation for Kids K–12
Strategies for Calming Minds and Behavior

Self-Regulation for Kids K–12

Strategies for Calming Minds and Behavior

Patricia K. Tollison

Katherine O. Synatschk

Gaea Logan

pro·ed
An International Publisher

8700 Shoal Creek Boulevard
Austin, Texas 78757-6897
800/897-3202   Fax 800/397-7633
www.proedinc.com

© 2011 by PRO-ED, Inc.
8700 Shoal Creek Boulevard
Austin, Texas 78757-6897
800/897-3202   Fax 800/397-7633
www.proedinc.com

Library of Congress Cataloging-in-Publication Data

Tollison, Patricia K.
    Self-regulation for kids K-12 : strategies for calming minds and behavior / Patricia K. Tollison,
Katherine O. Synatschk, Gaea Logan.
       p. cm.
    Includes bibliographical references.
    ISBN 978-1-4164-0483-5
    1. Classroom management—Psychological aspects.   2. Problem children—Behavior modification.
3. Self-control in children.   I. Synatschk, Katherine O.   II. Logan, Gaea.   III. Title.

LB3012.2.T65 2011
370.15'28—dc22

                                                                         2010024360

Art Director: Jason Crosier
Designer: Vicki DePountis

Printed in the United States of America

2 3 4 5 6 7 8 9 10   19 18 17 16 15 14 13 12 11

Dedication

This book is dedicated to those children and adolescents whose life experiences have left them needing to learn to calm themselves so that they can make better choices. It is also dedicated to the mental health professionals, and others on the front lines, whose job it is to help these kids become healthy, competent people.

—————————————

Contents

Acknowledgments

Patricia K. Tollison

I want to express my gratitude to my co-authors, Kathy Synatschk and Gaea Logan. Our ongoing, exploratory conversation has written this book. I wish I could meet with each of the many researchers and clinicians whose work we cite throughout the text and express my gratitude. Discovering what each had to say has been a rewarding adventure and has provided the foundation for the strategies for self-regulation (SSR) model. I am indebted to colleagues Kris Downing, Roland Fellows, Steve Koppell, Joan Ransom, Seja Rachael, Jev Sikes, and Sydnor Sikes for sharing their experience and expertise, and for providing support and enthusiasm. I want to thank family and friends for their understanding during the writing process and especially thank Doug Glasgow for offering perspective and for his sustaining good humor.

Katherine O. Synatschk

I want to thank the many counselors I have been privileged to work with whose dedication to students with extreme challenges inspired this book. I extend my gratitude to my co-authors, Patricia and Gaea, for helping to bring together all of the best aspects of solution-focused counseling with what we are learning about how the brain is affected by trauma and attachment. I also want to thank all of the students I have worked with. They taught me the value of accepting and embracing their views and shared many creative ideas with me. Most of all, I want to thank my family for its calming support.

Gaea Logan

I would like to gratefully acknowledge my children, Eliot Logan Hines and Gina Burchenal, who teach me how to love and how to wonder with a beginner's mind each day. I thank Khen Rinpoche Tsetan, a Tibetan Buddhist monk, who, by example, has taught me so much about the power of mindful awareness. I am deeply grateful to co-authors Patricia Tollison and Kathy Synatschk and all the folks at PRO-ED, for without them, this book would not have been possible.

Introduction

How you stand here is important. How you listen
for the next things to happen. How you breathe.

William Stafford, "Being a Person"

Background

Research in interpersonal neurobiology suggests psychological trauma physically changes the brain. Furthermore, these changes are linked to long-term psychological vulnerabilities related to physical and emotional regulatory processes. How can healthy maturational processes that strengthen a child's capacity for self-regulation be restored? How can children learn to cultivate calm in the storm?

One caring adult who can remain calm and attentive to an at-risk child—even in the worst of circumstances—can make a profound difference in the developing mind of that child. The presence of a relationship characterized by care, calm, and reflection can grow the capacity for self-regulation and emotional intelligence in the child—ingredients needed for success both in school and in life.

From the field of interpersonal neurobiology comes the discovery of the powerful influence of the brain on an individual's capacity for regulating arousal and emotion. The strategies necessary for cultivating self-regulation emerge from these findings and focus on the development of skills that calm the mind and behavior. These strategies cultivate pathways to improvement through somatic awareness and relational connection. Perhaps one of the most fascinating recent findings is the phenomenon of regulation within the attachment bond. A calm individual has a calming influence. Our children are better able to become regulated when we ourselves are calm and regulated. The best way to help children find their calm in the storm is to first find our own calm.

How to Use This Book

Self-Regulation for Kids K–12: Strategies for Calming Minds and Behavior describes a process for helping children and adolescents who experience difficulties with self-regulation.

In Chapters 1 through 3, we provide research-based information regarding the connection between emotional intelligence, somatic experience, emotional regulation, and the ability to self-regulate. In Chapter 4, we begin by becoming more aware of our own somatic experience and teach a set of skills to help students use awareness of their somatic experience to decide how to act. In Chapter 5, we link the concepts of solution-focused therapeutic approaches to the emotional/somatic concepts. In Chapter 6, we integrate theory and literature into a model for school and clinic use. Vignettes and case examples have been used throughout the chapters to illustrate typical experiences kids with self-regulation difficulties might face. Summaries of important points follow at the end of each chapter.

We provide several other features to assist mental health practitioners in developing their programs. They include the following:

- **Appendix A: Tools** includes an array of reproducible tools. It includes tools for assessment, individual counseling, group counseling, and crisis response. These reproducible items are included in the print version of Appendix A and are also available as pdfs on the enclosed CD.

- **Appendix B: Activities** includes lesson plans for use in individual and group settings. The activities in these plans teach skills to the caregiver and to the student in self-regulation (grounding, mindfulness, and tracking sensations), along with the CASEL skills areas (self-awareness, social awareness, self-management, responsible decision making, and relationship skills). Lessons are available for students from 5 to 18 years old. Many of the lessons include reproducible handouts for student use. All of the lessons and the student handouts are included in the print version of Appendix B. The reproducible items are also available as pdfs on the enclosed CD. Icons designate the items in the print version that are available as pdfs.

- **A Glossary** is included in the back of the book following Appendix B. The Glossary includes definitions of many of the terms used in the discussions in Chapters 1 through 6. Terms are shown in italic the first time they are used in the text. All terms in italic are defined in the Glossary.

It is our intention to provide both information about self-regulation and a step-by-step guide for developing a program to help children and adolescents. We have strived to integrate the theoretical material and focus it on practical applications for schools and clinics. We hope this book will be a helpful resource.

1

Connecting Emotional Intelligence and Self-Regulation to School Success

> The capacity to self-regulate is the foundation upon which a functional sense of self develops.
>
> Ogden, Minton, and Pain, *Trauma and the Body*

Self-regulation is basic to emotional intelligence, and significant research suggests that emotional intelligence is just as powerful a predictor of school success as IQ (Goldman, 1995; Rosenthal, 2002). *Self-regulation* makes it possible for us to know and manage our emotions, to recognize emotions in others, and to make use of these abilities in relationships. With an adequate capacity for self-regulation, we are able to control an immediate response to stimuli so that we can make choices about how to behave. For school success, kids need to be able to both regulate their emotions and accept help and direction for regulation from others (Ogden, Minton, & Pain, 2006). Teachers, administrators, and counselors across the country struggle with how to respond effectively to students whose serious difficulty with emotional and behavioral self-regulation creates chaos in schools. School personnel often wonder how to pre-empt extreme disruptions and de-escalate them when they occur (Carey, 2008).

A few years ago, a colleague of ours was a teacher in a private school. A particular student in the school was identified as "Trouble Boy" by faculty and staff. He was very aggressive and often out of control. At this school, the metal gate in front was not opened until school began. Each morning before the gate opened, Trouble Boy would come to the gate and look for our colleague, and she for him. Once they had spotted each other they would make eye contact. She described it as, "We stopped and found each other." Daniel Stern (2004) would call this a "moment of meeting." Before the day began, he was not Trouble Boy. He was simply a kid who sought out the experience of being seen in an attuned way by a calming adult, but also a kid who did not have the necessary skills of self-regulation to fill his day with such interactions.

Further support for the essential nature of the capacity for self-regulation comes from James Heckman, winner of a Nobel Prize in economics. Heckman's extensive

1

research, reported in the article "Schools, Skills, and Synapses" (2008), concludes that while IQ matters for school success, other traits are equally important in making this prediction. These include motivation levels, emotional stability, self-control, and sociability. The traits Heckman identifies can be found in the five skills, or competencies, defined by the Collaborative for Academic, Social, and Emotional Learning (CASEL) as making up emotional intelligence in children (Lantieri, 2008). CASEL's five competencies are self-awareness, social awareness, self-management, responsible decision making, and relationship skills. The capacity for self-regulation is basic to all of these competencies.

Chapter 1 highlights the characteristics of *emotional regulation*, the ability to self-regulate emotional responses, and *dysregulation*, the experience of being physiologically out of control with an inability to calm. It also introduces topics addressed in greater detail throughout the book: the interaction of self-regulation with complex trauma and the ongoing relationship of the mind and body. Finally, it introduces a model of intervention for helping kids improve self-regulation and, therefore, their chances for success.

Emotional Regulation and Dysregulation in Kids

No matter what the origin, chronic difficulty with self-regulation creates problems for kids and those who work with them. The following sections offer a picture of the kid who has adequate ability to self-regulate, the kid who is emotionally regulated, and the kid who has difficulty with emotional regulation (emotionally dysregulated). It is important to remember that even extremely dysregulated kids are not dysregulated all the time. Each kid presents with his or her own unique pattern of regulation and dysregulation.

Defining what an emotionally regulated kid looks like helps us define goals for kids who are emotionally dysregulated. Saxe, Ellis, and Kaplow (2007) use the following characteristics to describe the differences in the regulated kid and the dysregulated kid:

The regulated kid . . .

- spends most of his or her time in control of emotional responses
- self-soothes by using internal and external resources
- re-engages in activities and with others with relative ease when he or she has become upset
- almost never engages in dangerous behavior when stressed

The dysregulated kid . . .

- has difficulty controlling his or her *emotional states*—those relatively stable, repeated patterns of specific activity, cognition, affect, and relatedness
- often expresses negative emotions such as anger, fear, shame, guilt, or anxiety
- has difficulty with self-soothing, returning to calmness, and re-engaging with others and/or activities after he or she has become upset

- has intense changes in awareness (consciousness), affect (emotion), action (behavior), and relatedness (sense of connection to others) when faced with a stressor
- becomes dysregulated at least once a month, causing social, academic, or other problems
- may become behaviorally dysregulated and engage in dangerous behavior if stressed and in the midst of an episode of emotional dysregulation

All of us can become dysregulated at times. Usually, we know what the source is, but sometimes we do not. The same is true for kids.

Self-Regulation and Complex Trauma

Complex trauma is a useful concept that helps to explain unpredictable emotional and behavioral dysregulation in kids. It also helps lead the way toward more effective interventions. Trauma is not an event but a response to a stressful experience or chronically stressful experiences. In a traumatic situation, one's ability to cope is overwhelmed. Ninety percent of trauma with kids occurs within a family setting. In the words of a former child-abuse detective, interviews with children were not about "the monster under the bed, but about the monster in the house" (Sanders, 2008, p. A1). Each year in the United States, more than 3 million children are reported to authorities for abuse or neglect; about 1 million of these cases are substantiated (U.S. Department of Health and Human Services, 2004).

Many thousands of children suffer from chronic illness, undergo traumatic medical and surgical procedures, are victims of accidents, have parents who leave for war zones, or experience the death of a parent. Significant numbers of young children and adolescents witness violence in their homes, schools, or communities, or have parents who are incarcerated or homeless. However, trauma is not always the result of one extreme experience—it can be the cumulative result of ongoing fear and unpredictability in a child's environment (Lawson, 2009).

The impact of traumatic events is affected by the frequency, severity, duration, persistence of threat, proximity to threat, and factors—such as intelligence and resiliency—that are unique to a particular child. The impact of an event that is traumatic to one child's life cannot be assessed in isolation. Similar events may be traumatizing in one stage of life and not traumatizing at another. For example, being left alone for too long may overwhelm an infant's capacity to physically adjust, whereas an 11-year-old may only feel distressed and miserable.

A foremost determining factor of impact is whether a person is able to protect himself or herself from a threat. Children are rarely able to protect themselves, which makes them more vulnerable to being traumatized (Levine, 1997). Caregivers who aid or comfort a child during or following a traumatic event can make all the difference. Unfortunately, too many children are left without support—that is, without the *internal* or *external resources* to help them. Traumatized children may present with unmodulated aggression and impulse control, attentional problems, and difficulty negotiating relationships (van der Kolk, 2006); these and other emotional and behavioral difficulties are often misidentified as conduct problems.

The Complex Trauma Taskforce of the National Child Traumatic Stress Network (NCTSN) has adopted the term *complex trauma* to describe the response of a child to multiple, chronic, and prolonged developmentally adverse traumatic events, most often of an interpersonal nature (Ford & Courtois, 2009). Complex trauma interferes with neurobiological development (Ford, 2009) and the neurological capacity to integrate sensory, emotional, and cognitive information into a cohesive whole. Limited capacity for integration negatively affects an individual's capacity to regulate stress, creating the subsequent dysregulation of emotion and behavior (Rothschild, 2000; van der Kolk, 2006). For many kids who experience difficulty with self-regulation, there is no known exposure to traumatic events. However, they experience the same or similar serious emotional, behavioral, social, and learning difficulties. In the following section, several lists detail how specific trauma and complex trauma present in kids.

Symptom Patterns

Van der Kolk (2006) does an excellent job of describing the physical and emotional symptoms that can appear in children with complex trauma. These include the following:

- Disruption of *affect regulation*
- Disturbed attachment patterns
- Rapid behavior regressions and shifts in emotional states
- Loss of autonomous strivings
- Aggressive behavior against self and others
- Failure to achieve developmental competencies
- Loss of bodily regulation of sleep, food, and self-care
- Altered schemas of the world
- Anticipatory behavior and traumatic expectations
- Multiple somatic problems, from gastrointestinal distress to headaches
- Apparent lack of awareness of danger and resulting endangering behaviors
- Self-hatred and self-blame
- Chronic feelings of ineffectiveness

Tanya is an overweight 14-year-old girl who is in the 8th grade. Her school performance is below average even though her tested IQ is above average. There is no specific trauma in her reported history, but she has been a chronic discipline problem since elementary school. She finds herself in some kind of physical and/or verbal fight at least once a week. Most go unreported. When Tanya is asked to describe what happens, she always explains that the other person is at fault. She reports that she feels attacked and feels the need to act to defend herself. When adults are present and attempt to intervene, Tanya resists and frequently the situation escalates. While she has come to the attention of mental-health professionals in the schools, her problems have continued.

Trauma symptoms present differently in children and in adults. How they present depends on a combination of factors, including level of reasoning and perceptual, brain, and personality development. According to Levine and Kline in their book *Trauma Through a Child's Eyes* (2007), children may either "act out," making it clear that there is a problem or "act in," giving subtle clues that something is wrong. Levine and Kline list four symptoms as the distinguishing signs that a life experience, or experiences, has been greater than could be tolerated while still maintaining normal rhythm. Not every child will demonstrate all of these symptoms. The symptoms are *hyperarousal*; *constriction*; *dissociation*; and feelings of numbness, shut down, or *freeze*, with subsequent feelings of helplessness and hopelessness.

All four of these symptoms and, specifically hyperarousal and freeze, are normal responses to an overwhelming experience. They are built-in survival mechanisms. When the brain and body are working normally, they are time-limited (Levine, 1997). But when a child's experience is more than he or she can tolerate, and when he or she is left alone with the distress, the body's natural ability to return to normal levels of arousal is disrupted. These normal responses then become problematic, enduring symptoms (Perry, 2006).

Along with these primary symptoms, Levine and Kline (2007) list secondary symptoms that may develop when kids are not helped. (Notice the parallels in Levine and Kline's list with van der Kolk's list of complex trauma symptoms.)

Hyperarousal is greater than normal arousal. *Arousal* refers to physiological activation, including respiration and heart rates. Hyperarousal may present as one or more of the following:

- Exaggerated emotional response
- Guardedness
- Compulsive talking
- Anxiety and phobia
- Agitation
- Fidgeting
- Darting eyes
- "Restless leg"
- Distractibility
- Hyperactivity
- "Out-of-seat" behavior
- Frequent crying and irritability
- Temper tantrums
- Abrupt mood swings
- "Looking for a fight" and rage reactions
- Increased risk-taking behavior

Dissociation is a psychological response in which there is a disconnect between present awareness and the present physical and emotional experience. Dissociation is a natural response to extreme stress, but it is problematic when it is not time-limited. Dissociation may present in the following ways:

- Daydreaming
- Distractibility and inattentiveness

- Reduced ability to organize and plan
- Easily and frequently stressed out
- A blank stare
- Excessive shyness
- "Head in the clouds"
- Living in an imaginary world
- Inability to connect to others

Constriction is a physiological and psychological response to extreme stress. Attention, breathing, muscle tone, and posture constrict. **Freeze** is a brain/body automatic response to inescapable extreme stress in which emergency energy gets bound up. Constriction and freeze may present in the following ways:

- Muscle tension
- Fatigue
- Headaches, stomachaches, and other physical complaints
- Feelings of shame and guilt
- Diminished curiosity
- Feelings and behaviors of helplessness
- Eating disorders
- Avoidance behavior

Although there is always underlying hyperarousal with complex trauma, some children may show *hypoarousal* in their behavior and musculature (Rothschild, 2003). These children look physically weak and have slowed cognitive and emotional responses. They may have special difficulty with focused attention and connecting with their inner physical experience. These kids are frequently missed or are identified as depressed instead of traumatized (Ogden, Minton, & Pain, 2006).

Long-term stress wears down a child, causing an erosion of health, vitality, and confidence. In school, children's traumatic experiences can impact neurological, language, and cognitive functioning, interfering with school performance. The following lists are adapted from a number of sources, including Perrin, Smith, and Yule (2000), and Levine and Kline (2007). Areas affected for kids of all ages include the following:

Neurological impact

- Hyperarousal
- Difficulty with self-regulation of emotion and behavior
- Impaired *executive function*: adaptive decision making, including planning for the future, anticipating consequences, and inhibiting inappropriate responses
- Auditory processing disorders
- Verbal memory

Language difficulties

- Receptive/expressive language problems
- Diminished use of language for social/affective exchange

- Little experience with using language in problem solving and the use of anger and rage to maintain distance

Cognitive structures

- Poor understanding of cause/effect relationships
- Difficulty taking another's perspective
- Organizing narrative material and other sequential memory difficulties
- Impaired ability to read social cues

Some symptoms present differently at different ages. Examples follow.

Kids Ages 5–11

Symptoms of trauma in this age group often have a behavioral component. These kids will sometimes…

- re-enact the traumatic experience during play
- want to tell a story over and over again
- exhibit disorganized or agitated behavior and lack of ability to self-regulate
- worry about what happened to others who experienced the same events and carefully monitor adults to see if there is a reason to fear
- be frightened by their own grief and/or their wish for revenge
- show a lack of ability to concentrate, complete tasks, and efficiently process new information
- be easily distracted, subsequently impairing learning
- exhibit hyper-vigilance, fidgeting, inability to stay seated, quick startle response, and compulsive talking
- initiate fighting
- display inattentiveness, fatigue, and daydreaming
- misinterpret cause and effect; fail to see their contributions to what happens to them and failing to enlist allies
- have gender differences, with boys acting out anger through aggressive behavior and girls turning anger inward with depressed affect, somatic symptoms, anxiety, and self-denigration

Kids Ages 12–18

Symptoms of trauma in adolescence are like adult symptoms of trauma, but trauma in adolescence has greater potential for a long-term impact on a kid's sense of self. The completion of major developmental tasks of adolescence, specifically autonomy and identity, may be adversely affected (Levine & Kline, 2007). Traumatized adolescents may…

- re-experience traumatic events through flashbacks and may take steps to avoid situations, thoughts, and feelings that might trigger recollections
- become detached and withdrawn

- suffer more from sleeplessness than younger kids; in addition, they may show more irritability, depression with suicidal thoughts, anxiety, and inattentiveness (leading to truancy, poor grades, and defiant behavior that can be confused with oppositional behavior)
- make abrupt changes in relationships
- make radical changes in attitude and appearance
- shift to dependency on drugs and alcohol
- demonstrate sexual promiscuity and other risk-taking behaviors
- show a sudden disinterest in hobbies and sports that they previously enjoyed

The Complex Trauma of Disrupted Attachment

Kids have an innate need to be attached. They are born with the equipment for social engagement with a primary caregiver, and as they develop mobility, they seek physical closeness with *attachment figures* and turn to them when in distress. *Attachment figures* are the individuals in the child's environment on whom the child depends for safety and emotional connection. Children who have repeated experiences in which their attachment figures provide these things are able to internalize their relationships. Such internalized relationships provide children with resilience, which they can utilize even when they are physically distant from their caregivers (Siegel, 2003).

A predictable, calming, and consistent caregiver is the most critical factor in the acquisition of self-regulatory abilities (Schore, 2003). If a child has repeated success in coping with mild, brief episodes of fear, self-regulation is enhanced. Chronic early experiences in which the child internalizes the sense that he or she cannot count on caregivers for comfort and safety create *disrupted attachment*, and can be the source of difficulties with self-regulation (Schore, 2003). This kind of disruption in the primary relationship results in complex trauma when it prolongs, exacerbates, or prevents the learning of ways to behaviorally and physiologically modulate emotion. Furthermore, it severely hampers a child's development of self-regulation. For example, for the child who is not helped with her fear of the unfamiliar, novelty may become a lasting source of unmanageable distress. This occurs, not because fear or novelty itself is toxic, but because of the child's failure to learn how to regulate the body when experiencing fear of the unfamiliar (Ford, 2009). If the primary caregiver does not help a child to calm himself or herself, the child cannot internalize the experience and never learns to *self-soothe*. The term *self-soothe* refers to the ability to use our internal and external resources to calm and regulate ourselves.

Tony is 5 years old and in kindergarten. His family lost their home, and they have been living in shelters off and on for 2 years. Tony's father has never been involved in his life. His mother has problems with drug addiction, and Tony has witnessed her involvement with violent, threatening people all his life. School authorities are not certain of everything that has happened to him, but he has all of the symptoms of complex trauma. While Tony made significant progress in a preschool program, upon entering kindergarten, he had regular temper tantrums. The precipitating events of his explosive behavior are not predictable. Even when he is emotionally regulated, he is unable to consistently make eye contact with his teacher and/ or to listen to and follow instruction.

Attachment Patterns

We include a description of attachment patterns both to encourage you to consider what an individual kid's attachment style is and to facilitate more effective interaction. Knowing the characteristics of secure attachment helps us to see the direction in which we want to aim. Each of the following four attachment patterns has specific self-regulation tendencies (Allen, 2001; Cassidy & Shaver, 1999; Cozolino, 2002; Main & Solomon, 1990; Ogden, Minton, & Pain, 2006; Schore, 2003; Siegel, 2003). Although we are presenting these patterns as discrete groupings, often we will find that kids are not purely in one group. A kid may show a range of responses with stronger tendencies toward one of the patterns. The characteristics of each pattern follow:

Secure attachment

- Emotional flexibility and competent social functioning and cognitive abilities
- Resilient, even in the face of adversity
- Developmentally appropriate ability to self-regulate and to accept, with little or no resistance, help with regulation from others
- Optimal ability to evaluate safety and danger and ability to shift adaptively from dysregulated arousal to a regulated state

Insecure attachment

- Emotional rigidity
- Difficulty understanding the minds of other individuals
- Impairment in ability to reason
- At risk for dysregulation in the face of stressful situations

Insecure–avoidant attachment

- Expression of little need for proximity and apparently little interest in adult overtures for contact
- When contact is made, makes no effort to sustain the contact
- Following contact, may appear either more physically "armored" or passively withdrawn
- A lack of emotional expression and eye contact, and a lower level of arousal
- A preference for self-regulation that does not depend on another person's presence

- Although generally compliant, lacks flexibility in interactive regulation and the social engagement skills necessary for resolving interpersonal conflicts
- Disconnected from his or her internal experience: may appear to be physically uncomfortable but will smile and report being "fine"

Insecure–ambivalent attachment

- Dysregulated emotion and behavior
- Actively seeks proximity and contact with others one moment and the next acts angry or rejecting
- Tendency toward intense expression of emotion and negative mood responses
- Poor impulse control, fear of abandonment, and difficulty with stressful situations and change in general
- Compared with the kid with insecure–avoidant attachment, there is more congruence between internal and external states
- May tend toward focusing on internal distress, often frantically pursuing relief
- Low threshold of arousal and difficulty maintaining emotional and physiological activation
- Increased signaling for attention and escalating distress to solicit help
- Seeking of social engagement and simultaneous difficulty with being easily calmed and soothed either through self-regulating or through the help of others

Disorganized–disoriented attachment

Main and Solomon (1990) gave the term "disorganized/disoriented attachment" to a group of children with enduring negative affect and confusing behavior. These kids have frightening and/or frightened primary caregivers, many of whom have unresolved trauma in their own histories. They may abuse and/or neglect their own children (Siegel, 2003). The pattern is expressed in young children by the following:

- Contradictory actions, such as proximity seeking quickly followed by withdrawal or other disconnection
- Simultaneous contradictory action, such as avoidance and proximity seeking
- Incomplete and undirected action, such as expressing distress and moving away from caregiver
- Mistimed and strange actions, such as stumbling when there is no reason to stumble
- Freezing, becoming still, shutting down movements and expressions
- Postures that indicate apprehension of the caregiver, such as fearful expressions and hunched shoulders
- Disorganized or disoriented action, such as aimless wandering around, rapid mood changes, and dazed and confused expressions

- Arousal levels that tend to be too high or too low, with characteristic difficulty expressing needs and responding to others

Disorganized attachment may be expressed in an older kid by the following:

- A tendency to have both underdeveloped and ineffective self-regulation, with neither an ability to self-regulate or make use of help from others
- Expressed hostility toward peers, with an increased potential for interpersonal violence as he or she matures

Daniel, a 10-year-old boy living with both his parents in a middle-class neighborhood, was bitten by a dog unknown in the neighborhood. A neighbor ran to Daniel's house to alert his mother. Daniel sat on the ground holding his bleeding arm. He had not been able to run away from the dog or to fight back. When his mother got there, she examined his wound. She told him to stand up and walk back to their house. She did not comfort him; rather, she discouraged the tears that came to his eyes when he saw her, saying that crying was not going to help this. She also questioned what he had done to the dog.

Daniel's mother took him to an emergency room near their home, where he was given medical treatment for his wound. After they left the hospital, she carefully provided the follow-up treatment recommended by the medical staff, but did not talk about what had happened with Daniel. When Daniel's father got home, he told Daniel that he needed to stay away from dogs he did not know. Following this incident, Daniel began crying at school and not wanting to go out at recess. His schoolwork suffered as he began spending most of his time "daydreaming" in class.

The Mind–Body Connection

In this book we refer to the *mind–body connection* as the ongoing interaction between neurobiology and the rest of our physical body. A Yale University study reported in the journal *Science* by Williams and Bargh (2008) illustrates this important connection. The study began before participants realized it had. Half of them were handed a warm cup of coffee, half an iced cup of coffee. They were asked to hold the coffee only for moments as a "favor" to the assistant while getting on the elevator to go up to the fourth floor to fill out study questionnaires. On the fourth floor, participants were given a description of a hypothetical person and asked to evaluate the person's personality. Those who had held the warm coffee briefly rated this person as more generous, happier, and better natured than did those who had briefly held the iced coffee. In a follow-up study, participants were asked to evaluate a hot pad or a cold pad for treating injuries and were later given the opportunity to choose a reward for participation. Additionally, they were asked to choose to keep the reward or to give it to a friend. Those who had held the hot pad were more likely to choose a gift for a friend, and those who had held the cold pad were more likely to choose the reward for themselves.

Apparently, in these studies, the physical experience of holding something warm caused participants to feel more generous. The studies support the tight connection between our minds and our bodies. The researchers concluded that the early physical experience of being held by a warm body becomes linked in the brain with positive emotional responses. All of our life experiences are held in the mind–body memory system. The strategies for self-regulation (SSR) model makes use of the mind–body connection for effective intervention.

An Intervention Focused on Self-Regulation

We use the mind–body connection to help a kid learn self-regulation by teaching him or her to use *somatic awareness*, consciously noticing his or her body's response in the moment. The foundation for learning self-regulation in the SSR model is the creation of a calming relationship with the student. Our own healthy practice of self-regulation, a practice that also helps us not to take stress home, is essential to this work. In the counseling relationship, we recognize that even more important than the essential ability to care for the student is our ability to be a calming presence. We move out of focusing on the content of the student's distress and shift our focus to teaching him or her to re-regulate arousal and emotion.

For self-regulation to improve, sensorimotor, emotional, and cognitive processing must be integrated (Levine & Kline, 2007; Ogden & Minton, 2000; Saxe, Ellis, & Kaplow, 2007). In the SSR model, once kids can identify their own regulation and dysregulation, we teach them to use somatic awareness to slow down and think. Teaching kids to use somatic awareness in this way shifts the locus of control from external (Others are in charge of my emotions and behavior.) to internal (I am in charge of my emotions and behavior.). Van der Kolk (2006) argues that effective treatment of complex trauma includes this shift in locus of control. The solution-focused component of the SSR model also supports this change as it shifts responsibility for problem solving to students through helping them define goals. Throughout this goal-setting process, we actively seek input from teachers and other school staff and offer them our support by giving them tools to intervene before major "meltdowns" or violent acting-out occurs. Giving school staff this kind of help more effectively supports change (Levine & Kline, 2007).

Changing Perceptions

Many of the problem behaviors that traumatized children exhibit can be understood as their efforts to minimize perceived threats and regulate emotional distress. Unless we understand the nature of such responses, we are likely to label children as oppositional, rebellious, unmotivated, or antisocial (Pynoos, Frederick, & Nader, 1987). The SSR model of intervention addresses the necessary traits for school success to which James Heckman's research points and to the needs of schools looking for better models for addressing the difficulties of emotionally and behaviorally dysregulated kids. We use the descriptive term "complex trauma" throughout this book to include kids with known trauma, disrupted attachment, and difficulty with self-regulation with unknown cause. With this model there is no need to identify the origin of emotional and behavioral dysregulation.

The focus is on helping students set goals for improvement, learn to self-regulate through the use of somatic awareness, and develop the five competencies of the CASEL areas of emotional intelligence.

We are inviting you to join us in a new way to view these students' emotional and behavioral difficulties. The SSR model changes our perception away from viewing kids as "bad" and toward viewing them as kids experiencing dysregulation. The literature tells us that, just as kids can be negatively affected by traumatic experiences, they are affected positively by interventions (van der Kolk, 2006).

In the next chapter, we further our discussion of the mind–body connection by looking at the way the brain responds to trauma. The brain controls both regulation and dysregulation of behavior and emotion. Understanding how that works helps to change our perception of dysregulation and makes us more effective in helping kids learn to self-regulate.

In Summary

✧ Self-regulation is basic to emotional intelligence. Emotional intelligence matters as much as IQ when it comes to success in school.

✧ Complex trauma does not have to be the result of extreme events, but rather may be the result of chronic, prolonged stress of an interpersonal nature, including disrupted attachment.

✧ The impact of childhood traumatic stress is wide ranging, interfering with normal development.

✧ Hyperarousal, dissociation, constriction, and freeze are universal symptoms of trauma.

✧ Dysregulated emotion and behavior can be the result of complex trauma and unidentifiable sources.

✧ Pinpointing the occurrence of a specific traumatic experience is not necessary for effective intervention with the SSR model.

✧ Viewing difficult behavior as possibly resulting from complex trauma opens the door for more effective interventions.

✧ The SSR model focuses on a calming relationship, somatic experience, and building on the kid's strengths and goals to shift the locus of control to the kid.

2 Exploring Somatic Experience and Emotional Regulation

Traumatic symptoms are not caused by the triggering event itself. They stem from the frozen residue of energy that has not been resolved and discharged; this residue remains trapped in the nervous system where it can wreak havoc on our bodies and spirits.

Levine, *Waking the Tiger: Healing Trauma*

Our brains are perfectly organized for survival: We read our environment instinctively, assessing danger even before our ability to think or use language. Stressed by what is perceived as a threat, the brain knows just what to do and does it automatically. Stress hormones are released into the blood stream to supply the additional emergency energy the body needs in order to respond to the threat. We *upregulate* for fight or flight. The needed energy is utilized by the body and then discharged. Once a real threat has passed, the excess stress hormones are re-absorbed and, eventually, the body calms, or *downregulates*. This is a natural cycle that, under normal circumstances, completes itself, enabling an individual to mobilize resources in the face of stress and to metabolize the dysregulated experience at the physiological and emotional levels. While this process for managing stress is built into the brain, children require help from caregivers to develop its use for self-regulation. This chapter explores how complex trauma causes disruption in normal brain functions, affecting brain circuitry and the ability to self-regulate.

Children are particularly vulnerable to becoming overwhelmed and dysregulated by stress. They are dependent on their caregivers for providing soothing and safety until they are able to care for themselves. The plasticity of children's developing brains makes them significantly more vulnerable than adults to the impact of *unresolved stress*: the normal *arousal energy* that is not released and remains trapped in the body (Lawson, 2009; Siegel, 2003). "Arousal energy" is the physiological and mental activity that is an automatic response to a threat to survival. In children, if the stress is too extreme and/or chronic, and their caregivers are not available to calm them, the brain's natural capacity to downregulate arousal energy is inhibited and problems arise.

The Brain's Emergency Response System

There are two emergency response circuits within the brain. Under normal circumstances, these two circuits work together for survival. Understanding how these survival circuits

Figure 2.1 A Cross Section of the Brain

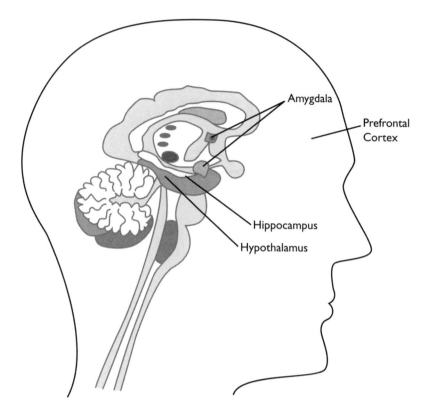

Note. From *Overcoming Attention Deficit Disorders in Children, Adolescents, and Adults, 4th Ed.* (p. 41), by D. R. Jordan, 2006, Austin, TX: PRO-ED. Copyright 2006 by PRO-ED, Inc. Adapted with permission.

work is invaluable in implementing the SSR intervention model. We include a brief explanation of their pertinent aspects in Figure 2.1.

The Low Road: The Rapid Survival Circuit

When something or someone is perceived as life threatening, a signal is sent straight to the *amygdala*, a small, almond-shaped structure in the midbrain that initiates an emergency response (LeDoux, 1998; Levine & Kline, 2007). The sensory processing sequence of the *low road survival circuit* does not attend to the details, subtleties, or the context of the situation. There is no stopping, thinking, or considering when this sequence is activated (Saxe, Ellis, & Kaplow, 2007). The absolute focus of the low road's path and the amygdala is to maximize the chance of survival.

In its effort to maximize survival, the amygdala initiates an emergency response and releases extra energy in the form of stress hormones. The body goes into its most extreme state of arousal: fight and/or flight. Blood flows away from the skin and into the muscles for quick movement. Heart rate, blood pressure, and respiration rates rise to provide more oxygen. We begin to sweat, and our eyes dilate to improve distance vision (Cozolino, 2002; Rothschild, 2003; Saxe, Ellis, & Kaplow, 2007). The brain's automatic responses are organized for fast, effective action. When this emergency response is to real danger, it is time-limited, life-saving, and highly adaptive (Levine & Kline, 2007).

Once the amygdala initiates the emergency response, extra stress hormones are released, even if neither fight nor flight is an option. Our neurobiology is organized to engage the freeze response when neither fight nor flight is possible and when survival is perceived to be at stake (Levine & Kline, 2007). The brain sends the message to the body to freeze all action. The muscles become slack or stiff, the heart and respiration rates slow, blood flows back to the skin, and the pupils constrict. Freezing is a biological survival response, and it is an excellent survival mechanism when it is time-limited. Once a threat has passed and freezing has been the best option, our bodies can literally shake off the experience. We release the excess survival energy.

The High Road: The Survival Circuit With a More Considered Approach

A moment behind the signal sent to the amygdala, the brain that has not been affected by previous trauma initiates the slower, more deliberate *high road survival circuit* when it perceives a life-threatening signal. This survival sequence activates the areas of the brain responsible for assessing danger and the degree of threat.

In the high road process, the brain gathers the details of the threatening situation and engages long-term memory, where experience with similar stimuli are found. The threatening stimulus is given a context of time and place. Finally, the information is made available to the *explicit memory system* or *working memory*. Working memory provides the information we use in the here and now to make decisions about what action to take. Like the low road, the high road's purpose is survival in the face of threat, but it is organized to determine adaptive responses and to regulate emotion (Saxe, Ellis, & Kaplow, 2007).

Joseph, a 16-year-old boy, was walking home alone in the early evening when out of the twilight a large figure came running toward him. Joseph's heart and respiration rate went up, and he felt afraid. He froze in place. As he focused on the figure heading his way, he saw a jacket he recognized as his older brother's, and he remembered that his brother was going to be home that evening for dinner. Soon, a voice he recognized called out. It was his brother.

Joseph's heart and breathing slowed to normal, and he shook off the tension in his body as he let out a big sigh. His brain had let him know there was no reason to be afraid. Happy to see his brother, Joseph ran toward him, yelling, "Hey, man. I thought you were somebody else!"

The Brain's System for Calming Down

When the low road and high road circuits are working together and a perceived threat has passed, the brain has a system for calming. As a part of the high road, the brain structure called the *hippocampus* provides information to place the threat in the context of the present time and place. Once the situation is perceived as no longer life-threatening or as a false alarm, the hippocampus sends the message to the amygdala to calm down. The brain and the body *re-regulate*. Returning to a baseline level of calm, they go back to "business as usual" (Cozolino, 2002; Saxe, Ellis, & Kaplow, 2007). The calming effect of downregulation moves the mind and body out of hyperarousal and helps them relax.

When There Is No Help Coming

Children do not initially have the ability to self-soothe. They need and require help. Without reliable help with calming, and with chronic threat in the environment, a child's brain can become conditioned to automatically connect to the rapid response of the low road survival circuit when there is a perceived threat. A frozen reservoir of trapped emergency energy comes to reside within a child's nervous system and becomes a source of dysregulation (Levine & Kline, 2007). The child is put at risk for the development of a chronically activated amygdala. Chronic activation of the amygdala floods the hippocampus so that it is unable to do its job of downregulation (Siegel, 2003). The high road survival circuit is bypassed.

Internally, kids with complex trauma come to live in an underlying state of chronic hyperarousal and have brains that react as if every fender bender in the city requires the EMS, the police, and fire trucks. Ogden and Minton (2000) compare individuals who have been traumatized to infants who lack the ability to use thought to guide action. "Similarly, traumatized people frequently experience themselves as being at the mercy of their *sensations*, physical reactions, and emotions, having lost the capacity to regulate these functions" (p. 4). ("Sensations" are physiological happenings in the body, such as trembling, pressure, tension, and vibration.) Kids with complex trauma have lost access to the natural slow-down-and-think response of the high road.

For these kids, when the mind and body experience stimuli that are neurologically connected with traumatic events, trapped emergency energy heightens and dysregulates arousal and emotion. Arousal and emotion are not the same thing, but they are often confused because they occur simultaneously. *Arousal* is physiological activation experienced as sensations in the body. Damasio (1999) defines *emotion* as the awareness of a feeling state of the body. Both arousal and emotion then are somatic experiences, meaning they are happenings within the body. The difference is that the sensations of emotions have thoughts associated with them, and the sensations of arousal are simply signals of physiological activation. Arousal and emotion interact in this way: Unattended, dysregulated arousal leads to escalating emotion. With no consistent help with calming and no opportunity to discharge emergency energy, the brain's survival system, which is organized for protection, can become too easily triggered. There is a loss of volume control for arousal and subsequent emotional responses (Bloom, 1997; Ogden, Minton, & Pain, 2006; Siegel, 2003;).

Leo is an 8-year-old boy. His mother and father were divorced when Leo was 2, and his mother abandoned the family. He lives with his father, an alcoholic, who rages at Leo almost daily. Their home is a small inner-city apartment, and Leo's father has had many girlfriends come and go from Leo's life. His father financially supports the family, and Leo does not show any obvious signs of abuse.

On this particular day, Leo's father is angry after stumbling on the backpack that Leo has left by the door. Leo's father yells for Leo to pick up the backpack, threatens him, and then slaps him. Leo is terrified. His brain releases excess energy for survival-in-the-moment, but he does not have the option to flee or fight. Leo does not move. He freezes and expresses no emotion. When the incident is over, there is no safe outlet to discharge this energy and no safe adult to help him. Events like this are repeated over and over in Leo's life. His brain works every time, but the energy that is naturally released remains trapped, creating and re-enforcing trauma symptoms. At school, Leo reacts in unpredictable ways to perceived threats from both authority figures and classmates. At times, there is no response and other times, he is extremely reactive and disruptive.

Emotion Becomes a Disloyal Guide

We notice physical feelings in our bodies. The sensations get our attention, and we have thoughts about those sensations. In response, and depending on the situation, we might decide to move closer, walk away, or stop. The brain is organized to use emotions to guide action. Our personal histories influence the kinds of thoughts we associate with the particular sensations of different emotions. Given similar sensations of emotion in the body, such as tightness in the stomach area, one child may associate the sensation with thoughts connected to hiding, while another child may associate the sensation with the need to retaliate. Fear, anger, sadness, grief, depression, and terror all register in our bodies first as physical sensations. Rothschild (2000) and Ogden, Minton, and Pain (2006) describe typical physical sensations associated with different emotions in the list shown in Table 2.1.

Table 2.1

Physical Sensations Associated With Emotions

Anger	Muscular tension (particularly in the jaw and shoulders), pursed lips, clenched fists, narrowed eyes
Anxiety	Fidgeting, restless appearance in body movements, frequent tense sighing, rapid breathing
Disgust	Nausea
Fear	Racing heart, trembling, hunched shoulders, held breath, a pleading look in the eyes, moving away from the frightening stimulus
Grief	A heavy feeling in the chest
Happiness	Deep breathing, relaxed sighs
Panic	Change in size of pupils, eyes darting, either extreme increase in body tension or decrease (muscles becoming limp)
Sadness	Wet eyes, "lump in the throat"
Shame	Rising heat (particularly in the face), sinking feeling in stomach area

"Emotional difficulties generally begin as a combination of thoughts and sensations" (Levine & Kline, 2007, p. 113). In kids with complex trauma, chronic underlying hyperarousal makes emotion too easily activated or, when hypoarousal has become the defense, too difficult to access. They cannot use their emotions to guide their actions (Ogden, Minton & Pain, 2006). What seems to be a neutral action or event can trigger a completely unexpected response in the traumatized kid. There is a "hostile takeover of consciousness by emotion" (LeDoux, 1998, p. 226). When activated, the traumatized child is unable to find within the self, or seek from others, the resources for calming, that is, downregulating the level of arousal. It is as if the water is turned on in a bathtub and left unattended. If no one is minding the tub, at some point the water will overflow (Levine & Kline, 2007).

Fear and Stress Circuitry and the Effect on Memory

Again, trauma is the memory captured in the circuitry of the brain, not the event itself (van der Kolk, 2007). The low road survival circuit takes in only enough information to respond with fight, flight, or freeze. These bits of incomplete information regarding threat, including body sensations, are not stored in working memory. They are stored in the *implicit memory system*, and they motivate emotion and behavior (Rothschild, 2003). This memory system is highly important to the brain's survival plan. It stores what is perceived as life-threatening stimuli in a way that makes the implicit memory rapidly available. When those stimuli are encountered again, the survival-in-the-moment state can be instantly activated (Ogden, Minton, & Pain, 2006; Saxe, Ellis, & Kaplow, 2007). Without unresolved trauma, this is highly adaptive; but with complex trauma, it can cause intermittent emotional chaos.

"The fascinating feature of implicit memory is that when it is retrieved, it lacks an internal experience that something is being 'recalled,' and the individual is not even aware that his or her internal experience is being generated from something from the past" (Siegel, 2003, p. 22). When implicit memory is triggered, our internal experience is that our responses are a result of the present situation. These responses may not make sense to others given the present situation, but they make sense to the brain's survival system.

Brain research has found that emotions such as fear have specific neural circuitry corresponding to specific physical sensations (Siegel, 2003). Fear can become paired with virtually anything, making it one of our most potent ways of learning. A sight, sound, smell, taste, or touch can become fear-conditioned, and a network of connections develops (Bloom, 1997). The implicit memory of an original threat, or threats, can be evoked by an innocent gesture from someone. This innocent gesture can engage the *fear and stress circuitry*, a network of neural connections activated by the perception of threat. It is as if the original real threat is happening again. Fear mobilizes physical response (Porges, 2007). A triggering event may have no associated explicit memory. It is the fear and stress circuitry that activates implicit memory of threat and motivates a physical response of fight, flight, or freeze (Levine & Kline, 2007).

The responses and behaviors produced by fear and the activation of implicit memory by the stress circuitry, may seem disturbing and difficult to understand and therefore manage. Kids can act as if there is a threat when there isn't. They are not aware of what is motivating them, and they fully believe that their present action is a response to the present situation. The fight, flight, or freeze responses associated with situations from the past invade the present. There is intense arousal without a meaningful context or the benefit of high road emotional regulation and cognition. "These images, sensations, and emotions can all be provoked, but without engagement of the explicit memory system, they cannot be narrated (cohesively recounted) or understood" (Rothschild, 2003, p. 11). The child keeps replaying past experience without awareness.

Cassandra is 13. When she was a year old, circumstances made it necessary for her to live with her maternal grandmother for an extended period of time, with only occasional contact with her mother. She returned to live with her mother at age 3.

Cassandra began refusing to go to school at age 5, when she was to begin kindergarten. In the last 8 years, her school attendance has continued to be a significant problem. She has unsuccessfully started the school year in regular settings numerous times, and she has now been diagnosed as emotionally disturbed. Other attempts to educate her have included a special school and homebound school program.

Cassandra has no memory of her mother's leaving her or of the time she lived with her grandmother. Her complaints have centered on stomach pains and other symptoms of anxiety when she is away from home. All of this has created great stress on an already stressed family system. Her school refusal is a specific source of frustration for her mother. Cassandra has been seen by a number of counselors off and on over the years. No one has been able to change this pattern of school refusal.

The Loss of Connections for Healthy Neural Integration

When the low road and high road survival circuitries are functioning normally, actions motivated by fear and stress circuitry and implicit memory can be moderated. The brain centers communicate; there is healthy *neural integration*. Siegel (2003) describes neural integration as the key process that is impaired in trauma. When emergency systems are chronically activated, the low road survival system effectively disables executive functioning—the use of cognition to make adaptive decisions—in favor of fight, flight, or freeze.

The brain is organized to function as an integrated whole with different brain centers communicating through neural connections. With healthy neural integration, the low road and the high road work together, enabling us to contextualize and put memory and experience into language. There is a healthy balance in the nervous system between upregulation and downregulation, which manages and maintains optimal arousal levels, even in the face of threat. We are able to access and assess details of the situation and use past experiences to make decisions about how best to respond. Neural integration enables whole brain processing and emotion to be modulated by a wedge of cognition; that is, it creates the opportunity for reflection and adaptive response to guide action (Saxe, Ellis, & Kaplow, 2007). Siegel (2003) describes in detail the functions of healthy neural integration. They include the following:

- **Regulating the body's physical reactions.** Example: We decide how hard we want to touch something, and our brain tells the hand to touch it that hard. We decide we want to stay in our seat, and we do.

- **Regulation of emotion.** Example: We have a disappointing experience in a public place, like school. Tears come to our eyes, but we realize that this is not the worst thing to happen. We decide to do something about it or to get help.

- **Emotionally attuned interpersonal communication, often involving eye contact.** Example: We are speaking directly with someone about something important to them. Though we are in a hurry to do what we want to do or are otherwise distracted, we slow down and look directly at the person, listening to what he or she is saying.

- **Creating a sense about other people's subjective experience.** We watch another person and consider how what is happening to her is affecting her. Example: The teacher is reprimanding a fellow student, and, rather than laughing at him, we think of how it feels when we're in trouble with the teacher.

- **Having response flexibility, taking in information, thinking, considering options, and producing an adaptive response.** Example: We usually eat lunch with a particular group of friends. We walk into the cafeteria and see there are no more seats at their table. We look around the room, noticing other people we know, enjoy, or might want to talk with today. Using all this information, we decide to ask a particular person if we can join her.

- **Creating self-awareness and autobiographical memory.** Example: We can observe ourselves in a variety of situations, and we notice our reactions and how others respond to us. We can remember our own lives and what has happened to us and what we have done.

- **Morality.** We bring our action into accord with standards of rightness and wrongness. Example: A set of circumstances makes it possible to cheat on a test to get the right answer. We choose not to cheat.

To illustrate, consider a classroom situation in which kids are standing in a line, and one kid accidentally bumps into another kid. A number of things might happen. Given normal, healthy neural integration in each of the two children, they will experience the physical sensation of bumping and being bumped and not immediately experience being under threat. Each kid's lower brain centers and higher brain centers will be connecting and communicating, making it possible to take in the details of the situation, put the event into the current context, and act accordingly. Even if they are not the best of friends, they will move on without incident.

If one of these kids, or both, had brains dominated by fear and stress circuitry that impairs neural integration, the situation could change dramatically. The somatic experience of being bumped could trigger fear and stress circuitry and implicit memory of past physical trauma. The amygdala would take over, escalating an accident into a battle. This condition of not being able to access and use knowledge across contexts and emotional states also affects the *sense of self*. The kid who loses it in this situation ends up feeling worse about himself or herself. In the SSR model, interventions are aimed at improving self-regulation by helping kids make connections between somatic experience and executive functioning. This enhances the kid's sense of self and self-mastery. *Sense of self* refers to the sum of the internal pictures we carry of ourselves and important others, the feelings we have about those pictures, and how they guide our capacity to act in our environment.

Vincent is 15 and a sophomore in high school. He has participated in the gifted and talented program since the first grade. His divorcing parents are extremely busy professionals. Vincent is handsome and has excellent verbal skills and a history of outstanding academic performance. Although he is painfully shy, he has never stood out as a problem until now. Even though Vincent does not meet the diagnostic criteria for depression, there is clearly a problem.

Since his parents announced their impending divorce, Vincent has avoided eye contact and just stops in his tracks when he perceives he has made an error. He frequently crumples up the paper on which he has been working. His past academic successes do not exist for him. It is as if he never experienced them.

While we cannot pinpoint a particular traumatic event, we can hypothesize that Vincent's parents' pending divorce has triggered his unconscious implicit memory system with its stored bits of confused, fragmented early memories. His lower brain functions are now in charge of his emotional responses. Any current real or perceived mistake appears to trigger a sense of being completely unworthy. His brain has become a house divided against itself.

Complex Trauma and Emotional States

Emotional states are relatively stable, repeated patterns of specific activity, cognition, affect, and relatedness. Even without trauma and with healthy neural integration, experiencing negative emotion temporarily shifts our emotional state. For example, a student thinks he has done well on a test. When the paper is returned, he finds that the grade is much lower than anticipated. In response to the lower grade, the student feels a little down but is able to continue to engage normally with friends and with class work. Though the grade initially stimulates troublesome thoughts, he can also turn his thoughts in a positive direction, even to what might help on the next test. For this student, there is no significant emotional disruption. He is not dysregulated, and there has been no sustained shift in his emotional state.

Now compare the same situation with a different kid. Imagine a student who is laughing and joking with friends in class. Her paper is returned, and when she sees the grade, suddenly everything changes. She is triggered. She becomes anxious, stops interacting with friends, can only think of the consequences of the grade, is unable to engage in completing current assignments and go on normally with the day. She feels the physiological sensations of emotion in her body. Her attention fills with negative thoughts, further triggering anxiety. The shift in her emotional state is both reflective of dysregulation and is itself dysregulating.

Regulated and Dysregulated Emotional States: When Punishment Does Not Work

It is valuable to remember that the regulated emotional state is "where traumatized kids spend most of their time" (Saxe, Ellis, & Kaplow, 2007, p. 53). In this state the kid is (1) relatively calm, (2) seems in control of his or her emotions, (3) is oriented to the environment and others, and (4) has continuity in his or her responses. When we speak of regulation of emotional states, we are referring to the process of learning to recognize emotional shifts and to use cognition to calm and/or direct emotional responses and reactions.

"The dysregulation of emotional states is a defining feature of child traumatic stress" (Saxe, Ellis, & Kaplow, 2007, p. 46). In a dysregulated emotional state, a kid's emotions become intense; his or her behavior becomes unpredictable; and his or her attention, affect, action, and relatedness shift together to a source of stress. There is a discontinuity in responses.

Adults often see a kid whose emotional state has just dramatically shifted into survival-in-the-moment as simply acting out. Adults might attempt to get a kid to behave by punishing him or her or threatening punishment. Punishment and threats of punishment do not work with these kids at these times. To use punishment as a corrective experience requires a capacity to integrate cognition and relatedness, and to regulate emotion when faced with a stressor. To be dysregulated is a neurological problem that has behavioral consequence. In order to effectively respond, interventions have to take this into account. The same is true of attempting to use cognitive behavioral techniques for anger management when the actual problem is emotional dysregulation. Valuable tools for re-regulating, such as counting to 10, taking deep breaths, or considering options, can be very effective if the student is frustrated or irritated (Levine & Kline, 2007). The same tools will not be effective once the metaphoric bathtub is overflowing. Traumatized kids can be taught to effectively use these tools once they are able to make use of their own early somatic signals of dysregulation and to allow a wedge of cognition to help them calm (Saxe, Ellis, & Kaplow, 2007).

The good news is that kids' brains are still developing and major growth will continue into their mid-twenties. Neuroscience tells us that children's day-to-day experience sculpts their brains during this period of growth. Of significance here is the finding that teaching kids how to calm down when they are upset seems to strengthen their brain's circuits for managing distress long term (Lantieri, 2008). The foundation of the SSR model is the calming relationship developed between the counselor and the kid. We will explore this in detail in Chapter 3.

In Summary

- The brain is organized to respond to threats to survival through rapid action followed by cognitive assessment.

- Complex trauma creates survival-in-the-moment circuitry in the brain that overrides normal cognitive functioning.

- A chronically activated amygdala overwhelms the hippocampus's capacity for downregulation and the ability to return to calm following a real or perceived threat.

- Children are particularly vulnerable to the impact of chronic stress in their environment.

- Complex trauma interferes with the brain's survival circuitry and memory. The implicit memory system, and fear and stress circuitry evoke threats from the past as if they were happening now.

- Dysregulated arousal leads to escalating emotion.

- Trauma interferes with children being able to use their emotions to guide their actions.

- Complex trauma disrupts connections between brain centers, impairing healthy neural integration and whole brain functioning.

- An emotional state is a relatively stable, repeated pattern of specific activity, cognition, affect, and relatedness.

- Students with complex trauma experience dramatic shifts in emotional state, affecting their awareness, affect, action, and relatedness.

- Cognitive behavioral techniques alone are not effective when a student is physiologically and emotionally dysregulated.

3 Building an Alliance for Change

> The roots of resilience and the capacity to withstand
> emotionally aversive situations … are to be found in the
> sense of being understood by and existing in the heart
> of a loving, attuned, and self-possessed other.
>
> Fosha, *The Transforming Power of Affect*

In a 2007 workshop, Bessel van der Kolk, pioneer in the field of trauma, told a story of a friend's 5-year-old son. The young boy's school was across the street from the World Trade Center. He had seen the first plane go into the tower on September 11, 2001. He had seen the flames and the smoke. He had seen the towers go down. He also had seen people leaping out of windows many stories above the ground. Some weeks after the tragedy, Dr. van der Kolk was visiting the family and saw a drawing the young boy had created. In the drawing, figures were falling from a tower. At the bottom of the drawing there were some undefined forms. When he was asked what they were, the boy said in a calm, matter-of-fact manner that they were trampolines. He further explained that the trampolines were placed there to catch the people who had jumped out of the windows.

Dr. van der Kolk did not detail how the boy's parents had responded to their son in the days since the traumatic events he had witnessed. Yet, from the description of this drawing, we find evidence of resilience in the image of the trampoline—a creative and hopeful symbol of resolution in which the world became safe again. Those upon whom the boy depended could be trusted to supply what was needed. The trampolines were placed in just the right place where the people who were falling could be caught. According to D. W. Winnicott, British pediatrician and child analyst, the deepest insecurity of children is the fear of falling through space and not being caught (Winnicott, Shepherd, & Davis, 1989). In this boy's drawing, we see him imagining a powerful way to resolve the frightening feelings stirred within him as he witnessed the tragic events. Somewhere within him he was also able to draw upon basic trust. The term *basic trust* refers to the psychological stage of development in which, under good enough conditions, children internalize the sense that important others will provide them with reliability, support, and protection (Erickson, 1950). We can speculate that the child in van der Kolk's story had internalized this sense of basic trust through his relationships with his attachment figures, making it possible for them to help him process the arousal and emotion created by such traumatic events.

Calming Intervention and Self-Regulation

The quality of the client–counselor relationship as perceived by the client is one of the best predictors of counseling success (Bedi, Davis, & Williams, 2005; Martin, Garske, & Davis, 2000). The strategies for self-regulation (SSR) model is founded on the relationships we develop with students and, in turn, the relationships they develop with others.

While the SSR model is designed as a brief counseling model, we make use of compelling interdisciplinary research suggesting that attachment patterns have the potential for change as relationships change. Although a student may not have had the opportunity in his or her home environment to develop secure attachment, we intentionally offer a relationship based on what is known about the interaction of secure attachment and self-regulation. We offer a positive, reliable source of calming connection, a *corrective relational experience* (Ogden, Minton, & Pain, 2006; Rutan & Stone, 2001). The intention is to enhance a student's capacity for holding a positive, calming, internal sense of another when his or her developmental history with relationships has been less than optimal.

In our effort to offer a corrective relational experience, we work toward what Fosha (2007) calls an *attachment stance*—a working therapeutic or helping alliance characterized by calm, reliable, emotionally responsive interaction. This kind of relationship improves the capacity for self-regulation (Siegel, 2003). In an attachment stance, the mental health professional (MHP) is playing the usual role, only with an intentional shift in focus from caring to calming.

Essential Elements of SSR Corrective Relational Experience

The first and most essential intervention to help kids learn to self-regulate is to find a calm place within ourselves from which to interact with them. Our self-regulation is the beginning point of the SSR model. This requires us to be self-reflective; to notice our own level of arousal and emotional state; and to observe our thoughts, actions, and our impact on others. Fosha (2003) refers to evidence suggesting that just one relationship with an individual who has a well-developed capacity for self-reflection can enhance resilience in a child. "Trauma can be transformed and its effects neutralized or counteracted" (Fosha, 2003, p. 223). Beginning with our initial contact, we work to establish a helping alliance students can trust: one in which they experience us as safe, strong, calm, and knowing what we do (Fosha, 2007; Ogden, Minton, & Pain, 2006; van der Kolk, 2007).

"The quality of earliest interpersonal relationships sculpt the brain's survival circuits to make the child more or less able to regulate emotion when faced with stress" (Saxe, Ellis, & Kaplow, 2007, p. 44). The attachment and interpersonal neurobiology literature offer us valuable information regarding the impact of early relational experience on self-regulation. In this chapter, we highlight this literature and its useful implications for successful intervention. The following are basic elements to be considered when building an alliance for change with kids with complex trauma.

- Basic trust and containment
- Interactive affect regulation
- Relational attunement
- Responsive communication, reflective dialogue, and interactive repair
- Improving relationships with others
- Recognizing difficulty and celebrating small successes

Basic Trust and Containment

Early in life, kids develop what Bowlby (1969) refers to as an inner working model of self in relation to others. These cognitive and emotional representations are normally outside of conscious awareness and include basic trust or mistrust, a sense of how safe the world is, and whether others are trustworthy (Kinsler, Courtois, & Frankel, 2009). A significant role in the development of basic trust is the quality of *good enough* assistance by caregivers in modulating arousal and emotion. As the term *good enough* implies, good enough caregivers are not perfect, but what they offer is good enough calming, reliability, and responsiveness. This quality of interaction between caregivers and children supports the growth of healthy neural connections between emotion and calming.

Containment refers to an environment that reflects the competency of the caregivers and offers a reliable presence. Offering safety in a student's relationship with us is our most basic and essential task. We provide containment by creating an interpersonal environment that allows a child to feel safe, seen, and understood. At the same time, we remain calm and effective in our efforts to intervene to improve a child's self-regulation.

Maintaining a consistent schedule with the student is a good place to start. To the extent possible, we meet in the same place at the same time and provide an environment capable of responding to intensity and vulnerability. Our effort to offer reliability to our students also focuses on following through with our agreements with them, and while we will never be perfect, our goal is to plan sessions well enough to present a calm, competent consistency.

Alex is 9 years old, and his older sister, Carson, is 12; both children score in the superior range on intelligence tests. Their parents are both respected professionals and offer their children many opportunities. An outside observer would not see this family as a problem in any way. However, Alex is a chronic underachiever who has trouble staying on task and can be mildly disruptive by incessant talking in class. His parents and school have tried numerous disciplinary approaches with little success. Carson, on the other hand, is a high achiever and a strict rule follower. Her only signs of stress are her distress when others do not follow rules and her voice, which has a noticeable constricted quality.

In private, and beginning with Carson's birth, the parents' relationship has been extremely problematic, with chronic arguments and intermittent emotionally explosive fights, often in the middle of the night. The parents do not actively involve either child in their battles, and there is no physical violence in this family.

At the beginning of the new school year, Alex's teachers suggested a referral to the counselor. His parents, who were as confused by his problems as his teachers, agreed. After an assessment using the SSR model, the counselor suggested that Alex's difficulties were at least in part unexplainably due to emotional dysregulation. She focused her attention on developing a calming, reliable relationship with Alex; he had an immediate positive response to her efforts. Accepting the interactive regulation she offered, he was also able to make use of the somatic skill development she has worked on with him. His behavior in class and his grades have dramatically improved.

Interactive Affect Regulation

Interactive affect regulation is the emotional regulatory activity of one person's nervous system affecting the emotional regulatory activity of another's. The arousal, thoughts, emotions, and actions of one individual can affect the internal regulation of another (Fosha, 2003). It is hypothesized that brain cells called *mirror neurons* precisely reflect and anticipate the neural activation patterns of another brain and are involved in interactive affect regulation. Mirror neurons are at least in part responsible for the significant impact of the caregiver on the child (Rothschild, 2006).

"Born with limited capacities for self-regulation, human infants are dependent on . . . the interactive affective regulation of their primary attachment figures to maintain their arousal within the *window of tolerance*" (Ogden, Minton, & Pain, 2006, p. 41). The term *window of tolerance* refers to the range of emotional and physiological activation a child can tolerate without becoming dysregulated, either by too much or too little arousal. Kids who have problems with self-regulation often come to counseling with a narrow window of tolerance and benefit from "borrowing" our more regulated nervous systems to assist them in increasing their tolerance for a wider range of arousal and emotion. As a responsible adult in a kid's life, our interaction potentially "enables the child's brain to regulate itself in increasingly sophisticated ways" and encourages the capacity to self-organize (Siegel, 2003, p. 33). Effective interactive affect regulation requires face-to-face interaction between us and the student (Tatkin, 2009). The recognition of the powerful regulatory potential of interactive affect regulation underlies our intentional efforts to provide a calming presence as we assist students in developing more adaptive regulatory capacities (Ogden, Minton, & Pain, 2006; Siegel, 2003).

Interactive affect regulation can have an impact between adults and kids, as well as between kids and other kids, and between adults and other adults. Kids who are emotionally and behaviorally dysregulated can create chaos and unconsciously induce everyone around them to experience the same emotional dysregulation. To assist students and others who work with them, at times we have to re-regulate, or calm ourselves, in order to offer positive interactive affect regulation. Through our self-regulation, we can provide calming experiences, modulating the arousal of those around us (van der Kolk, 2007).

How Calm Creates Calm

Oxytocin is a biochemical critical to human life. It is specifically critical for healthy attachment. It is naturally released by the brain during safe, caring interpersonal contact and causes a sense of calmness (Saxe, Ellis, & Kaplow, 2003). Saxe and his colleagues summarize research done at the National Institute of Mental Health in which images of participants' amygdalae were taken while they were being shown frightening photos. The amygdalae were activated at the sight of the photos. When the same participants were given a dose of oxytocin and were shown the same frightening photos, the amygdala was no longer active, indicating that oxytocin calms by regulating the amygdala.

A regulated amygdala takes us out of the survival-in-the-moment circuitry and makes it possible for the higher cortical areas of the brain to be in charge. Again, the brain naturally releases oxytocin in the context of calm, safe, caring relationships. Staying calm in the face of traumatic events with kids who are traumatized clearly makes a significant difference in trauma intervention.

The results of a 2008 UCLA study looking at the impact of friendships between women on their stress levels found oxytocin to be an important ingredient in the physiological value of these friendships. When women in the study were under stress and actively engaged in friendships with other women, there was an increase in their oxytocin levels with a subsequent calming effect. Findings support the idea that, in addition to fight, flight, or freeze, women's brains have another possible response to stress, defined by researchers as *tend and befriend* (Taylor et al., 2008).

Relational Attunement

The term *relational attunement* refers to the way in which a caregiver observes a child and attentively responds to his or her signals of comfort and distress. Relational attunement drives the developmental process toward secure attachment and self-regulation. A significant proportion of our interaction with kids is through right brain–to–right brain communication (Schore, 2003). Right brain communication is primarily nonverbal communication and includes facial expression, tone and volume of voice, body posture, movement, and the instant appraisal of another's facial expression. The brain's right hemisphere has more reciprocal connections with the emotional response system than the left area of the brain. The right hemisphere is dominant in the human stress response and holds autobiographical memory. We communicate right brain–to–right brain through physical and emotional attunement, gaze sharing, face-to-face contact, entrained vocal rhythms, and play. This kind of communication can be used to help a child maintain positive emotions, rapidly metabolize negative affects when they occur, and maximize positive emotional states (Fosha, 2007; Ogden, Minton, & Pain, 2006).

We recently observed Lisa, a young mother, with her baby, Sean, at a large social gathering. Sean was extremely distressed, and Lisa's presence was required in the formalities of the evening. She was desperate to calm Sean. Despite her best efforts, he continued to scream. A wise relative went into the kitchen and found a smiling older woman who gladly agreed to help. Within a minute or two of Lisa entrusting this "grandmother" with Sean, he was quiet and soon asleep. What we observed was a calm caregiver offering (1) containment through her own regulated arousal and her sense of knowing what to do and (2) right brain–to–right brain communication of relational attunement through her soft smile, eye contact, and infinitely slow, gentle movement with Sean.

In the previous example, we see the direct, immediate benefit of a caregiver engaging even a very young child through face-to-face contact. From birth, children interact with caregivers through what is called the *social engagement system* (Ogden, Minton, & Pain, 2006). The social engagement system is innate and makes it possible for infants and young children to learn to communicate their needs and to respond to others. This essential system is activated and shaped by relational attunement. Through research in interpersonal neurobiology, we know that as the caregiver learns the child's signals and responds, neural connections are created. With good enough caretaking, the child becomes increasingly able to purposefully signal his or her needs and respond to others (Siegel, 1999; Schore, 1994).

As the caregiver attunes to the child's signals and the child has increasing ability to signal, the caregiver can provide a responsive amount of calming and/or stimulation. This contingent interaction increases the child's ability to tolerate differing levels of emotional and physiological activation: The child internalizes the positive expectation "help is coming." Neural circuitry is created, increasing the child's ability to transition from distress to a state of calmness, a sign of developing healthy neural integration. (Neural circuits are like paths. Paths taken frequently between one place and another become the brain's natural choice.) We aim for good enough relational attunement with the awareness that we will make mistakes (Ogden, Minton, & Pain, 2006).

Over time and with successes, these contingent interactions, along with interactive affect regulation, lead to a widened window of tolerance and a competent social engagement system (Ogden, Minton, & Pain, 2006). The child develops a sense that he or she can predictably expect a response to his or her expressions of need, making it possible to tolerate a lack of immediate response and increasing the ability to self-soothe. The widened window of tolerance, the capacity to self-soothe, and the internalized secure sense of a responsive, available caregiver lead to good enough self-regulation. With good enough self-regulation comes the ability to postpone immediate responses. The ability to postpone responses is critical. It allows a child to slow down and think about alternative responses, engaging executive functioning (Saxe, Ellis, & Kaplow, 2007).

Interactive Regulation

Kids with complex trauma more often than not have compromised social engagement systems and subsequent difficulty with making use of relationships. In building an alliance for change, we focus on improving the student's capacity to utilize us for *interactive regulation*. *Interactive regulation* is the ability to self-regulate using help from another person. Some students will need extra time and intention to develop the ability to accept help to self-regulate, continually turning away our efforts to assist them. On the other hand, another group of students will turn continually to others for help. These students need our extra time and intention to learn more productive ways to self-regulate without help from others. This group of students tends to be more emotionally expressive, demanding our attention. Our observations and relational attunement help us determine the best interventions with any particular student.

Traumatic Transference

A student's initial response to us may be distrust. Kinsler, Courtois, and Frankel (2009) talk about *traumatic transference* occurring when the student, expecting that the counselor will be yet another abuser, is vigilant to that likelihood. When counselors do not behave in abusive, exploitive, or retaliatory ways, they provide a different model for relationships in which abuse is not the inevitable outcome. In an effort to offer a corrective relational experience, we measure out our verbal and nonverbal interactions in response to our perception of the student's level of trust and tolerance for connection. Kids do not always make any of this easy, but we have "a responsibility to serve as a role model, co-regulator, and guide by using self-regulation skills not only to 'talk the talk' but also to 'walk the walk'" (Ford & Cloitre, 2009, p. 78).

Responsive Communication, Reflective Dialogue, and Interactive Repair

Responsive communication, reflective dialogue, and interactive repair are three useful elements of verbal and nonverbal communication that further operationalize a relationally attuned attachment stance and a corrective relational experience (Fosha, 2003; Siegel, 2003). *Responsive communication*, both verbal and nonverbal, intentionally sends the message to the student that he or she is seen and that his or her needs are being taken into account. This kind of communication encourages the sensation of "feeling felt." The student experiences this through eye contact, facial expression, tone of voice, physical gestures, and the timing and intensity of response. *Signals of care*, a term used by Saxe and his colleagues (2007) fits into the category of responsive communication. Usually nonverbal, signals of care express warmth, empathy, and positive regard and are as simple as a smile, a gesture indicating support, or a wink at the right moment.

Responsive communication offers an empathic connection and respects the need for psychological distance when necessary. Offering students this kind of communication calls on our capacity for considering the student's subjective experience in the moment. A student's feelings are acknowledged, soothed, and not contradicted. When we are able to do this, over time students can learn to identify their own emotional experience and to identify with themselves. This process gives them the opportunity to express their needs and in so doing, to self-soothe.

The following example illustrates a situation where responsive communication could be used. A student comes into a counseling session with a story of a classroom experience in which he or she had a melt down. As the MHP, we may well have already heard about this event from the teacher's perspective. We could easily feel disappointed that the student did not use the skills we have been working on together. Our response might well be to skip listening and immediately focus on skill development. However, our relationship with a student in a situation like this will benefit from holding the goal of responsive communication. When we can calm ourselves first, it is easier to smile, make good eye contact, and listen to the student's version of events before moving to skill development.

Reflective dialogue is interaction and conversation about thoughts, feelings, sensations, perceptions, memories, attitudes, beliefs, and intentions. Reflective dialogue is the foundation for the development of *mindsight*, or self-reflection: the capacity to perceive our own subjective experience and that of others. We cannot overemphasize the value of helping kids develop the ability to be self-reflective in order to improve their ability to self-regulate (Ford & Cloitre, 2009). When we engage in reflective dialogue with kids, we encourage sharing both positive and negative emotions. This increases the awareness that emotions can be tolerated internally and provides an opportunity for a kid to deepen his or her capacity for self-observation and self-understanding. Effective reflective dialogue with students is highly dependent on our own capacity for self-reflection and our ability to lend a hand in the management of high stress. Continuing with the example scenario, once we have listened to the student's experience, we could engage in conversation to encourage self-reflection. Continuing and using our own calm to calm, we could invite the student to talk about his or her feelings and to wonder with us about the experience of the others involved.

Our capacity for self-reflection and for reflective dialogue can be called on unexpectedly. While we are observing kids, they are observing us as well. They will see our bias and our judgments whether we want them to or not. At our best, we can acknowledge to ourselves what these are and listen to students' reactions to what they experience with us. In schools, staff members are often confronted with significant cultural differences between themselves and students. Ford and Courtois (2009) offer an innovative and valuable approach to cultural differences, suggesting that we not hide from them but rather acknowledge the existence of these differences as they occur, engaging in reflective dialogue. This model is useful in any situation in which students have specific reactions to us.

Interactive repair refers to the action taken following a disruption to interpersonal connection. In these instances, we acknowledge the disruption and make an effort to move forward and reconnect. Working with kids with complex trauma, there are plenty of opportunities for interactive repair. Fortunately, each time we take the time to repair it, we increase the student's window of tolerance for arousal and emotion by encouraging an increased sense of security in the relationship (Fosha, 2007; Ogden, Minton, & Pain, 2006). The message of repair is essential: There will be disruptions, but our relationship will continue. Effective interactive repair depends on our ability to be mindful, observing, and regulating of our own emotions.

In the scenario where the student reported a meltdown, an MPH may be tempted to take the teacher's side. When there is this kind of disruption and the student expresses disappointment with us either verbally or nonverbally, there is the opportunity for interactive repair. We repair by doing the following:

- Staying calm and being nondefensive regarding the student's perception
- Acknowledging the student's sense of the disruption in our connection
- Engaging in a dialogue regarding what the student needs in order for us to move forward together

When a student experiences a disruption, often he or she will not say anything, but there will be a change in the student's arousal and/or emotional state. In these cases, it is particularly important and useful to acknowledge the change and inquire about the student's experience. Even if the student cannot identify or acknowledge any change, we are sending the message that we are paying attention. Addressing disruption in the counseling relationship encourages the development of the student's social engagement system, specifically improving the ability to express needs. The inability to express needs is a major source of dysregulation.

Improving Relationships With Others— Being in a Group

We recommend group counseling as an essential part of helping kids improve their ability to self-regulate. As group leaders, we continue from the starting point of our own self-regulation and focus on providing a corrective relational experience for all group members. We offer the same calming, attuned relationship we have worked toward in our individual work.

Moving into a group will make the strengths and weaknesses of a kid's social engagement system and window of tolerance quickly apparent. Being a part of a group provides a student with situations that resemble those in the classroom. Offering members interactive affect regulation, relational attunement, and interactive regulation, as needed, in difficult interactions in the group will carry over to improved self-regulation in the classroom.

The following list of benefits from being in a group are based on a number of sources, including Glading (2003), Malekoff (2004), Rutan and Stone (2001), Tollison and Synatschk (2007), and Yalom and Leszcz (2005). This list focuses on the benefits of group counseling for kids who need help with self-regulation.

Benefits of Group Counseling

The professional literature suggests that group counseling is helpful to students (Whiston & Sexton, 1998), and that group counseling offers many benefits in the school setting.

In order to promote and organize groups effectively, we have to be sold on their unique benefits (Malekoff, 2004).

- In a group, we have the opportunity to experience students in an active relationship with us and with their peers simultaneously. We can see the kinds of situations that stress a kid's ability to self-regulate and can offer contingent assistance in the form of coaching and practicing different responses.
- Being in a group provides the opportunity to have to share attention, to feel disappointed, to become angered, to get excited, and/or to celebrate.
- Students have the opportunity to make mistakes and to learn from them with help from us and other group members.
- In a group, students learn others share their difficulties. This helps them learn empathy for themselves as well as for others.
- Problems similar to the ones they have in their classrooms occur in the group. In the group, we offer a calming relationship and cultivate a mindsight culture. We can offer practice at do-overs: opportunities to repeat and improve actions and/or exchanges. In real time, we are able to interrupt and/or extend experiences, offering opportunities to slow response times and to cultivate the use of a wedge of cognition.
- We can observe and support progress, noticing when strengths are demonstrated.
- Specific to corrective relational experience, group work gives students the experience of a secure connection, extending their relationship with us to other group members.

Jessica is in the first grade and is a member of an SSR counseling group. All the members of the group were referred because of their difficulty with self-regulation. Jessica has been an additional concern to school staff because of her apparent lack of concern when she is unkind to other students. The counselor has focused her attention on developing a relationship with Jessica by encouraging Jessica to drop by the office on her way to her classroom each morning. In group interactions, the counselor watches for specific opportunities to ask Jessica how she thinks another member might be feeling. In this way, the counselor can help Jessica become more empathic toward others.

When Group Is Not Recommended

There are specific reasons why some kids should not go into a group, and we define these reasons in Chapter 6. When group is not a good option, the SSR model suggests more individual sessions with focused attention on a corrective relational experience and practicing skills. Activities such as role playing can provide practice for improving interaction in other relationships.

Recognizing the Difficulty and Celebrating the Successes

When we are aware that our neurobiology is interacting with the neurobiology of others, providing a calm, responsive, confident stance only makes sense. The kind of calm we want to cultivate in kids comes from our own regulated arousal. Remaining calm does not require us to be disconnected from our natural responses to difficult events and/or kids. It does require that we work to re-regulate as needed and be self-reflective—mindful of what we want to express and what we do not want to express.

Staying calm and offering relational attunement will pay off ultimately, but be prepared for resistance in the beginning. As mentioned previously, initially the promise of closeness and relational attunement may elicit negative reactions. Survival circuitry may well be evoked, and this circuitry might include defending against close relationships with adults (Ogden, Minton, & Pain, 2006; van der Kolk, 2006). Some subtle interpersonal signals can lead to emotional regulation, while others can lead to dysregulation (Saxe, Ellis, & Kaplow, 2007). You certainly cannot always predict what you will be triggering. The good news here is that we build resilience in our relationships with students through our mistakes and through our efforts to mend the disruption with interactive repair.

With kids who have self-regulation difficulties, our focus naturally goes to the times when they are dysregulated and creating problems for themselves and others. It is extremely important to also notice and celebrate successes with them and with ourselves as we work together. In Chapter 5 we will discuss specifically how to use compliments to empower kids and increase their awareness of what they are doing to contribute to their own solution. A significant aspect of building an alliance for change is remembering the value of the real or virtual pat on the back. It is beneficial when kids do not succeed, to place the focus on the reality that they are working to learn to self-regulate and to find what there is to be learned from this particular moment of difficulty.

In Chapter 4, we describe skills that help kids use somatic awareness to improve their self-regulation. Learning to use these skills ourselves has been useful both personally and professionally. We encourage you to learn and use the somatic awareness skills you will be teaching kids and to actively participate in the training experience we offer through the exercises in Chapter 4.

In Summary

✧ Self-regulation develops through interaction with primary caregivers. We can make use of the basic elements that support the development of self-regulation as we interact with students.

✧ Our own self-regulation is the most basic foundation in helping kids learn to self-regulate.

✧ Through interactive affect regulation, our ability to be calm has a calming effect on others.

✧ We encourage students' basic trust by providing safety through containment.

✧ Relational attunement is primarily conveyed through right brain–to–right brain communications.

✧ Students' ability to self-regulate is facilitated through improving their social engagement system and their window of tolerance.

✧ In offering a relationally attuned attachment stance and a corrective relational experience, we focus on responsive communication, reflective dialogue, and interactive repair.

✧ Group work offers an opportunity for students to practice self-regulation in the moment and extends a healthy relationship to others.

✧ Initially, our offers of connection may well meet with resistance.

✧ We should celebrate successes, small or large.

4 Facilitating Healthy Neural Integration

> Perhaps integrative capacity is at the heart of mental health.
>
> Siegel, "An Interpersonal Neurobiology of Psychotherapy"

Our focus is helping kids learn to calm themselves so they are able to access the high road circuitry. This makes it possible for them to choose adaptive behavior responses when stressed. In the three previous chapters we examined the problematic outcome of deficits in neural integration and the lack of communication between brain centers. Chapter 4 addresses this source of dysregulation by introducing a set of skills to help students make the connection between their somatic experience—including emotional responses—and their actions.

A colleague shared a moment she experienced recently with a 10-year-old with whom she was using a somatic counseling approach. We will call this student Charlie. Charlie had a pattern of explosive temper tantrums, and on this particular day, he was in an extremely dysregulated emotional state. As they began to work, the counselor asked Charlie what would help him re-regulate. He stated with authority, "It's not going to be talking about it!"

Dysregulation disconnects a child from his or her words. The impact of complex trauma lives underneath and between words, and sometimes where there are no words. Charlie's response speaks to the reality that, more often than not, our attempt to use words to help a kid re-regulate increases, rather than decreases, arousal.

Our somatic experiences are affected by our emotions, the *sensorimotor activity* in our body, and the cognitive processing of our emotional and sensorimotor experience. *Sensorimotor activity* refers to body sensation, physiological arousal, and motor functioning (Ogden, Minton, & Pain, 2006). The consensus from recent research in trauma treatment is that to improve capacity for self-regulation, somatic experience is the vehicle through which traumatized individuals can be helped by teaching them to carefully observe "the ebb and flow of internal experience" (van der Kolk, 2006, p. 277). According to Ford and Cloitre (2009), the common therapeutic goal for all of the many complex forms of somatic dysregulation is to enable children (and caregivers) to recognize, label, and use input from their bodies as a guide to managing their emotions. In this way, they draw on their cognitive competencies and make purposeful, consequence-sensitive behavioral choices that help them to feel and be healthy.

The skills taught in the SSR model encourage the interruption of patterns of emotional and behavioral dysregulation and make a wedge of cognition possible, opening the door to increased executive functioning. Again, executive functioning refers to adaptive decision making and includes planning for the future, anticipating the consequences of actions, and inhibiting inappropriate responses. Even at 5 years of age, most kids are developing these functions. For kids with complex trauma, hyperarousal overwhelms executive functioning. In these situations, the development of adaptive decision making is significantly compromised (van der Kolk, 2006).

We teach kids to use their own somatic signals of heightened arousal to figure out when to stop and think. Each time they are able to identify these signals, they are connecting brain centers, facilitating neural integration, and strengthening a sense of self (Ford & Cloitre, 2009; Levine & Kline, 2007; Ogden, Minton, & Pain, 2006; Saxe, Ellis, & Kaplow, 2007; van der Kolk, 2006).

The elementary counselor, Kathy Smith, received a distress call from a second-grade teacher regarding a student named Jonah, who was transferred into her class mid-year. There were minimal school records for him, and in a conference, his mother seemed surprised to hear about a problem. The problem the teacher was experiencing was Jonah's serious difficulty staying in his seat for more than 5 minutes without jumping up and moving away from his desk. The behavior was disruptive to his work and to the work of those around him. Listening to the teacher's description of the problem and gathering other assessment data, Ms. Smith felt confident that using the SSR model would be helpful to Jonah.

An Exercise in Somatic Experience

There is an old saying, "You can no more teach what you haven't learned than you can come back from where you haven't been." In this chapter, we offer exercises to use the SSR somatic skills for our self-regulation. We want to promote beginning the day in a calm state and to calm and re-regulate as necessary during the day. Take a few moments now to experience using somatic awareness.

EXERCISE

First, if you are not sitting down, do so. Is your back resting against the back of the chair? Feel your feet firmly planted on the ground; place particular attention on the sensation of your heels touching the floor, noticing how that feels. Check your posture. Are your shoulders raised or fallen? Do you notice any little unexplained internal physical feelings (tension, pain, relaxation, tingling, warmth, etc.)? What is your skin temperature (cool, warm, hot, cold)? By checking in with yourself and your body, you have allowed yourself to become more aware of your somatic experience in the moment.

Let's go a step further and find the somatic experience of emotion. Take a breath and remember a time when you felt safe and happy. Where were you? What was happening? Were you alone, with one person, or with a number of people? What were you wearing? Remember as much as you can from that time with as much detail as you can. Now return to an awareness of your body. Do you notice any changes? Are you more relaxed? Is there less tension in your muscles? Are you smiling? Enjoy this moment and just notice how it feels in your body.

Take a slow breath and remember the last time you were angry with someone. What happened and with whom were you angry? What did you say, or think? As you remember being angry, notice any physical feelings (tension, heat in your belly, heart rate, etc.). Do you notice any leftover angry thoughts from that experience? Again, drop your attention down into your body; observe the sensations. What happens to them? Usually, sensations begin to move and change when we observe them. Can you feel any differences? Take another slow breath.

Now choose a memory of an event that was only somewhat disturbing to you, but when you felt fearful. As you remember the time and place of this event, notice what is happening in your body. Do you notice your heart rate going up? Is there a feeling of wanting to physically pull back or move away? Are you breathing differently? Just notice what you are feeling in your body separate from thoughts. Notice any sensations, and notice what happens when you observe them.

Take a long, slow breath. Then slowly and completely allow yourself to return to the memory of being happy and safe. Notice what you feel in your body now. As you are ready, come back into the here and now.

The Basic Somatic Strategies

The previous exercise included the use of the three essential SSR skills: *grounding, mindful awareness,* and *tracking sensation. Grounding* is a technique and a practice that helps us to connect or re-connect with our physical body. It helps our body connect to our physical surroundings and to the ground beneath us. *Mindful awareness* is the experience of a neutral mind or wise mind: the compassionate, nonjudgmental observation of what is arising in the moment in our environment and within ourselves. *Tracking sensation* refers to a range of interventions using somatic experience, all intended to increase our awareness of physical feelings and to use them as signals to alert the need to stop and think.

In the somatic experience exercise, we asked you first to experience the connection of your body to the ground beneath you, and then to become a witness to your experience through the use of a *body scan.* We then asked you to identify sensations as distinct from emotional thoughts and to watch sensations change. This distinction between sensation and emotion is a significant factor in the use of somatic awareness as an intervention (Ogden, Minton, & Pain, 2006). A *body scan* is a simple technique we can use to check in with our physical status—going from head to toe and noticing places of relaxation and/or tension.

We asked you to leave a memory of feeling fearful and return to a memory of a time when you felt happy and safe. When we did that we were asking you to use *somatic memory* as a resource to assist with shifting from one emotional state to another. *Somatic memory* is a body memory of sensations associated with certain times and events. In teaching the use of somatic memory, we always begin with a positive experience. A positive somatic memory is a valuable tool for calming.

The ability to recognize internal experience facilitates self-regulation (Saxe, Ellis, & Kaplow, 2007). The three SSR skills, grounding, mindful awareness, and tracking sensation, facilitate a process for students that leads to (1) an improved ability to focus, (2) an increased awareness of somatic signals of regulation and dysregulation, (3) an understanding that internal experience changes when it is simply observed, and (4) an experience of calming themselves. Together, improvement in these abilities leads to an increased ability for self-regulation and an engagement of executive functioning.

Relational Attunement in Teaching Somatic Strategies

Although the SRS model focuses on the student's physical experience, the first step is always to stimulate social engagement. We observe and respect what the child or adolescent can take in from us, using that to gauge what we offer. We pay special attention to communicate our interest and engagement through eye contact, tone of voice, and posture (Ogden, Minton, & Pain, 2006).

Touch is not necessary for this work, but rituals that include shaking hands to begin and end meetings or agreements for holding hands at important moments can be extremely valuable. Depending on the kid, teaching him or her to use touch can be useful. For example, asking a student to place his or her hands over the heart area of his or her chest can help to get in touch with positive feelings. To assist a student with containing intensive negative emotion, the act of pressing the fist of one hand into the palm of the other can offer help with bringing his arousal back into his window of tolerance. Another containment exercise is to ask the student to be seated; to place his hands on the inside of the opposite knees (right hand left knee, left hand right knee); then to press out with his hands and in with his knees; and to continue this until his arousal is within his window of tolerance (Ogden, 2010).

John is a counselor in a high school where an athletic team was involved in a tragic bus accident. A number of members of the football team were seriously injured, and one died. John has been trained in the SSR counseling approach to trauma. In the hours after hearing the details of the accident, and before the beginning of school the next day, he made the time to connect to his own somatic and emotional experience of loss. He first took a few moments to breathe deeply to calm and de-activate the hyper-arousal he was experiencing. He created the space to mindfully track the physical sensations in his body, and he allowed the tears of grief to come. When John met with the faculty to present his plan for helping them and the students, he was still processing the shocking loss himself, but he was calm and grounded.

How We Take the Stress Home

Emotions are energy. An individual in the vicinity can literally experience the emotion being experienced by another individual. In Chapter 3 we discussed the positive potential impact that our regulated nervous system can have on our students. Again, researchers are investigating an explanation for this through the concept of mirror neurons: the brain cells that reflect the activity of another's brain cells (Rothschild, 2006). Unaware, this activity can have a negative effect on us as helpers when we are in the midst of another's dysregulation. We are not just thinking about the experience of those we help, we can experience this shared emotion as empathy in our mind–body. The way we listen can affect us physically. Rothschild refers to this as *somatic empathy*.

According to Daniel Stern (2002), "One of the real questions is not, 'How does this happen?' We're beginning to have a really good idea. The real question is 'How do we stop it from happening?'" And you might ask, why would we want to stop it? After all, being empathic is the business of helpers. Indeed, this is true, but it does not mean we need to take the emotions of those with whom we work into our own bodies, quite literally carrying the burdens of their lives on our shoulders and in our hearts. This kind of empathy is a double-edged sword and can lead to what has been called *compassion fatigue*. This mind–body state is characterized by feelings of incompetence, as well as difficulty maintaining a level of emotional detachment needed to work with students who are emotionally and behaviorally dysregulated. Without attention to our self-care, we can also experience symptoms commonly seen in traumatized children: hyperarousal, nightmares, anxiety, and depression.

Self-Care Through Increased Awareness

When we are aware that emotion is energy and accept that we can internalize it, we can develop practices to use daily in our work to consciously not accept emotions that are not ours. Making a conscious decision not to do this is a good starting point for self-care. We develop daily practices, such as always starting the workday with grounding. You can use your body awareness to *gauge* your level of arousal, that is, to inform yourself how strongly you are identifying with students' emotional states throughout the day. (To *gauge* in this context means to notice your physical and emotional arousal level.) Dysregulated arousal interferes with our ability to think clearly. Rothschild (2006) suggests for self-care we not emotionally identify with stories or picture them in our minds. She suggests when confronted with a story of traumatic events, we remind ourselves through our internal dialogue that "this has happened to this kid and not to me, and I am here to help him or her." We are more helpful when we are energized and calm. We are less helpful if we are over-identified. Signs of hyperarousal signal that we are overidentified. In the following list, Rothschild (2006) describes some noticeable signs.

- Faster respiration
- Quicker heart rate
- Increased blood pressure
- Speedy internal feelings
- Dilated pupils
- Pale skin color
- Increased sweating

- Cold skin (could be clammy to touch)
- A decrease in digestion

Somatic awareness helps us to be more effective in our self-care. When we do regular check-ins with our body, we get to know the signs that indicate our arousal level is too high or too low. Observing what is going on in our body is the best gauge of how our day is affecting us (Rothschild, 2003). We are better able to make sense of our experience and make good choices for ourselves if we use somatic awareness. When you experience hyperarousal, stop and take a *calming break*. A *calming break* may be as simple as grounding by slowly taking three deep breaths or noticing if you feel tension or pain somewhere in your body. We can relax and re-regulate by simply bringing our awareness into the places of tension and/or pain and focusing relaxing breath into the area or areas.

Hypoarousal is another way our body can respond to stress. Checking in with your body, you may notice areas that would benefit from more muscle tone. The following technique for bringing more tone into your body is recommended by Brantbjerg (2007).

EXERCISE

In a sitting or standing position, bend your right knee and lift it as you are bending your left arm, raising it with your fist heading up. Then reverse this with your left knee and right arm and fist. (This does not have to be a big movement. Our muscles do not gain strength from being pressured to work too hard. Slow activation works best.) If you are standing and concerned about balance, use your free hand to balance yourself by holding onto something. We can also increase muscle tone by using our breath. Breathe more deeply and slightly increase your rate of respiration. Using your intention, bring more tone into muscles until you find a tension level that feels more energized.

Through increasing our somatic awareness, we access valuable interpersonal information that we can use both for self-care and for helping students. For example, a student enters your office and the calm state you were experiencing is immediately disrupted. You notice a tight feeling in your chest and a slight feeling of nausea. Once you take a breath and re-regulate, you can then use this somatic information in your interaction with the student. For example, you might consider whether there is something unusual happening for the student that day or wonder if this happens regularly. We might ask the student to check in and notice what sensations he or she is experiencing in the current moment. Depending on the details of the situation, this could be information we can use to better understand both the student and the responses he or she evokes in others.

In our work, we celebrate small victories and avoid self-criticism. Negative self-talk is destructive to a positive sense of self and makes us more vulnerable to chronic stress (Rothschild, 2006). We will decrease our level of stress by simply making a practice of paying attention to even small positive changes in ourselves and in those with whom we work and by interrupting self-criticism.

Calm Creates Calm

The most basic intervention is simply our own emotionally regulated state. Our calm creates calm in our interaction with both students and our colleagues. Whether we are sitting with one individual or a group, our calm emotional state has the potential for calming and re-regulating others. Learning to use grounding, mindful awareness, and tracking our own sensations makes it possible to remain in a calm state for more of our day.

Ford and Cloitre (2009) suggest that while working with a student, we repeatedly ask ourselves this question: "How can I communicate an understanding of this child's state of mind and body that will be meaningful and validating, while also moving him or her gradually toward greater integration, self-awareness, and self-control across all aspects of experiencing?" (p. 63). This particular internal dialogue is actually self-regulatory and parallels the internal activity we are teaching the student to use.

Grounding Practice

There is another old saying: "Keep your head on your shoulders and your feet on the ground." The practice of grounding is a reflection of that traditional wisdom. Grounding is the experience of using our mind to move into our body and to connect with our physical being—our somatic experience in the moment. Psychotherapist Yvonne Agazarian, and those who use her Systems Centered Therapy (SCT), start meetings by asking each participant to move into his or her somatic experience and his or her physical body's connection to the ground. A grounding practice is used in SCT with individuals and with small and large groups (Agazarian & Gant, 2000).

Ogden and her colleagues (2006) refer to grounding as a core somatic resource, giving a feeling of both physical and psychological solidity and stability. Grounding affords us a sense of self-support and integrity through the back, legs, and feet and their connection to the ground beneath us. Levine and Kline (2007) suggest that grounding gives a kid the feeling of the solid connection to the earth and facilitates being directly connected to his or her body's sensations. We make grounding practice the beginning point for our somatic work in the SSR model. Learning to ground makes the use of mindful awareness and learning to track sensations possible and more effective.

Grounding Practice for the MHP

You had a brief grounding experience in the somatic exercise when we asked you to notice the connection of your feet on the floor and your back against the chair. While grounding is not complicated and with practice will take you only seconds, experiencing this firm connection to the ground can be a challenge. We all too easily find ourselves drifting away into a proliferation of thoughts about the past or future. It is often difficult to stay in the present, to feel our feet on the ground, or even to notice that we have feet. But to be connected to our own bodies is crucial if we are to effectively care for others and ourselves. In mythological terms, the symbol of touching the earth represents gathering sensory resources, namely the strength and compassion to do this challenging work.

Remember, there is no right way to become grounded. For some, simply stopping to take a slow, deep breath and noticing our feet's connection to the floor will work. You will find your unique way, and once it is your regular practice, like all habits, it will become automatic. We recommend you include a grounding exercise at the beginning of each day and at any other time when you feel it would be beneficial. Being connected to our own body with "our head on our shoulders and our feet on the ground" makes the work of assisting others with self-regulation possible without bringing stress home. Developing our own practice brings a specific authenticity to the work of teaching students to ground. Grounding is a positive somatic experience and an intervention on its own.

Do the following two exercises while sitting, standing, or walking. The exercise of grounding is often accompanied by a deep sigh—the body's way of surrendering or letting go of tension patterns—stabilizing attention, and regulating arousal. Gaea Logan has coined the term *sensory stabilization* to describe a mind–body state that is characterized by deep relaxation, mindful awareness, *panoramic attention* or widened attention, and the sense of being calm and connected to our bodies (Homan, Logan, Meyer, & Tsetan, 2008). Grounding is basic to the possibility of being able to interact with students from this place.

EXERCISE

Begin by taking a few deep breaths. If you are seated, find a comfortable position. Gently notice the contact of your body: your buttocks, thighs, and lower back with the chair. Notice how the chair supports you. Bring your attention to your feet and your contact with the floor. Feel your heels, the balls of your feet, and your toes. Feel each toe and notice its contact with the floor. Notice how the sense of connection moves up your legs and into the core of your body.

If you are standing, find a comfortable stance and bring your attention to your feet. Notice your in breath and your out breath. Now, bringing your attention back to your sensory experience, pay particular attention to the connection between your heels and the ground. Feeling that firm connection with the ground, notice how that sense of connection moves up your legs and into the core of your body. Feel how your attention to your sensory experience deepens a sense of stabilization, a sense of being rooted and grounded.

If you are walking, simply shift your attention to your feet and slow your steps. Take a moment and bring attention to your sensory experience. Pay particular attention to the connection between your heels, the balls of your feet, your toes, and the ground. Once you feel the firm connection to the ground, continue to take slow steps, and notice how the sense of connection moves up your legs and into the core of your body. (You can ground yourself using a walking practice as you walk down a hallway.)

EXERCISE

Breathe in slowly. Breathe out slowly. Breathe in. Breathe out. Notice the contact of your feet with the ground. Imagine that you have roots growing from the soles of your feet stretching deep into the earth. Even if you are on the top floor of a tall building or on a jet 30,000 feet up, imagine your roots grounding you. Contemplate the quiet power of these roots. Feel yourself firmly planted; flexible yet strong against the wind. Notice and feel the sense of connection to the ground with each inhale and exhale.

Teaching Students to Ground

We encourage you to use your own experiences with grounding to develop plans for your students. Matching your language to the developmental level of your students, the concept can be introduced as the best way to keep physical and emotional balance. Kids at different ages and/or developmental stages will need more or less structure to facilitate grounding. All students benefit from the experience and the confidence gained through a regular grounding practice.

For kids with complex trauma, any activity that invites quiet and greater connection to an internal experience has the potential to facilitate the release of a residue of frozen emergency energy. This release can surface as strong, overwhelming sensations. Knowing this possibility, we can prepare to be the calming voice that the student needs. With our awareness and confidence, we can normalize the experience and provide containment (Levine & Kline, 2007).

An MHP working with an 8-year-old student with hyperactivity was using Tai Chi exercises to teach the boy to ground. *Tai Chi* is a system of slow, meditative physical exercise that facilitates relaxation, balance, and health. It is a useful intervention for improving self-regulation. The movements the student was learning involved slowing down both breath and physical motion. After mastering one of the simple movements, they boy said, "I should do this every night. I've never done anything this slow in my life." He was clearly encouraged by the experience of feeling connected to his body and his sense of mastery in slowing his movements.

We offer a variety of grounding techniques. We believe it to be such a useful tool that we suggest you improvise until you find the grounding technique that works best for you and your students. One grounding exercise will work for one individual but won't work for another. In all grounding practice, we basically ask kids to mentally connect to their physical experience in the moment and notice their connection to the ground beneath them. Detailed directions for introducing grounding to students and numerous grounding activities are in Appendix B: Activities, Grounding.

Mindful Awareness

Siegel (2007) describes mindful awareness as a teachable skill with five definable elements. Read through the list and consider how helpful each of the elements will be to the student who has difficulty with self-regulation (and to us as we work with the student). Try to . . .

- be a witness to experience as it is happening
- be non-reactive or come back easily to emotional equilibrium
- be more receptive to what is happening or to what is being offered through letting go of judgments. (Siegel suggests that it is impossible not to judge, but it is possible to let judgments go.)
- label and describe your own internal experience
- observe your own mind in the moment

Mindfulness involves intentionally remembering to be aware, to pay attention, and to untangle the self from troublesome thinking and emotional reactions. We press the pause button on our automatic and habitual responses, which enables us to move toward more creative and discerning choices. In situations that can feel threatening to a kid, learning to observe somatic experience offers the opportunity to "fire up" the brain's high road circuitry. The practice of mindful awareness offers useful interventions for a variety of problems (Singh, Wahler, Adkins, & Myers, 2003). For example, an individual with mild intellectual disabilities who had problematic angry outbursts was successfully taught to use mindful awareness to manage outbursts. He learned to shift his attention to the soles of his feet whenever he noticed he was starting to feel angry (Siegel, Gerner, & Olendzki, 2009).

Mindful awareness harnesses the same neural mechanisms as secure attachment, that is, the neural activation that freely utilizes the whole brain. This allows us to step back and observe, rather than going to fight, flight, or freeze when we are triggered (Siegel, 2007). Damasio (1999) states that the use of mindful awareness makes it possible for traumatized brains to make the necessary connections for improved neural integration and more adaptive decision making. Its practice strengthens the capacity for self-regulation, giving us the option of using the information that our body gives us (Fisher & Ogden, 2009; Siegel, 2007).

Although the benefits of the training and practice of mindful awareness has been well-researched and documented for adults (Kabat-Zinn, 1991), in more recent years, research with mindfulness training has also been carried out with kids. Findings support the value of mindful awareness training for improved resilience, decreased aggression, decreased opposition toward teachers, increased attentiveness in class, and increased expression of positive emotions, including optimism (Lantieri, 2008). In a study at the Mindful Awareness Research Center (MARC) at UCLA, adolescents diagnosed with ADHD were taught mindfulness techniques. The findings support that these techniques lead to reduced anxiety and improved ability to focus (Zylowska et al., 2008). Preschool kids in another MARC study who were taught mindful awareness showed a marked increase in their ability to use stop, breathe, focus, and think to improve classroom behavior and participation (Flook et al., 2008). Mindfulness training is central to a number of therapeutic projects and approaches with kids, including the Inner Kids program (Goodman, 2005) and the structured training model used in Dialectical Behavior Therapy (DBT) (Miller, Rathus, & Linehan, 2007).

Mindful awareness and mindfulness meditation originates in the 2,500-year-old tradition of Buddhism. Similar practices can be seen throughout most contemplative traditions. In recent years, numerous psychotherapeutic approaches have focused on developing mindful awareness skills to help individuals improve their abilities to monitor emotional reactions. The goal is to help them choose more adaptive responses. Marsha Linehan calls the mindful awareness skills developed in DBT the "psychological and behavioral versions of meditation skills" (Linehan, 1993, p. 144). To be mindful makes it possible to observe what is happening around us and inside of us without needing to act. In DBT, mindful awareness is taught as a set of skills defined in terms of two areas: the "what" skills and the "how" skills (Spradlin, 2003).

The "what" skills include the following:

- **Observing.** We bring our clear intention to observing what is happening without attempting to change what we observe.
- **Describing.** We find words to silently describe for ourselves our experience as it is occurring.
- **Participating.** We fully engage and give our attention to what is happening and how we are experiencing this moment.

The "how" skills are the way the "what" skills are practiced. They include the following:

- **Being nonjudgmental.** We observe, describe, and participate in the moment. When judgments come up, we let them go.

- **Being one-mindful.** We focus our attention completely on one activity at a time. When thoughts or concerns about something other than this activity come up, we gently push them away. This is not easy, so we give ourselves lots of chances.

- **Being effective.** We do our best to handle things as they come our way, knowing we won't do it all perfectly.

Mindful Awareness Practice for the MPH

A recent study in Germany suggests that when counselors practiced mindful awareness, their clients made significant therapeutic progress over those clients whose counselors did not (Grepmair et al., 2007). When we are mindful, we are more regulated and regulating. As with grounding, developing our own capacity to use mindful awareness will bring confidence to the task of teaching students to use mindful awareness. Developing the ability to step back mentally and be a witness to our somatic experience makes it possible for us to know when we are dysregulated. We can then use grounding techniques to re-regulate.

A natural beginning point for developing mindful awareness is making it a daily practice to pay close attention to a regular activity, such as washing hands. Simply slow your breath and carefully observe yourself in the activity. We observe what we are experiencing, mentally, physically, and emotionally. Using the DBT "what and how skills" helps develop this practice. Once mindful awareness has been experienced in a specific activity, the practice can be expanded to other parts of the day, and particularly to situations that are dysregulating. Breath is a good *anchor* for both grounding and for mindful awareness, and it helps us return to calm attention. We use the term *anchor* to refer to anything that can be used as a focus to assist with nonjudgmental observation of the moment. We use an anchor whenever necessary and as frequently as needed.

Learning to use mindful awareness is like developing a good serve in tennis: The more we practice on the court, the better we become at serving. We train our muscles and hand–eye coordination to know the feeling of the serve, the height of the ball as we toss it in the air, and the feel of the arc of the serve overhead. The training occurs through repetition. The brain develops neural pathways that correspond to the motor skills. Mindful awareness training is no different and, with daily practice, becomes a useful tool. Through mindful awareness, we can intervene on our automatic mental and emotional tendencies of planning, reacting, worrying, predicting, or ruminating. We can step back to simply notice what is going on inside us and around us. We create the mental space for our own executive functioning.

In the film *The Class* (Benjo, Scotta, Lettelier, & Arnal, 2008), a sequence of events leads to a student being expelled from school. The teacher, who normally does a good job of interacting with this class of inner city adolescents, makes a mistake and becomes defensive rather than repairing with the students. When emotions begin to escalate, the teacher further "loses his cool," and a student particularly vulnerable to dysregulation engages him verbally and physically. The exchange results in the student unintentionally injuring another student.

The committee that determines punishment for the offending student defines the problem as the student's inability to control his emotions and actions. Watching the film with an understanding of the power of relational repair and interactive affect regulation, the problem becomes more multi-faceted. We can imagine a different outcome for all concerned had the teacher known how to ground, become mindful, and re-regulate.

Teaching Students to Use Mindful Awareness

Brain research has found that although the brain can switch attention from one thing to another quickly, it only attends to one thing at a time (Schumacher et al., 2001). This bit of science underlies why mindful awareness is such a useful tool for kids. When kids are taught to stop and observe their somatic experience at the first signals of dysregulation, in that moment they are not focusing on what they believe is the source of their distress. They get the opportunity to have a moment to think instead of reacting emotionally.

To really understand mindful awareness, we have to experience it (Siegel, Gerner, & Olendzki, 2009). Lantieri (2008) says when first introducing kids to a mindful awareness practice, it is best to do so through exercises that mirror daily life, such as mindfully eating. Exercises using guided imagery to introduce the experience work well with many students. With practice, mindful awareness can help students become familiar with the indicators of their own emotional states. We teach students to become witnesses to their own actions: to stop and think. In this way it is possible for cognition to interrupt dysregulation. When students learn they can make better choices, their self-confidence increases and their sense of self improves. Appendix B: Activities, Mindfulness, offers activities to teach students mindful awareness skills.

Tracking Sensation

Tracking sensation refers to a range of interventions using somatic experience. Sensations are physiological happenings in the body not associated with thoughts. The lower brain does not include cognitive functions and only understands sensations. When our reactions are only based on sensations, we do not stop and think. Fisher and Ogden (2009) call this "bottom-up processing." Sensations offer important information about our current arousal and emotional state. When there is potential for becoming dysregulated, mindful awareness makes it possible to observe sensations and then engage the upper cognitive areas of the brain to make decisions using "top-down processing" instead. In this way we are using bottom-up processing to enhance top-down processing (Fisher & Ogden, 2009). The sensations of hyperarousal, for example, can become signals for a student to slow down and think, making it possible to master situations that previously only caused trouble.

Again, although sensations are signals of emotion, they are not emotions or conscious actions. While we are usually unfamiliar with observing our own sensations, they are not difficult to get to know. It does take time, attention, and intention. Levine (1997), Saxe (2007), Ogden (2006) and their colleagues suggest the pathway to recovery from trauma and indicate that the prevention of trauma resides in cultivating the capacity to track sensations. The capacity to track sensations becomes an internal resource kids can use to alert themselves to the need to ground. The calming that comes with grounding assists with down-regulation of arousal and the subsequent regulation of emotion, leading to increased ability to shift emotional states.

It is helpful to become more familiar with the language of sensations. Pressure, temperature change on the skin, vibrations, warmth, racing heart, jitters, nausea, hunger, muscular tension, constriction or spaciousness, tingling or trembling, gut feeling, dizzy feeling, cold or heat, calm or excited, energetic or tired are all examples of sensations (Ogden, Minton, & Pain, 2006; Levine & Kline, 2007). Specific sensations can give us information about what we are feeling emotionally. "Butterflies in the stomach send a message of excitement, a heavy feeling in our chest speaks of grief, tension in the jaw informs us we are angry, an all over tingling feeling indicates fear" (Ogden, Minton, & Pain, 2006, p. 12). Some important characteristics of sensations include the following:

- Sensations offer information about our current level of arousal.
- While sensations are not emotions, they are vehicles for recognizing internal emotional states.
- Sensations are often vague and can appear to be without a clear precipitating event.
- Sensations are free of interpretations and judgments that can come with emotion (Levine & Kline, 2007).
- Sensations never remain static (van der Kolk, 2006).
- While sensations are not conscious actions, we can have conscious control of them through self-awareness, conscious thought, and self-management (Rothschild, 2003).

Working with sensation rather than the student's current emotional state is a new way for us to think, and an important step in helping kids to improve self-regulation. We often need to interrupt strong expression of emotion and direct the student's attention back to their somatic experience. For example, if a student begins to experience strong emotion, giving him the instruction to put aside the fear, anger, or whatever the emotion is and to begin to identify and notice the sensations, offers an immediate opportunity to practice. After the student's attention has been directed to somatic experience, wait for a sign that the child's arousal is within his window of tolerance before going forward. Self-regulation precedes problem solving (Ogden, 2010).

An Exercise in Tracking Sensation

Tracking our own sensations makes us more effective in both our own effort to re-regulate throughout the day and to teach students how to use their somatic experience to self-regulate. The following exercise was adapted from Levine and Kline (2007). We invite you to take this opportunity to experience tracking sensation.

Find a sensation in your body. For example, it might be tension in your shoulders or your neck or a slight pain somewhere. Just notice the way the sensation changes simply by observing it. Place your awareness there long enough, and it may relax on its own.

An emotion may emerge as you observe the sensation. Along with the emotion, a memory of some event from the past, a concern about the future, or thoughts about something that is happening right now might emerge. Let go of any thoughts and just notice the sensations. Sitting with the sensations offers the opportunity to observe that at this moment these feelings are all coming from inside you. Predictably, as you notice this, you will also notice a shift in your body and a change in how you are feeling in your body. When we are able to spend a little time with this activity, often this shift is accompanied by an idea for some kind of positive action and/ or a sense of relief.

Teaching Students to Track Sensations

The SSR model suggests four types of tracking sensation interventions. However, as you work with kids using this model, you will undoubtedly create others. The interventions we suggest come from a variety of sources including Ogden, Minton, and Pain (2006); Levine and Kline (2007); and Fisher and Ogden (2009). They include the following: (1) calm creates calm, (2) sensation conversation, (3) activation and de-activation training, and (4) moment-to-moment tracking. When we keep in mind that the most problematic emotional responses kids have originate from survival-in-the-moment, we are better able to avoid running straight into their emotional defenses. Rather than pointing out what they are doing wrong, we do our best to shine a light for them on the usefulness of increased somatic awareness to improve self-regulation. For each type of intervention listed, you will find exercises in Appendix B: Activities.

Sensation Conversation

This type of intervention invites students to experience what is happening in their bodies and to expand their *sensation vocabulary*. The term *sensation vocabulary* refers to the words an individual has available to describe physiological happenings. It is essential to begin sensation conversation—as with other somatic awareness activities—with positive, calming experiences. By doing this, you offer safety and hopeful possibilities.

An example of a sensation conversation intervention would be noticing when a student takes a relaxing sigh and then doing the same thing yourself. Follow up by exploring the experience. Questions might include "When you do that, what do you notice happening in your chest?" "Do you feel warm in your middle?" "What happened to your shoulders?" The intention is to encourage students to first become aware of the positive somatic experience of a gesture or series of movements and then to use it to increase their sensation vocabulary. When students are aware of a positive somatic experience, they can learn to use it to contrast with sensations of dysregulation. They will also have words to help them.

Developing a positive somatic memory is a useful intervention on its own and can serve as a vehicle to increase sensation vocabulary. As we work with students to help them remember times, situations, and places in which they felt safe, comfortable, and comforted, our conversation will focus on the somatic experience and specifically on developing sensation vocabulary.

Activation and De-Activation

When students can use words to describe their sensations and are at least familiar with observing somatic experience, we can teach them to activate and de-activate their physical experience. The reliable use of this technique alone can improve self-regulation, and for some students, may be all that is needed. We start with de-activation because it is the down-regulated, calm position. Depending on the student, you might use his or her preferred grounding technique to find the experience of calm. A positive somatic memory can also be used to assist the student with calming.

Once a student can reliably de-activate him or herself, we introduce activation. Activation involves finding the sensations associated with the student's experience of upset, tension, or distress in his or her body and the ability to practice creating it. The student practices being dysregulated. When he or she can do this, we teach the student to move back and forth between sensations of activation and de-activation. Developing this capacity offers a sense of mastery and confidence in their ability to re-regulate themselves. With practice, students come to recognize the first signals of activation and can call up de-activation. See Appendix B: Activities, Establish Body Awareness for an example of how to use activation and de-activation with kids.

Moment-to-Moment Tracking

Depending on a student's developmental level, we can teach him or her to find sensations in his or her body and to use mindful awareness to observe sensations as they move and change. This specific type of tracking sensation requires becoming aware of the physical experience of sensations in the body and being able to mindfully observe and describe the physical feelings as they change and slowly progress throughout the body. Simply observing a sensation changes it, and even sensations evoked by specific stressors will change and eventually diminish when observed. Again, we are working to separate the physiological experience of sensation from emotion.

In order for students to use moment-to-moment tracking sensations to re-regulate, we have to help them identify the first small sensations associated with their own dysregulation (Levine & Kline, 2007). Once they are familiar with these first signals of internal agitation, they will have a number of options. They can track the sensation as it changes. Rothschild refers to this particular process of tracking sensation as "making friends with sensations" and it becomes a resource (Rothschild, 2000, p. 106). The initial sensations of dysregulation can be observed and then grounding and mindful awareness can be used to calm before emotions escalate. Rothschild calls this "putting on the brakes" (Rothschild, 2000, p. 113). When students can do this, they can have positive experiences of intervening with themselves and calming. Mindful moment-to-moment tracking sensation allows arousal to be observed and to "eventually come to rest, rather than utilizing behavior, such as aggressive outbursts" (Ogden, Minton, & Pain, 2006, p. 60).

Developing Resources for Self-Regulation

Ogden, Minton, and Pain define and describe resources as "all the personal skills, abilities, objects, relationships, and services that facilitate self-regulation and provide a sense of competence and resilience" (2006, p. 207). In the SSR model, through skill-development exercises and practice, we work to re-instate resources, develop new resources, and strengthen existing resources. A kid's internal and external resources are the best predictors of recovery from complex trauma (Ford & Cloitre, 2009).

Children are born with internal resources that require adults (external resources) to mirror and nurture the children. In this way, children's internal resources develop (Levine & Kline, 2007). We can find a student's particular resources or potential resources through observation, conversation, and information from others. As a MHP, we may have lots of resource ideas and suggestions for students, but in order for something or someone to be considered a resource by a student, it has to be experienced as helpful, comforting, or pleasurable to him or her. Something we offer as a resource may be helpful to one student, but not to another. For example, listening to music may be calming to one student and aversive to another. A grounding technique may work wonders for one student and not work at all for another.

Our goal is to help students develop resources that they can internalize and experience as being useful and creating confidence. An effective resource can be used as an anchor that can be called on to help with self-regulation in stressful or emotionally overwhelming times. Such a resource might be a positive somatic memory, the use of mindful awareness to help with slowing down, or an adult to go to for help.

Lea is 5 years old and in kindergarten. She is extremely quiet, and even though she has an average vocabulary for her age, she rarely speaks. Lea does anything that is requested of her, but responds slowly to activities and questions from her teacher or her peers. Her teacher noticed that she had to remind herself to interact with Lea and decided to refer her for evaluation by the counselor. The counselor met with Lea and experimented by teaching her to ground. Lea was enlivened by the activity.

Using Somatic Awareness as an Internal Resource

To gain confidence, kids benefit from developing a variety of resources. Anchors and the ability to identify and track sensations can become dependable internal resources.

We can increase a student's somatic awareness through activities to shift somatic experiences. A simple activity that illustrates how to create such a shift is: (1) think of a problem you have; (2) imagine yourself really big; (3) notice how you feel about the problem when you are very big; (4) imagine yourself really small; (5) notice how you feel about the problem; and (6) get really big again (Ogden, 2010). Any activity like this may need to be expanded or have more time taken with each step. If any particular activity does not work for a student, simply discontinue.

Improvement in posture is an important somatic resource for numerous reasons and specifically for increasing positive social engagement. The kid whose typical posture includes his chest pushed forward and his head looking down does not invite friendly exchange. Usually, it is not helpful to attempt to change posture by suggesting changes in muscular compensation, but rather to use visualization (Ogden, Minton, & Pain, 2006). For example, with this student we could use the following exercise: (1) ask him to stand as he usually does; (2) ask him to notice how his body feels and to describe it; (3) ask him to think of someone he would really like to see and to hold that person in mind; (4) ask him to shift his position so that the other person will know he is glad to see him.

Observe the child's body to learn how he processes information, including what he expects from others. Use this information to teach strategies to address negative patterns. For example, the child is observed to slump whenever he is given instruction. An intervention strategy might be to: (1) bring the child's awareness to the somatic experience of slumping; (2) ask him to imagine a string or ribbon attached to the top of his head helping his whole body to rise up while his feet are firmly planted on the ground; and (3) bring his awareness to the difference in how he feels as he hears the instruction.

Using Somatic Memory as a Resource

We can help children in problematic situations use positive somatic memory to shift from a negative somatic experience to a positive one. In the following exercise we ask that you practice calling up somatic memories of positive and negative experiences. (This is a similar process to activation and de-activation.)

EXERCISE

Remember or imagine a time when you felt a sense of competence. Drop your awareness into your body and notice any sensations. Hold that sense of competence in your awareness. There might be warmth, or a feeling of being energized or increased muscle tone. You may feel an overall sense of strength. Just notice what the sensations are. Take time to become familiar with the sensations.

Now take a nice, slow breath. Shift your thoughts to a recent experience when you felt a negative vulnerability. An example might be a disagreement with a friend or being stuck in traffic when you were on a tight schedule. Notice the sensations in your body as you bring up the memory of this experience. Again, take a nice, slow breath. Shift back to the memory of the experience of feeling competent and once again notice those sensations.

Developing the ability to move back and forth between sensations in this way builds resilience. The next time you feel a negative vulnerability, call up this sense of your own strength.

Internal and External Resources

The following is a list of internal and external resources adapted from suggestions by Rothschild (2000, 2003); Ogden, Minton, and Pain (2006); and Levine and Kline (2007). Examples of **internal resources** include the following:

- The capacities to ground, and the use of mindfulness to observe sensations of dysregulation and not act on them
- Somatic memory of sensation that is experienced as stimulating, calming, soothing, and/or comforting that can be used in problematic situations to maintain emotional regulation
- Using body awareness to anchor, gauge arousal, put on the brakes to maintain emotional regulation, and/or shift from dysregulation
- A kid's abilities, unique skills, talents, and interests, such as verbal or math skills, artistic ability, leadership skill, athletic ability, and other nonverbal abilities
- Physical abilities, such as sight, hearing, smell, touch, large and/or small motor agility and balance, healthy body, and energy
- Personality qualities, such as initiative, generosity, kindness toward others, dependability, sense of humor, ability to make and keep friends
- Action that is experienced as establishing personal boundaries, and the strength to defend oneself
- The ability to ask for help

Examples of **external resources** include the following:

- Caring and involved parents
- Adults who can be depended upon, including teachers, counselors, and all members of the school staff
- Extended nurturing family, friends, pets, and a larger community of people and activities such as coaches; scout leaders; and cultural, social, athletic, and/or religious opportunities
- Access and opportunities to experience the natural environment
- Access to an environment enriched with books, art supplies, toys, and music
- Objects and other experiences that offer either stimulation or calming and soothing comfort for the senses, such as music, color, textured materials, soft blankets, and stuffed animals

Creating an Internal Resource
From an External Resource

David is a 12-year-old boy with multiple physical problems who has to undergo regular medical procedures, including surgery. David's grandmother is a warm, comforting person who always goes to medical procedures with David. At school, David was extremely reactive if he felt he was experiencing a real or perceived physical threat. He was referred to Mr. Johnson, the counselor.

Mr. Johnson first worked to bring David into greater connection with his own body through the use of grounding. He taught David the use of mindful awareness and how to track sensations. Through assessment, he found David could feel a warm, calming sensation around his heart when he thought of his grandmother's presence. By developing the "imprint" of this sensation as a resource, Mr. Johnson taught David how to use this somatic memory when he felt threatened. This internal resource made it possible for David to feel more competent in stabilizing his own emotional state when he felt physically threatened.

An Exercise to Identify Your Internal and External Resources

We have adapted the following exercise from one offered by Levine and Kline (2007). This exercise can also be adapted to use with students. Helping identify the resources a student already has, values, and can make use of is beneficial. We invite you to experience identifying your own internal and external resources.

EXERCISE

Using a blank a piece of paper, make two lists vertically down the page. On one side, list what you consider your external resources. On the other side, list your internal resources. If something is not clearly one or the other, include it in both lists.

When your lists feel complete, look them over and notice which resources stand out as offering you the strongest support in times of stress. With each of the resources you listed, take the time to notice what sensations and emotions emerge. Notice where you experience them in your body. You might notice a sense of being held in your back and shoulders, a feeling of strength in your muscles, a smile coming to your face, a feeling of warmth in your chest area, or a sense of feeling grounded in your trunk and legs. In some way note those experiences, either on this page or another, in an effort to form stronger somatic memories of these resources.

Going back over your lists, do you notice the need for developing or adding resources? If you do, note what you might do to make that happen. For example, it might be in such areas as interpersonal relationships, meditation practice, or physical activities.

In Summary

✧ Teaching students to ground, to practice mindful awareness, and to track sensations increases their ability to connect with their somatic experience and their own signals of regulation and dysregulation. This opens the door to executive functioning.

✧ Our own confidence and ability to improve our students' somatic awareness is found in developing the skills of grounding, mindful awareness, and tracking sensation in ourselves. These skills also are beneficial for our own self-care.

✧ Self-care decreases the possibility of developing compassion fatigue.

✧ Our calm creates calm.

✧ Simply learning to ground can give students a sense of greater connection to their surroundings and confidence in their ability to calm themselves.

✧ The practice of mindful awareness makes it possible to step back and observe current experience and to re-regulate as needed.

✧ Teaching students to track sensations involves at least four different types of interventions.

✧ Learning to distinguish and notice sensations opens the door to improved self-regulation.

✧ A positive somatic memory can be used as an anchor to assist with re-regulating.

✧ Developing internal and external resources helps students improve their sense of competence and confidence for self-regulation.

5

Using the Solution-Focused Approach

By paying attention to the skills and abilities children already have, we can uncover and build on them, rather than try to make up for the child's deficits.

Berg & Steiner, *Children's Solution Work*

In dealing with kids who have experienced complex trauma, Ford and Cloitre (2009) recommend maintaining a consistent, strengths-based approach, with a rigorous focus on identifying and building on a child's or adolescent's capabilities. Typically in the schools, especially with kids with severe dysregulation difficulties, helpers rely on a problem-focused approach. An important difference in the strategies for self-regulation (SSR) model is a solution-focused component. In previous discussions, we described the calming relationship and the skill development aspects of the SSR model. These give students specific skills to help them connect their somatic experience to their ability to decide how to act. With the addition of the solution-focused approach, we purposely focus on a kid's strengths and successes, no matter how small, and accommodate his or her goals to develop solutions to school problems. In Chapter 5, we describe the basics of the solution-focused approach as it is applied to the SSR model.

Solution-Focused Therapy

Steve de Shazer and his colleagues at the Brief Family Therapy Center in Milwaukee, Wisconsin, created the solution-focused therapy approach in the 1980s (de Shazer, 1985; de Shazer, et al., 1986). This approach is used effectively, even with young children (Berg & Steiner, 2003) and in the schools (Metcalf, 2008; Murphy, 1994; Tollison & Synatschk, 2007) because of its practical emphasis on cooperation, solutions, student strengths, and efficiency. At the same time, the solution-focused approach is a perspective, a way of interacting, and a way of listening—staying curious and open to the kid's solutions. With this approach, we are oriented primarily to the present and the future, and we emphasize discovering what kids are doing about their problems that works. We can then help them use that knowledge to make changes. Counseling focuses on solution-related details and possibilities rather than the problem history and presumed causes. Note the critical differences between problem-focused and solution-focused counseling in Table 5.1.

Table 5.1

Comparison of Problem-Focused and Solution-Focused Counseling

Problem-focused counseling	Solution-focused counseling
Focuses on weaknesses, deficits, and problems	Focuses on strengths, resources, and solutions
Focuses on the past	Focuses on the future
An interview serves an assessment and a diagnostic function	An interview serves an intervention and a solution-building function
Client is viewed as sick	Client is viewed as stuck
Services are counselor driven: Goals and interventions emerge from counselor's preferences and model	Services are client driven: Goals and interventions emerge from client's preferences, theories, and resources
Counselor is the expert and teacher: Client follows the counselor's lead	Client is the expert and teacher: Counselor follows the client's lead
Intervention failures and client's uncooperativeness indicate that the client is resistant and needs to adapt to the counselor and the intervention approach	Intervention failures and client's uncooperativeness indicate that the counselor and the intervention approach need to be adapted to the client
Assumes a direct relationship between problems and solutions: Solutions emerge from the assessment of problem history, origins, and presumed causes	Assumes no necessary relationship between problems and solutions: Some solutions fit any type of problem, regardless of its history, origins, or presumed causes
Solutions are seen as resulting primarily from the counselor's skillful application of counseling models and techniques	Solutions are seen as resulting primarily from a strong alliance and from accommodations of the client's ideas, resources, and feedback

Note. From *Solution-Focused Counseling in Schools* (2nd ed., p. 42), by J. J. Murphy. Copyright 2008 by the American Counseling Association. Alexandria, VA: American Counseling Association. Reprinted with permission.

With the solution-focused approach, we shift our attention from what's wrong to what's working. In this way, we accommodate a kid's goal for change; tap into a kid's strengths, resources, and ideas; and collaborate on an intervention based on those ideas. In the SSR model, we combine these strategies with teaching somatic awareness skills and social–emotional learning skills to help kids reach their goals for improved self-regulation. Because we accommodate their goals and their ideas for solutions, the locus of control shifts from external to internal. We have the added benefit of encouraging self-responsibility in kids. The approach results in a positive, culturally sensitive, strengths-based intervention for behavior change.

In using the solution-focused approach with kids with complex trauma, we remember to use fewer words, rather than more, and to make the calming relationship primary as we help kids find their own solutions. While working to understand a kid's perspective and not to impose our view, we keep in mind that at times a kid may need help with ordering his or her thoughts and focusing on the task at hand.

Assumptions of the Solution-Focused Approach

Several seemingly obvious assumptions undergird the solution-focused approach (Murphy, 2008). With each, consider how the ideas described compare to the usual way of working with problem situations in schools.

1. If it works, do more of it. If it doesn't work, do something different.

2. Every client is unique, resourceful, and capable of changing.

3. Cooperative relationships enhance solutions.

4. No problem is constant.

5. Big problems do not always require big solutions.

In the following discussion, we will apply these assumptions to practical strategies for helping students with self-regulation difficulties.

The Three A's of Solution-Focused Approaches

The Three A's of solution-focused approaches are Acceptance, Acknowledgement, and Accommodation. What this means is we accept kids as they are, acknowledge their experience, and accommodate their goals for change.

Acceptance and change are the essential components of solution-focused work. In the tradition of Carl Rogers (Evans, 1975), we accept kids where they are right now, and we help them accept themselves. But then we add a little twist. We communicate, "Where you are now is a valid place to be, and you can change."

Our calm relationship with the student is fundamental to the SSR model and offers an external resource for him or her. We build on that relationship by letting kids know we have heard and understood their suffering, concerns, experience, and points of view without closing down the possibilities for change. *To acknowledge* means to notice and allow whatever is there to be there. Instead of trying to get rid of it, hide it, analyze it, or judge it, we just let ourselves be aware of it. We do not have to like it—just accept that this is what is happening for the student at this time. The simple act of not arguing or invalidating what the kid says is a form of acknowledgement. But acknowledgement is only half the job. We work both to acknowledge and to keep the possibilities for change open. We do this through matching the kid's language and position and by using some useful language-based techniques.

In dealing with a kid with complex trauma, we accept his or her view of the problem (while keeping in mind the needs of the referral source and setting) and come to a common goal of improving the kid's capacity for self-regulation. For example, a kid who regularly falls apart during transition times in the classroom might report the cause of the problem is others bugging him. His or her defense is that other people are causing the trouble and he or she doesn't have any power. (Notice the attribution to an external locus of control.) We acknowledge this perception of being bugged by others and keep possibilities open. Later, we can explore times when he or she has coped with others bugging him or her and managed to make a smooth transition. We then ask him or her to consider how this was done. It is in considering these times that we can learn how to help him or her do more to improve behavior. The key difference is that this information is coming from the kid's experience and is not being imposed by another person. The likelihood that the student will be able to improve his or her behavior is increased when the option comes from a personal repertoire.

Possibility Language

O'Hanlon and Beadle (1997), in *A Guide to Possibility Land*, call language that communicates to individuals that we accept them and that they can change *possibility language*. Small changes in how we speak about a problem can "unstick" the situation and facilitate change. Counselors and other helpers are accustomed to reframing when reflecting a client's position. Using possibility language is similar to reframing except the intention here is very simple: We open up the possibility for change rather than challenging an individual's perception. The test of acknowledgement is that the kid (or the adult) feels acknowledged. We judge the success of what we have said by the kid's response rather than how right our word choice may seem to us. We pay attention to the kid's verbal and nonverbal language to determine if we achieved what we were after. When a referral comes from an adult who is experiencing the explosive consequences of a kid's dysregulation, we acknowledge the adult's view (just like we would the student's) and validate his or her ideas for improvement.

As we acknowledge a kid's or an adult's statement, we can use simple language techniques to closely capture what the person has said, but open up the possibility for change. These techniques include reflecting the individual's description of the problem in the past tense, from global statements to partial statements, or from truth or reality assertions to perceptions. In real exchanges, several of these strategies may be combined; however, for the purpose of illustration, we will discuss each technique separately.

Reflecting a Problem in the Past Tense

Changing the present tense verb to past tense sends a subtle and powerful message: We acknowledge there have been serious difficulties but suggest they do not have to continue into the present or future. There is a very real possibility for change. The intent here is to match the language and position of the person rather than refuting it, and then to add the possibility for change. We do not seek to change or lessen the feeling, but to help the student, teacher, or other referring adult become a little more optimistic about change. For example, for the kid who says, "I get in trouble all the time!" the counselor might reflect, "You've been getting in trouble" or "You've been in trouble in the past" or "You were in trouble all the time." We might hear from a teacher or an administrator, "This child has meltdowns every day!" The counselor might reflect, "He's had meltdowns every day!"

Reflecting Global Statements as Partial Statements

When we can subtly suggest to a kid or adult a less all-encompassing, partial-sounding term in place of a global, very stuck-sounding term, we assist him or her in considering other possible descriptions of the situation. When a kid says, "I fail at everything," a counselor might reflect, "You've failed at most of the things you have tried." Or when a teacher says, "She's always out of control," a counselor might reflect, "She's out of control practically all the time." Again, we pay attention to the response from the kid or the adult to gauge whether we have adequately acknowledged his or her view. If a student's feedback indicates we have moved too far from his or her position, we simply ask him or her to tell us more about the situation so we can understand. We then try again to acknowledge his or her experience.

Sometimes kids (or adults) will let us know we missed the mark by saying something like, "No, you don't get it, I really do mean always!" This does not mean that we have failed, merely that we should ask more about the kid's viewpoint by saying something like, "You're right, I missed it. Help me understand what's going on for you." Implicit in this exchange is a valuable message of relational repair. It signals that what we most care about is hearing about the kid's view and position. At times, acknowledging the difficult circumstances and experiences of our students can be stressful and dysregulating for us. These are excellent times to remember to re-regulate as we build a calming relationship.

Reflecting Truth or Reality Claims as Perceptions

We perceive things in our environment through our eyes, ears, touch, and emotions. When we reflect truth assertions as perceptions, we can reflect with sensory words again with the intention of acknowledging the kid, validating his or her perspective, and opening up the possibilities for change. It is an acknowledging, encouraging stance. For example, when a kid says, "It's totally impossible to get along with her!" A counselor might respond, "Wow, it sounds like it's totally impossible to get along with her." Or a referring adult might say, "He's just like his father, and there's nothing you can do about it!" A counselor might reflect. "He appears to be just like his father with seemingly nothing to be done about it."

O'Hanlon and Beadle (1997) call this the "teeter-totter" of acknowledgement and possibility. We figuratively step down on one side of the teeter-totter as we listen to the kid's or adult's concerns, then step down on the other side as we reflect and step into "possibility land." Our calm, neutral, invitational way of reflecting a kid's or an adult's statement keeps the exchange from becoming confrontational. Instead, the exchange is curious and concerned. Inflection, emphasis, and tone of voice, as well as our encouraging nonverbal language, help a student feel heard and a little more open to the possibility of change. Keep in mind that our goal is for the student to feel acknowledged and for us to learn more about the situation.

Action Talk

When we receive a referral about a student who is having trouble with self-regulation, it is likely the problem or complaint will be described in global terms. While we acknowledge the experience of the person giving us the referral, we usually do not learn much specific information about the problem. Getting *action talk* allows us to gain a clear, behavioral description of the complaint. This is referred to as the "doing" of the problem. Action talk helps us focus very specifically on changing behaviors, as opposed to making diagnoses or relying on assumptions. To get this kind of information from the referring person, it is helpful to ask questions to get a more specific, behavioral description of the difficulties. For example, when a teacher says, "This child is defiant!" we can respond by asking, "What is the child doing that tells you he or she is defiant?" In response to a parent who says, "My child has total meltdowns!" we can reply, "Tell me what it looks like when your child has total meltdowns." Getting action talk, or a more behavioral description, helps us better understand what is going on. Once we can talk in concrete terms about the problem, we can discover what would constitute a slightly improved situation.

Clarifying Solution Attempts

After acknowledgement, dialogue with the student (or referring person) can focus on learning about previous attempts to solve the problem. Implicit in this is the idea that the student has already tried to alleviate the situation and has undertaken some measures on his or her own, even if those efforts have been less than successful. Asking and listening carefully to what the student says about previous solution attempts gives us valuable information about the student's ideas of an improved state, his resources, and his supports. In this, we are also sending the message we are respectful of the attempts made by the student, implying that we believe he has the ability to create the best solution for himself. We can get this information by asking questions like the following:

- *What have you tried so far? How did it help?*
- *Of all the things you've tried, what worked the best?*
- *How have you handled similar situations? How might that help in this situation?*

Building on Exceptions

As we listen to the description of the problem and previous attempts at resolution, we may hear about times or situations in which the problem seemed a little less challenging or did not exist at all for a time. These times are referred to as *exceptions*. One of the most effective ways to identify and build on capabilities is by finding exceptions to the problem (Murphy, 2008). An *exception* refers to a specific event or situation in which the problem does not occur or occurs less often or less intensely than usual. It is much easier to increase existing successes than it is to eliminate problems. Simple questions we can ask to identify exceptions include the following:

- *When is the problem absent or less noticeable?*
- *When is the improvement happening already, if only for a little bit?*
- *When have you been able to manage this behavior?*
- *How were you able to do that?*

Once exceptions have been identified, exploring and elaborating them gives us valuable information about strengths and resources. We can then ask questions about related features and circumstances under which those exceptions occur.

- *What is different about those times when [the problem] didn't occur?*
- *Who was there?*
- *What else was going on?*

Goal Setting

The process of developing goals is often overlooked in the push for quick solutions. This is especially true in work with students and school problems when the referring person already has a definite goal. In the SSR model, we work to identify a kid's goal for change. Our deliberate focus on a kid's goal shifts the locus of control and communicates respect and confidence in the individual. The goal we arrive at should encompass a kid's solution ideas. Murphy (2008) attributes most counseling failures to ineffective goals, resulting from one of the following: (1) failing to explicitly develop and revisit goals throughout the counseling process, (2) invalidating or minimizing a student's goal in deference to the goals of a counselor or other adults, and (3) placing one's own theories above those of the student. Developing goals in collaboration with kids, parents, and teachers can be a challenging task. However, it is well worth the effort, because goals keep our work on track and provide clear criteria for evaluating its effectiveness. That said, in working with kids who have significant difficulty self-regulating, it may be helpful to postpone goal setting. Instead, introducing somatic awareness skills and giving students the opportunity to feel some success with self-regulation can facilitate their involvement in goal setting.

Solution-focused goals are significant, specific, small, self-manageable, and define a place to start. Table 5.2 summarizes the characteristics of effective goals. The solution-focused approach includes a number of effective techniques to help kids articulate their goals. These include the *miracle question*, the *difference question*, and the *scaling technique*.

Table 5.2

Characteristics of Effective Goals

Characteristic	Description	Useful questions
Significant	Relevant and important to the client	*What do you want to work on? What can you do at school to move closer to being a decent and caring person?*
Specific	Clear, concrete, specific, observable, described in videotalk	*If I videotaped you being less depressed, what would I see? What will you be doing differently when you have higher self-esteem?*
Small	Reasonable and attainable	*What will be the first small sign that things are getting better? You said that school was a 3 on a 10-point scale. What will a 3.5 or a 4 look like?*
Start-based	The presence or start of something desirable	*What will you be doing instead of being depressed? What should this student be doing instead of goofing off?*
Self-manageable	Within the client's control	*How can you get your teachers to be nicer to you? How willing are you to try something different to make things better?*

Note. From *Solution-Focused Counseling in Schools*, (2nd ed., p. 98), by J. J. Murphy, 2008. American Counseling Association. Alexandria, VA: American Couseling Association. Reprinted with permission.

Miracle Question

The miracle question was developed to help kids envision and describe life without the problem. It is worded as follows: "Suppose one night, while you were asleep, there was a miracle and this problem was solved. How would you know? What would be different?" (de Shazer, 1988, p. 5). Insoo Kim Berg demonstrated asking the miracle question in a fun, dramatic way by inviting kids to enjoy the fun and fully describe a future without the problem (Berg & Steiner, 2003). For example, asking the question slowly with inflexion to encourage imagination and creativity allows kids to visualize in detail their preferred better state. It helps kids define more precisely what they want from counseling. The miracle question also helps parents and teachers translate broad goals and expectations into concrete behavioral descriptions. In addition to shifting the focus from the problem to the solution, concrete goals offer practical criteria for use in evaluation. As well as helping students develop clear goals, the miracle question boosts hope by focusing on future possibilities.

Difference Question

Another technique to help define the goal for counseling is the *difference question* (Pichot & Dolan, 2003). *Difference questions* identify and accentuate the effects of a kid's changes or potential changes, providing a check to ensure the goals are realistic, feasible, and worthwhile. Difference questions heighten kids' awareness of the effect of their goal, thereby increasing their motivation. When we investigate what difference the change will make, deliberately and reflectively, we gain a more defined idea of the change. We ask questions such as the following:

- *What difference will it make for you when you are able to make friends?*
- *What difference will it make when you wait for your turn to speak in class?*
- *What difference will it make when you are able to avoid meltdowns in your classroom?*
- *What difference will it make for you when you can calmly let your teacher know you need help?*

Roberto is a third-grade student who had been in an SSR group for 4 weeks. At this group meeting, the counselor began with a grounding exercise in which members were asked to feel and observe their breath going down to their feet and into the ground beneath them. They had practiced this same exercise the previous week. Afterward, the counselor checked in with members about their progress toward their goals over the past week. The counselor asked Roberto what difference learning to calm himself was having. With a big grin on his face, Roberto said, "My teacher smiles at me."

Escalator Language

We can help students to articulate goals by using escalator language. This language technique acknowledges a student's perspective while leading him or her to a view of the future he or she would prefer. Escalator language makes the suggestion that the student is already headed toward such a future. Escalator language involves the following:

1. When students speak of a problem, reflect it in a way that states their concerns as preferred goals, rather than problems to be gotten rid of.

2. When reflecting, summarizing, or clarifying, use words that convey an expectancy that the preferred future will come about.

3. Reflect using words like *yet* or *so far* to suggest that sometime in the future, the problem will end or things will get better.

For example, when a student says, "I'm fighting all the time," we can respond, "So we'll know we're being successful here when you are getting along a lot better most of the time." Or when a student says, "I can't seem to stay out of trouble every day," we can respond, "So far you haven't managed to have things go well for a day."

Scaling

Most typically, scaling questions ask a kid to rank aspects of his or her life on a 10-point scale (Miller, 1997). Scaling provides valuable information about where kids are in relationship to their "miracle" or goal. Scaling empowers kids to explore exceptions and how they created them. When we are asking scaling questions, we need to remind kids there are no right or wrong answers and that the purpose is to obtain their perception of progress, regardless of what others might say. It is important to invite kids to elaborate on their ratings through follow-up comments and questions. For example, we might ask the following questions:

- *On a scale of 1 to 10, with 1 being the worst and 10 being the best, where would you say you are now toward your goal?*
- *What will the next number look like? What will you be doing differently when that occurs?*

Table 5.3 is a Solution-Focused Interview Guide and shows a sequence of sample interview tasks and questions to help students define a goal for counseling and to do the beginning work toward a solution. The interview guide is also available in a reproducible format in Appendix A: Tools, Individual Counseling.

Table 5.3

Solution-Focused Interview Guide

Task	Sample language
Define the student's goal Find out what needs to happen (kid's goal) in order for counseling to be useful.	*What needs to happen in our time together to make you feel it has been worthwhile? Or, How do you want things to be?*
Verify understanding Verify that the counselor's understanding of the goal is accurate by asking difference questions or scaling questions. If the goal is unclear, repeat Step 1.	*What difference will it make when _____ happens? Who else will notice? What difference will that make? On a scale of 1 to 10, with 1 being the not at all and 10 being completely achieved, where are you now in the achievement of this goal? (Adjust number scale for younger students.)*
Use the miracle question Ask the miracle question and get as many details as possible.	*Suppose tonight, while you are asleep, a miracle happens, and this problem is completely solved. What will be the first thing you notice when you wake up that will tell you it has happened? What difference will that make for you? Who else will notice? What difference will that make for you?*
Describe exceptions Listen for exceptions and follow up on them by getting as many details as possible.	*When is this miracle happening even a little? What are you doing to make that happen? How are you managing to keep things from being worse? When are you able to beat the problem, even a little?*
Use scaling Ask a scaling question to determine a kid's current progress toward the goal.	*On a scale of 1 to 10 (10 is your miracle has come true, and 1 is that your problem is the worst it has been), where are you right now? What lets you know that it is a _____ and not a _____ (lower number)?*
Identify successful efforts Referring to the previous scaling question; find out what the kid has done to reach and maintain the current level of progress.	*Wow! That number is pretty high. How have you been able to do that? Even though it has been tough, you have been able to do that? (Reinforce successful efforts to show it was not just luck.)*
Understand other people's ratings Find out where on the scale the kid thinks others would rate him or her.	*Where would your mother (father, coach, teacher, assistant principal) say you are on this scale of 1 to 10? What will (the referral source) be seeing when you are at a 10? What difference will it make when they are able to see that? What difference will that make?*
Understand other people's descriptions Find out what the kid thinks significant people would say about why they rated the kid as they did.	*If (referral source) was here, what do you think she would tell me that she currently sees in you that would make her rate you a _____ rather than a _____ (lower number)?*
Difference Ask the kid what differences he or she thinks significant others are noticing.	*What difference would you say those behaviors are having? What else does it tell her to see in you _____ (hanging in there)?*

Task	Sample language
Goal scaling Ask the kid where on the scale he or she hopes to be by the next session. Continue to ask questions about how the kid will know when he or she is at this specific place on the scale (e.g., *What will be different then?*).	*Where on the scale of 1 to 10 do you hope to be by the next time we get together? How will you know you are a _____? Suppose you are at a _____ (higher number). What do you think would have happened for you to be there? What will be different when you are there? Who else will notice? What difference will that make?*
Confidence scaling If high on the scale, use scaling questions for the kid to rate his or her confidence in the ability to sustain these changes (or to scale the referral source's confidence that the client can sustain the changes).	*On a scale of 1 to 10, with 10 being that you have complete confidence that you can maintain the changes you have made, and 1 being that you have no confidence at all, where would you put yourself?*
Task development Based on responses to questions 1 through 11, invite the kid to assign self-homework.	*I'm wondering as you think about being that _____(#) on your scale, what is the most important thing you did before coming here today that helped you to get there? If it was next week and you were telling me how you accomplished this, what would you be telling me?*

Note. From *Solution-Focused Brief Therapy* (pp. 30–42), by T. Pichot and Y. M. Dolan, 2003, New York: The Haworth Clinical Practice Press. Copyright 2003 by Haworth Clinical Practice Press.

Using the Solution-Focused Approach With Referral Sources

As we mentioned previously, we use the solution-focused approach with referring adults as well as with kids. The principles that guide our work with kids also facilitate working successfully with parents, teachers, and other school personnel. The following guidelines apply:

- Remember to accept, acknowledge, and accommodate the referring person, just as you would the kid.
  - *Sounds like Todd's meltdowns have been a disaster for your class.*
  - *It must have been so tough trying to manage Todd's behavior and teach the rest of the class. How have you been able to manage so far?*
- Solicit action talk—a behavioral description—with follow-up questions to their problem statements.
  - *What do you see that tells you Todd is having a meltdown?*
  - *What would I notice that would tell me Todd is having a really bad day?*
- Listen for exceptions to the problem.

- *Tell me about a time when Todd was able to avoid a meltdown or had a less severe reaction.*
- *What was happening that day? What seemed different?*

- Ask them about their goal for improvement.
  - *What can you see happening that would be an improvement, if even a little?*
  - *Of all the troublesome behaviors you're seeing, with which one would a little improvement make the most difference?*

- Compliment their effective actions or thoughts.
  - *It's unbelievable you could remain calm under those circumstances. Most people would have lost it, but you didn't. How were you able to do that?*
  - *I appreciate the way you are supporting my work with (student's name) by encouraging him/her to practice grounding in your classroom.*

There are many advantages to taking the solution-focused approach with referring parties. They include the following:

- We can acknowledge all they have been doing already.
- We can support them in continuing to work with a difficult situation.
- We change the viewing and the doing, so they can envision improved behavior and what that looks like for the kid.
- We can use their behavioral description to give us a much better idea of the problem and the solution.
- We are able to shift their focus to instances when the problem was not quite so bad, what they were doing when that was occurring, and what difference that will make in their interactions with the kid.

In Summary

◇ The SSR model makes use of a solution-focused approach while taking into account the difficulty that kids with complex trauma can have with executive functioning.

◇ Basic to the solution-focused approach is the idea that kids can describe the improvements they would like to see and draw upon their resources to achieve solutions.

◇ Acknowledging the kid's (or referring adult's) experience helps lessen resistance and helps the counselor discover what is working.

◇ Rather than spending a lot of time analyzing the problem, the solution-focused approach shifts attention to exceptions—the times when the problem isn't happening or is a little bit less severe.

◇ Goal setting occurs in a cooperative way, attributing to the kid what he or she has already done to improve and incorporating the small steps the kid believes are doable.

◇ The miracle question is an effective technique to help the kid describe the preferred state and identify an eventual target.

◇ The scaling technique allows incremental description of progress toward a goal.

◇ The solution-focused approach is also effective and helpful to the person referring the kid. The process assists with defining a behavioral description of the desired change, offers information about the kid's strengths and resources, and shifts the focus from the problem to the solution.

6 Integrating the Strategies for Self-Regulation (SSR) Model

> In order for children to thrive at school, they need to be able to function beyond a survival level. When trauma symptoms are addressed and strategies developed to intervene, students' energy is freed up to learn and to engage in pro-social behavior.
>
> Levine & Kline, *Trauma Through a Child's Eyes*

The strategies for self-regulation (SSR) model offers a structure to help kids who have trouble self-regulating move beyond a survival level. In so doing, kids can increase their adaptive behaviors and improve relationship skills. The SSR model is facilitated by our own calm, and it uses the strengths and resources of the student to set goals for behavior change. In addition, the model teaches skills to self-regulate, and it improves social–emotional competencies. These components are supported by Bessel van der Kolk's (2009) view that contemporary neuroscience research suggests effective treatment needs to include (1) learning to modulate arousal; (2) learning to tolerate feelings and sensations by increasing body-based, self-regulatory practices; and (3) learning that after confrontation with physical helplessness, it is essential to take effective action. This chapter integrates and describes the features of the SSR model in-depth and discusses practical logistics for implementation in individual and group counseling, crisis response, and classroom and school-wide practices.

Features of the SSR Model

In the SSR model, we begin by establishing a calm, secure relationship with the student. We work to shift the locus of control to the student by helping him or her set specific, measurable goals and by teaching the somatic skills to self-regulate: grounding, mindful awareness, and tracking sensation. These skills support the student's development of emotional intelligence in the areas of self-awareness, social awareness, self-management, responsible decision making, and relationship skills.

We Begin With Ourselves

As we have learned in previous chapters, our level of calm and self-regulation makes a significant difference in the success of our interventions with students who have trouble self-regulating. Our calm state and our relationship with the student actually promote self-regulation in the child. Therefore, no matter the situation—whether we are intervening in a crisis or doing the ongoing work of helping a student develop skills for self-regulation—first we start with ourselves. We recommend the following process:

- We use a body scan and breath to calm ourselves before we begin.
- We observe a student's emotional and behavioral self-regulation (or lack of) and notice how it effects our emotional state. We then consider how the student's self-regulation effects others.
- We take steps to re-regulate as needed throughout the day.
- We teach caregivers, parents, and teachers the techniques for calming themselves: grounding, mindful awareness, and tracking sensation. Activities for caregivers are found in Appendix B.

Candace Simpson is one of three counselors in a large elementary school. At the beginning of the new school year, she was given many administrative responsibilities. Every morning the top of her desk seemed to grow a few inches of paper. On this particular morning, she had just settled down to confront some of her paperwork when an angry teacher rushed in with a student in tears. Before standing up, Candace let her attention drop to her feet to feel the support of the ground beneath her and took a long slow calming breath. She did this five more times before the transaction with this teacher and student were complete that morning.

We Assess the Kid's Needs

Mental health professionals routinely assess the functioning and safety of the kids in their care, especially those kids who may have experienced trauma or abuse. The first priority is identifying and addressing any threat to a child's stability. Potential threats to safety include self-harm and suicidal behavior, ongoing family violence, abuse, neglect, substance abuse, psychopathology or behavior that places the child at risk for sexual victimization, community violence, abduction or kidnapping, life-threatening accidents, life-threatening illnesses, or legal problems and incarceration. When threats to safety are ongoing or imminent, assessment should concentrate on identifying the severity and monitoring change in these key indicators as services are delivered (Ford & Cloitre, 2009).

In the SSR model, along with the usual clinical assessment, we assess the child's various responses to dysregulation, the consequences of those responses, and possible behaviors that would be more adaptive in the school setting. Assessments include informal interviews, checklists, and observations from referral sources, the child, and us. Our intent is not to provide a formal diagnosis but to identify those aspects of dysregulation that are problematic for the child. We also want to pinpoint the child's internal and external resources for addressing them. Our goal is to describe a baseline of behavior and to establish priorities for our work. Through the use of solution-focused interviewing, we can gather information that focuses on exceptions to the problem, for instance, when it does not occur and what is already working, if even a little. We include quick methods of getting specific descriptions of behaviors from teachers, parents, or the other referring persons. In this way, we can focus our work on the most pressing needs. See Appendix A: Tools, Assessments.

Assessment continues throughout treatment so that we can monitor the process and the outcomes. Scaling techniques give us an easy-to-use method for assessing with the kid where he or she is in achieving goals. We get feedback continually as to what is working from the child and from the referral sources so that the process can be modified as needed. Scaling techniques can easily and effectively be used with adults as well as with kids. Ultimately, we are able to demonstrate improvements and a kid's progress toward his or her goals.

Yvonne is 15 and has a long history of discipline problems at school, primarily because of the difficulty she has with anger. She gets in verbal and physical fights with her peers and yells at teachers. Yvonne has been referred for counseling many times over her years in school but has been uncooperative with the counseling process. Recently, she was referred again. This counselor used the SSR model with Yvonne. Although Yvonne continues to be difficult, avoiding conversation with her about her problems at school and focusing on somatic awareness techniques has had some positive effect. It has helped to bypass her usual defensiveness.

One-on-One Intervention

Sometimes the first encounter you have with a kid happens after an event when the kid is actively dysregulated. Meltdowns and explosive situations are frequent in many classrooms. While de-escalating the situation is the first priority, Daniel Siegel, in *The Developing Mind* (1999), strongly suggests that there is therapeutic potential even in this first encounter. The kid's out-of-control state can be joined neurologically by reflective and supportive dialogue with you. This dialogue, and those that follow, can lead to a better information flow for the kid between his or her dysregulated emotional states and more adaptive thinking. This process will ultimately lead to an improved ability to self-regulate. It's not that kids will no longer be triggered, but that they will have skills to use when they are triggered.

Words spoken in a calm, firm voice are effective, as is a step-by-step plan to help the student out of the mess he or she finds himself in. In the following example, notice the dialogue between the kid's dysregulated emotional state and our adaptive thinking: *Antoine, you're out of control. You got angry so fast it took us all by surprise! You must have been really startled (annoyed, etc.). It's okay now. It's over. We'll work together to help you settle down.* Levine and Kline (2007) describe guidelines for de-escalating an agitated student. See their suggestions in the following list. We would add to this that to the extent feasible, maintain eye contact and use as few words as possible.

- Take a deep breath, step back, and ground yourself first. Let your energy settle into your feet and lower legs, feeling the support of the ground.

- Remind yourself you know what to do because you have memorized this list.
- Adopt a soothing tone of voice.
- Avoid threatening behaviors or gestures.
- State the behavior you observed without shaming or exaggeration.
- Show you understand your student by reflecting his or her overwhelming feelings.
- Avoid threatening punishment.
- Make a statement showing the student he or she is not alone.
- Make a statement showing the relationship can be repaired.
- Make a statement giving a choice to save face.
- Make a statement describing the misbehavior without chastisement.
- Make a statement describing correct behavior and/or what can repair the effects of the infraction.

Individually Scheduled Sessions

We recommend working with kids individually at first to help them improve their emotional regulation. In the SSR model, we teach the essential skills of working with somatic experience as a prerequisite to helping students talk about their experiences and emotions. Going back to the example of Antoine's active dysregulation, notice that there is no questioning of what is wrong or speculation about what happened. In individual and group work, we continue with this approach; by doing so, we avoid running into kids' defenses. We offer our own regulated emotional state and use fun, non-threatening activities to help teach grounding, mindful awareness, and tracking sensations. We teach the kid to use these skills if he or she becomes activated or dysregulated and make access to more adaptive thinking possible, improving neural integration.

Typically, we schedule three or so individual sessions to develop and practice the essential skills. Students will have additional opportunities to practice the skills later in group work. We watch to see how much of a *dose* of a lesson an individual kid can use. *Dose* refers to the amount of time, detail, frequency, and/or intensity offered in a session. We provide safety and the opportunity for corrective relational experience through containment, interactive affect regulation, relational attunement, and responsive communication. We aim for a pace that fits the kid's needs. We build a relationship that is a therapeutic intervention, and we offer kids our calm assurance that our teachings will be helpful.

Over the course of an individual session, we address the tasks listed below. Appendix B: Activities, includes an array of exercises and activities to support skill development. Using your judgment of the best dose for the kid, you can address one task or several in a session. It is not necessary for kids to achieve absolute proficiency with somatic awareness skills. We might focus on only one skill or two skills. We will continue to build upon these skills with most kids in group sessions later. We work longer with those kids who we decide not to place in group. Starting from our calm, regulated emotional state, we establish rapport, build a relationship, and address the following tasks:

1. Teach the basic self-regulation skills of grounding, mindful awareness, and tracking sensations

2. Identify the kid's internal and external resources

3. Teach how to use positive anchors

4. Practice using these skills with episodes of dysregulation

5. Assist the kid in articulating a goal for improved self-regulation

Joey is a 10-year-old boy whose father is in the military and is now away for a second year-long absence. There are three other children in Joey's home, and his mother has been overwhelmed in the role of a single mom. Previously, Joey had average achievement and apparently a good ability to self-regulate. However, this school year his achievement has slowly deteriorated and his teacher, concerned that Joey had undiagnosed attention deficit disorder (ADD), referred him to the counselor. After gathering assessment information, the counselor worked with the teacher to postpone a decision regarding testing for ADD and began using an SSR approach with Joey. He is learning to make use of the skills and he now signals his teacher when he is not able to concentrate. The teacher has created a place in the room where there are fewer distractions, and Joey goes there to do his work after he gives her the signal.

Individual Session Process Recommendations

We invite kids to work with us by offering to teach them skills that can make their situations better. We recommend first teaching kids to use grounding. Grounding is fun, easy to learn, and offers a safety net against the discomfort of hyperarousal. Grounding can immediately increase a kid's sense of competence regarding self-regulation. Sometimes grounding can be enough for some kids to manage their regulation.

As the student is beginning to use grounding effectively, we extend the experience to include training in mindful awareness. We help kids observe what they are experiencing internally and describe it to us. We encourage kids to describe the sensations in different terms than they might typically use for emotions or feelings. Instead, we ask questions directed at physiological experience using sensation vocabulary and listen for words such as *tight, hot, cold, tingly,* and so on. Through this work, kids learn that sensations are different from emotions. They learn to notice specific sensations that are signals of the beginning of dysregulation. In this way, they can calm themselves and then make better choices. The use of mindful awareness encourages focused attention on one experience at a time. Ultimately, this will serve a kid in the midst of situations that usually produce out-of-control hyperarousal.

Tracking sensations is the next skill to be developed. We teach kids that they can use mindful awareness to bring their attention to the sensations they feel in their bodies and use that to de-activate arousal and emotion.

Levine and Kline (2007) suggest developing and practicing sensation vocabulary and to include sensations that are pleasurable or neutral as well as those that are uncomfortable at first.

Some of the sensation vocabulary they suggest include the following:

- cold, warm, hot, chilly
- twitchy, butterflies
- sharp, dull, itchy
- shaky, trembly, tingly
- hard, soft, stuck
- jittery, icy, weak
- relaxed, calm, peaceful
- empty, full
- flowing, spreading
- strong, tight, tense
- dizzy, fuzzy, blurry
- numb, prickly, jumpy
- owie, tearful, goose-bumpy
- light, heavy, open
- tickly, cool, silky
- still, clammy, loose

Becoming skilled in tracking sensations helps kids identify and modulate the sensations that signal trouble and possible dysregulation. Refer to Chapter 4 for a discussion of sensation conversation, activation, de-activation, and moment-to-moment tracking.

The capacity to ground, use mindful awareness, and track sensations will make it possible for kids to use somatic awareness for re-regulating. Appendix B: Activities, contains exercises and activities to facilitate skill development in these three key areas. Following are three sample sessions to illustrate teaching these essential skills for working with the student's somatic experience. We use the term *couselor* here to refer to all mental health practitioners who may be fulfilling a counseling function. We invite you to notice the counselor's use of solution-focused language.

Session 1

Counselor	*I'm glad you came to see me today. Sounds like you've been having a rough time in your classroom.*	The counselor checks his/her own arousal level: breathes and grounds.
Student	*Yes, my teacher picks on me all the time.*	The counselor notices the child's level of arousal before continuing discussion of the problem.
Counselor	*That's rough. Your teacher has been picking on you.*	The counselor acknowledges the student by matching language and position, reflecting what the student has said in the past tense.
Student	*Yes, every time she does, I start to get all mad and frustrated because it isn't fair. Then I have a really hard time doing my work, and I get sent to the principal's office.*	The counselor notices the child's arousal and listens for details of sensations and behavioral descriptions.

Counselor	*That must be hard. I'd like for us to work together so that you can learn some skills to use when things get rough.*	The counselor acknowledges the kid's position and offers a calm relationship through which the kid can learn skills.
Student	*OK, I'd like to do that.*	
Counselor	*OK, let's start with some ideas about breathing. I imagine people have told you to take deep breaths when you are upset. Show me how you do that.*	
Student	*(Demonstrates rapid breathing in upper chest)*	
Counselor	*Let's try a different way of breathing.*	The counselor chooses from breathing exercises in Appendix B: Activities.
Counselor	*What difference will it make for you when you use breathing before you get upset?*	The counselor helps the student visualize using deep breathing in real situations that are likely to provoke arousal.
Counselor	*Now, let's learn something called grounding. We'll use the good breathing you were just showing me and put it together with grounding.*	The counselor chooses an activity from Appendix B: Activities, Grounding. Some kids may think that grounding is like "being grounded." In that case, work with the kid to come up with another name for the grounding technique.
Counselor	*What difference will it make for you when you use grounding before you get upset?*	The counselor helps the student visualize using deep breathing and grounding in real situations that are likely to provoke arousal.
Counselor	*Let's get together again on _____. Between now and then, what do you see yourself doing when you start to get upset?*	The counselor helps the student come up with his or her own task to do between now and the next session.

The counselor checks own arousal level, breathes and grounds self. |

Depending on the age and the arousal level of the child, you may choose to end the first session after the student has learned some grounding techniques. Paying attention to a kid's window of tolerance makes us more effective at increasing it. Allowing plenty of time to learn and practice these skills pays off when a kid begins to work on potentially dysregulating issues later.

Session 2

Counselor	*It's good to see you today. What's better or different since the last time we were together?*	The counselor is focusing the student on the specific work at hand, listening for actions the student has taken to improve the situation and exceptions to the problem. The goal is to find a reason to compliment the student on his/her actions and to get the student to acknowledge what he or she did to make the improvements happen.
Student	*Things are about the same with my teacher, but yesterday when she was picking on me and the other kids were laughing, I tried breathing and grounding. I managed to stay calm so I wasn't sent to the office.*	
Counselor	*Wow! That's really great! How were you able to use breathing and grounding in such a tough situation?*	The counselor is helping the student to examine how he or she was able to use the skills in a stressful situation and to realize that this is a difficult thing to accomplish.
Student	*At first I was about to get really mad, but I was kind of curious to see if breathing and grounding might work. I really didn't want to end up in the principal's office, because my dad and I had plans after school. So I gave it a try.*	
Counselor	*That's really impressive. Thinking about your dad was a resource for you also. Today, let's practice the grounding that you seem pretty good at.*	The counselor chooses from an activity in Appendix B: Activities, Grounding.
Counselor	*Now, while you're grounded, let's see what you notice in your body. Where in your body do you feel that? What are you experiencing now? What are the qualities of that sensation? What about the size, shape, color, weight, or temperature of the sensation? What words match the sensation?*	The counselor teaches mindful awareness through activities in Appendix B: Activities, Mindfulness. The counselor may also practice mindful awareness with an activity from Appendix B: Activities, Tracking Sensations.
Counselor	*What difference will it make for you when you are able to focus on what you are sensing inside your body when you get upset?*	
Student	*When I am paying attention to the sensations inside my body, I might be able to stay calm.*	

| Counselor | *Sounds like that can work for you. Let's get together again on _____. Between now and then, can you notice when you focus on sensations in your body, and how that affects your calmness?* | |

By using mindful awareness, we can train kids and ourselves to become more observant of sensations. It's a good idea to become acquainted with our own sensations in a variety of situations and to notice how we feel when we regain our equilibrium after an upset. The language of sensations is somewhat foreign to kids, so our own experience with identifying sensations brings confidence and authenticity to the training. We can help a kid add to his or her sensation vocabulary by adding words from our own repertoire.

Session 3

Counselor	*It's good to see you again. What's different or better since we were together last time? How are you using grounding, and how are you paying attention to your sensations?*	The counselor gauges his/her level of arousal and grounds before beginning.
Student	*I'm still having some bad times, but mostly I've been able to stay calm, even when other kids are bugging me. I've noticed that when I am about to yell at someone or hit someone, I get a really hot feeling in my stomach.*	
Counselor	*I'm glad you've noticed that. Let's practice a little of the breathing and grounding we've been learning.*	Once the student seems more relaxed, the counselor explores the angry sensation.
Counselor	*Think about being angry and that sensation in your stomach. What else can you tell me about how that feels?*	

Ava is a freshman in high school and experiences high levels of anxiety when she faces important exams. She referred herself to counseling, and she has learned to use grounding, mindful awareness, and tracking sensation to calm herself. She can now call upon the somatic memory of calmness when she gets ready to take an exam.

Deciding to Transition to Group Work

A lot of good work can be achieved individually with students. We believe, though, that the best opportunity for students to generalize their new abilities to self-regulate and maintain emotional stability comes from participating in a group. As the initial individual session goals are beginning to be met, it is time to consider group work. Because of the opportunity for groups to practice, our task as leader is to monitor the degree of self-regulation among group members. We start from the position that group work is beneficial to students, and then ask if there is some reason why the student would not benefit. Our own judgment regarding the student's suitability for group is paramount. Some considerations to inform the decision include the following:

- **Vulnerability to disclosures that could be detrimental.** Some students are not ready to talk about their personal issues in a group without disclosing information that could cause them embarrassment or ridicule.

- **Willingness to work in a group setting.** Some students do not want to be in a group. They will work toward goals privately, but are not ready to work on them with other students.

- **Ability to take turns.** The dynamics of the group setting require that members take turns talking and allow others to receive the attention of the group. Many students need modeling of this behavior and occasional reminders from the group. However, you might consider working individually for a longer period of time with students who seem to have a great deal of difficulty sharing attention.

- **Ability to relate to others positively.** It is critical that group settings be perceived as comfortable and safe for all group members. Group members learn to discover and build upon their strengths. They will also learn to encourage the same in the rest of the group. While group is a good place for kids to learn to respect and give each other support, students who demonstrate antisocial behavior can be harmful to other group members. Including these students in a group will simply give them targets for their misbehavior. We recommend you work with these students individually and include them only when they show the ability to relate positively to others.

- **Level and type of disability.** Students who have disabilities can do well in a group setting. When screening, consider carefully whether the disability will make him or her unable to participate fully or set him or her up to be disliked. When you include students with disabilities, construct groups that can encourage the student's full participation by modifying the material if necessary, selecting compatible group members, and arranging accommodations that support and include the student.

- **Single gender or mixed gender groups.** Consider the developmental age of the student and in which type of group he or she would be most comfortable. Weigh the effect of gender issues on the working of the group. Middle school and early high school groups are typically single gender groups.

Group Logistics

The standard recommendations for running groups in schools apply to SSR groups as well. We elaborate on these ideas in *SOS! A Practical Approach to Leading Solution-Focused Groups With Students K–12* (Tollison & Synatschk, 2007). We find it helpful to address these features when planning an SSR group: size, composition, setting, group agreements, informed consent, duration, communication, monitoring for effectiveness, and social and emotional learning.

Size

We recommend selecting a small group of three to five students. There is much to be accomplished in each group session: Limiting group size to four students, or no more than five, increases the likelihood that each student will receive attention.

Composition

Prior to moving into SSR groups and using the solution-focused approach outlined in Chapter 5, students should craft their goals for improvement for a variety of problem areas, including those affecting self-regulation. As group leader, you can select members of a group to balance needs and the severity of needs. Bringing students whose difficulties with self-regulation vary in intensity allows you, as the group leader, to facilitate students learning from each other while they are all learning new skills.

Setting

Group should be held in a private spot, especially for SSR groups, that allows for some space for movement without injury to the students or the facility. Group activities may generate some noise.

Group Agreements

Group agreements set the rules for member participation and are the foundation for establishing boundaries and safety. Confidentiality and other group rules should be carefully explained and agreement reached before moving a student into a group. It is helpful to have these agreements posted in the group space. Some group leaders have students sign an agreement as a part of their informed consent before participating in group.

Informed Consent

All students participating in the group should be informed prior to the first meeting about how the group will work, what kinds of activities will be included, and what kinds of interactions occur. Students of every age can understand when the explanation matches their development.

Duration

SSR groups are designed to be time-limited and are built on a 10-group-session format. Group members continue to practice self-regulation skills (grounding, mindful awareness, and tracking sensation) with the content focus on the CASEL competencies. We recommend a 10-session format so that each competency area is addressed in two sessions. You may choose to focus either two consecutive sessions on a competency area (or different area) in each of the first five sessions, followed by five sessions in which a higher level of each competency is taught. One method allows a more in-depth treatment of a competency area in a short time span. The other method allows the leader to address each area initially, then return later for more skill development. As with other aspects of the SSR model, the group format may be modified to fit your needs and your students' needs. For a group session planning form, see Appendix A: Tools, Group Counseling.

Communication About Group

As we believe that group is the best place to practice somatic awareness skills for self-regulation and for social and emotional learning (SEL), we usually begin talking with students about group from the first individual session. In addition, sharing the content focus of SSR groups with parents, teachers, and other referral sources helps to gain their involvement and support. See Appendix A: Tools, Group Counseling, for sample information sheets for teachers and for parents.

Monitoring Effectiveness

The solution-focused approach aspect of the SSR model encourages us to continually monitor the effectiveness of the group. We do this by scaling with each student as to his or her progress toward his or her goal and by discussing at each session what is working for the individual student and for the group. The use of scaling with referring adults is a quick way to exchange information and monitor their views of a student's progress. Additionally, we as facilitators have goals for ourselves to evaluate. See Appendix A: Tools, Group Counseling, for items to use in monitoring progress within the group.

Social and Emotional Learning

SSR groups incorporate self-regulation skills, solution-focused approaches, and social and emotional learning. The solution-focused approach provides the framework for helping each student identify a goal and a process to work toward its achievement. A portion of every group session is spent learning and practicing skills to improve each student's ability to self-regulate. In addition to practicing the skills of grounding, mindful awareness, and tracking sensations, we incorporate social and emotional learning (SEL). SEL is the process through which kids acquire the knowledge, attitudes, and skills to recognize and manage their emotions, set and achieve positive goals, demonstrate caring and concern for others, establish and maintain positive relationships, make responsible decisions, and handle interpersonal situations effectively. These critical social–emotional competencies involve skills to enable children to calm themselves when angry, initiate friendships and resolve conflicts respectfully, make ethical and safe choices, and contribute constructively to their communities (Collaborative for Academic, Social, and Emotional Learning, 2003). As mentioned in Chapter 1, the Collaborative for Academic, Social, and Emotional

Learning (CASEL) has identified five groups of inter-related core social and emotional competencies that SEL programs should address:

- **Self-awareness.** Identifying your thoughts, feelings, and strengths, and recognizing how they influence choices and actions
- **Social awareness.** Identifying and understanding the thoughts and feelings of others, developing empathy, and being able to take the perspective of others
- **Self-management.** Handling emotions so that they facilitate rather than interfere with the task at hand, setting long- and short-term goals, and dealing with obstacles that may come your way
- **Responsible decision making.** Generating, implementing, and evaluating positive and informed solutions to problems, and considering the long-term consequences of your actions for yourself and others
- **Relationship skills.** Saying no to peer pressure and working to resolve conflicts in order to maintain healthy and rewarding connections with individuals and groups

These competencies align with the American School Counseling Association (ASCA) National Standards for Students (Campbell & Dahir, 1997). Aligning with the ASCA Standards provides specific indicators of competence in these areas. These specific indicators allow us to be very focused in developing the skills' target for each group session. See Table 6.1 for an expanded list of the competencies as they align with the indicators within the ASCA Standards. In each group session, a skill from one of these five competency areas is taught, practiced, and applied to interactions in the group and to each student's individual goals.

Table 6.1

Alignment of CASEL Competencies With ASCA Standards

CASEL competency	ASCA Indicator—Personal/Social standards	
Self-awareness	A1.1	Develop positive attitudes toward the self as a unique and worthy person
	A1.2	Identify values, attitudes, and beliefs
	A1.5	Identify and express feelings
	A1.7	Recognize personal boundaries, rights, and privacy needs
	A1.10	Identify personal strengths and assets
Social awareness	A1.11	Identify and discuss changing personal and social roles
	A2.2	Respect alternative points of view
	A2.3	Recognize, accept, respect, and appreciate individual differences
	C1.3	Learn about the differences between appropriate and inappropriate physical contact
	C1.4	Demonstrate the ability to set boundaries, rights, and personal privacy
Self-management	A1.3	Learn the goal-setting process
	A1.6	Distinguish between appropriate and inappropriate behavior

(continues)

Table 6.1 *Continued.*

CASEL competency	ASCA Indicator—Personal/Social standards	
	A1.8	Understand the need for self-control and how to practice it
	A1.12	Identify and recognize changing family roles
	A2.6	Use effective communication skills
	B1.4	Develop effective coping skills for dealing with problems
	B1.5	Demonstrate when, where, and how to seek help for solving problems and making decisions
	B1.11	Use persistence and perseverance in acquiring knowledge and skills
	C1.5	Differentiate between situations requiring peer support and situations requiring adult professional help
	C1.6	Identify resource people in the school and community, and know how to seek their help
	C1.10	Learn techniques for managing stress and conflict
	C1.11	Learn coping skills for managing life events
Responsible decision making	A2.1	Recognize that everyone has rights and responsibilities
	B1.1	Use a decision-making and problem-solving method
	B1.2	Understand consequences of decisions and choices
	B1.3	Identify alternative solutions to a problem
	B1.9	Identify long-term and short-term goals
	B1.10	Identify alternative ways of achieving goals
	B1.12	Develop an action plan to set and achieve realistic goals
	C1.7	Apply effective problem-solving and decision-making skills to make safe and healthy choices
Relationship skills	A1.9	Demonstrate cooperative behavior in groups
	A2.8	Learn to make and keep friends
	B1.6	Know how to apply conflict resolution skills
	B1.8	Know when peer pressure is influencing a decision
	C1.9	Learn how to cope with peer pressure

The Role of the Group Leader

Creating a predictable, safe group environment that grows in self-awareness and has specific group skills is the foundation of effective group leadership. SSR group leaders follow good group principles. (For further information, see Schaefer, 1999; Schechtman, 2006; or Tollison & Synatschk, 2007.) Because our primary goal is for the kids to get better and better at self-regulation, in SSR groups we focus our attention on some specific group tasks. These include the following:

- Practicing the self-regulation skills on ourselves as our arousal level changes
- Being aware of the level of self-regulation of each kid

- Monitoring the need for re-regulation in each group member
- Helping group members to become aware of the early signs of their dysregulation
- Helping group members interrupt dysregulation to practice self-regulation skills
- Being aware of which self-regulation skills fit the kid best at this moment
- Amplifying the use of self-regulation skills when they occur
- Offering opportunities to integrate the use of self-regulation skills throughout the group session

While we are helping students develop the skills of self-regulation (grounding, mindful awareness, and tracking sensation), we are working to integrate these three somatic interventions to be used as one skill rather than separate ones. For example, we can ask kids, "What sensations will we notice that tell us we are grounded?" As leaders, we can facilitate each group member noticing how he or she is self-regulating and what might be useful to the fellow group members.

Group Sessions Overview

In the following section we describe typical SSR group sessions. There are small variations depending on where the session falls in the sequence of group sessions. Our goals are to involve the student in working toward his or her goal, promote interaction among group members, continue practicing and developing skills to improve self-regulation (grounding, mindful awareness, and tracking sensation), and promote SEL. The group is both a learning environment and a place to practice becoming self-regulated. Generally, the process in each session is very similar. See Appendix A: Tools, Group Counseling, for group session outlines containing scripts and discussion questions for Session 1 through the Booster Session.

Session 1

This first session focuses on orienting group members to each other and to the structure of the group. After roll call, we welcome the group members and have them introduce themselves. As with all sessions, we begin with a grounding activity this session. Depending on the particular group and each member's needs, you may also choose to focus on mindful awareness and tracking sensation. You may choose to always use the same practice activity to begin each meeting or vary the activity. (Encouraging members to share experiences helps to highlight the use of somatic awareness throughout each session and in their daily lives.) Next, we review group agreements. Then have members review their goals. Follow with an SEL activity. Apply the lesson to the individual member goals and have students discuss their plans for putting new ideas into action in the next week through specific task development. Use scaling for evaluation and planning. Dismiss the group and complete group notes and evaluation. Throughout the session, notice individual kid's level of arousal, inserting opportunities to practice self-regulation skills. As the leader, continue to monitor your level of arousal and re-regulate as needed.

Sessions 2–9

The following eight sessions start with roll call, a grounding activity, and status check-in: listening to each member's status in working toward his or her goal since the last session. Ask solution-focused questions regarding goals that include differences, exceptions, and scaling, and find ways to compliment students for efforts they have made since the last session toward accomplishing their goals. Watch for opportunities to practice re-regulation in the moment. Follow with an SEL activity, and apply the lesson to the members' goals. Inquire about the members' plans for the next week. Use scaling for evaluation and planning. Dismiss the group, and then complete group notes and evaluation.

Session 10

In the final session, repeat the procedures from Sessions 2–9 with a focus on members' plans for continuing to build on the skills they have learned. Add a celebration of successes and achievements and an acknowledgment of graduation from the group. Discuss plans for a booster session. Dismiss the group and complete group notes and evaluation.

Booster Session

We like the idea of building in a booster session at the end of the series of group meetings. We schedule it out a bit, separating it from the end of group by several weeks or a month. It is a scheduled meeting that allows ready follow-up for group members on the achievement of their goals. It also eases the transition for group members who are reluctant to end the group. The leader should follow the same format as with regular group sessions. Some ideas for discussion include the following:

- *Since we were last together, what have you noticed in your life (family, relationships, at school, etc.) that you want to continue to happen?*
- *What have you done to make that happen?*
- *What have you noticed about your ability to identify early signs that you may be getting dysregulated (revved up, triggered, etc.)?*
- *What has worked to calm yourself?*
- *How were you able to do that?*

Begin with a self-regulation activity that integrates grounding, mindful awareness, and tracking sensation. Select an SEL activity the kids enjoyed during group sessions and reinforce the skills taught with additional opportunities for practice. Ask the students if you may call on them in the future for their ideas and suggestions for helping others deal with situations similar to those they have successfully changed. Finally, offering students an open door for future contacts seems to reduce any apprehension surrounding the ending of group.

Marcus is 6 years old and was referred because of his frequent meltdowns and friendship difficulties. He is in an SSR group that has been meeting for 5 weeks. According to his counselor, his meltdowns are less frequent in the group, but he continues to have trouble getting along with the three other group members. During a recent group, Marcus began knocking his chair into the chair of another group member, a boy, who then began to retaliate.

The counselor took a calming breath to re-regulate himself and then made eye contact with the two members who were in conflict. He also asked that all group members stop and check in with themselves. He asked them to notice what sensations they were experiencing and to take a moment to just watch them. After a few moments, the counselor asked if members had noticed something they could share. Marcus spoke up and said he had felt his heart beating fast; other members joined with reports. The counselor came back to Marcus and asked what he thought they should do now. Marcus said simply, "Ground!"

Crisis Relief With the SSR Model

Throughout this book, we have discussed an approach to helping students who have difficulties with self-regulation: difficulties that seemingly came about as a result of previous (and, perhaps, long ago) traumatic experiences. Unfortunately, new crises occur daily for students in our schools, with no locality or school level immune. The following section will guide you through ways to respond to a crisis in the moment and in the aftermath, with individuals, small groups, and an entire class so that we can help prevent future trauma.

The SSR model's goal in responding to the aftermath of a crisis is to assist students with the discharge of traumatic energy so that the crisis does not become traumatizing. There is no focus on describing the details of the event. This is also the format of Levine and Kline's First Aid for Trauma Prevention (2007, p. 461). See Appendix A: Tools for a useful brochure version of these eight steps. When a child needs immediate attention in a crisis situation, such as when he or she has been exposed to a threatening, frightening, or painful experience, Levine and Kline recommend the following eight steps for action. (These may be used as soon as the child is in a safe, quiet place):

1. **Check your own body's response first.** Take time to notice your own level of fear or concern. Next, take a full deep breath, and as you exhale s-l-o-w-l-y feel the sensations in your own body. Repeat until you feel settled. The time it takes to establish a sense of calm is time well spent. It will increase your capacity to attend fully to the child. Your composure will greatly reduce the likelihood of frightening or confusing the child further.

2. **Assess the situation.** If the child shows signs of shock, do not allow him or her to jump up and return to activities. (Signs of psychological shock can be contradictory, including either little emotional expression or excessive crying. Other signs include hyperactivity; dissociation, not emotionally present; lack of focused eye contact, confused stare, fixed gaze, vacant or distant look; chronic posture or repetitive movement.) You might say something like, "We're going to sit (or lie) still for a while and wait until the shock wears off." Remember a calm, confident voice communicates to the child that you will help him or

her. Even if you do not observe any of the signs of shock, but have a sense that what has happened may be too great to be metabolized without assistance, continue the steps.

3. **As the shock wears off, guide the child's attention to his or her sensations.** Softly ask the child how he or she feels in his or her body. Repeat the answer as a question—*You feel okay in your body?*—and wait for a nod or other response. Be more specific in the next question: *How do you feel in your tummy (head, arm, leg, etc.)?* If he or she mentions a distinct sensation, gently ask about its location, size, shape, color, temperature, or weight (e.g., *heavy or light*). Keep guiding the child to stay with the present moment with questions such as, *How does the _____ feel now?*

4. **Slow down and follow the child's pace by carefully observing any changes.** This may be the hardest part for the adult, but it's the most important part for the child. Allowing a minute or two of silence between questions allows deeply restorative physiological cycles to engage. Too many questions asked too quickly disrupt the natural course. Your calm presence and patience are sufficient to facilitate the movement and release of excess energy. Be alert to cues that let you know a cycle has finished. If uncertain whether a cycle has been completed, wait and watch for the child to give you clues. Examples of clues include a deep, relaxed, spontaneous breath; the cessation of crying or trembling; a stretch; a yawn; a smile; or making or breaking eye contact. The completion of this cycle may not mean that the recovery process is over. Another cycle may follow. Keep the child focused on sensations for a few more minutes just to make sure the process is complete. Wait to see if another cycle begins or if there is a sense that the child has had enough for now.

5. **Keep validating the child's physical responses.** Resist the impulse to stop the child's tears or trembling, while reminding him or her that whatever happened is over and that he or she will be OK. The child's reactions need to continue until he or she stops on his or her own. Your task is to convey to the child that crying and trembling are normal, healthy reactions. A reassuring hand on the back, shoulder, or arm, along with a few gently spoken words as simple as, *That's OK* or *That's right. Just let the scary stuff shake right out of you* will help immensely.

6. **Trust in the child's innate ability to heal.** As you become increasingly comfortable with your own sensations, it will be easier to relax and follow the child's lead. Your primary function, once the process has begun, is to not disrupt it. Trust the child's innate ability to heal. Trust your own ability to allow this to happen. Your job is to stay with the child, creating a safe container. Use a calm voice and reassuring hand to let the child know that he or she is on the right track. To avoid unintentional disruption of the process, don't shift the child's position, distract his or her attention, hold him or her too tightly, or position yourself too close or too far away for comfort. Notice when the child begins to reorient to the environment. Orientation is a sign of completion.

7. **Encourage the child to rest, even if he or she doesn't want to.** Deep discharges generally continue during rest and sleep. Do not stir up discussion about the mishap by asking questions. Later, the child may want to tell a story about it, draw a picture, or play it through. If a lot of energy was mobilized, the release will continue. The next cycle may be too subtle for you to notice, but the rest promotes a fuller recovery, allowing the body to gently vibrate, give off heat, go through skin color changes, and so on as the nervous system returns to relaxation and equilibrium. These changes happen naturally. All you have to do is provide a calm, quiet environment.

8. **Attend to the child's emotional responses and help him or her make sense of what happened.** Later, when the child is rested and calm—even the next day—set aside some time for him or her to talk about his or her feelings and what he or she experienced. Normalize any feelings expressed and tell the child whatever he or she is feeling is OK and worthy of your time and attention. Drawing, painting, and working with clay can be very helpful in releasing strong emotions. Play works especially well with the preverbal or less verbal child.

SSR Crisis Relief Response

With the SSR model's combination of self-regulation skills, a relationship with a calming adult, and a solution-focused approach, we view the purposes of crisis relief response to be (1) monitored assistance to facilitate the release of excess arousal energy, (2) symptom relief through accessing resources to re-regulate, (3) acknowledgement of the experience and what the child is already doing that helps, and (4) accommodating goals for improvement. Like Somatic Experiencing® (successfully used with children in Thailand after the 2004 South Asian tsunami, and with survivors of Hurricanes Katrina and Rita in the United States), the SSR model is very different from some other crisis response methods, which are focused on gathering and disseminating information and asking kids to describe the catastrophe. Research is beginning to show that crisis response models that ask victims to talk about their experiences with no protocol for processing what gets stirred up cause the terror to be relived rather than relieved. Instead, a critical difference with the SSR model is that children are asked to share their post-event difficulties—not their memories (Levine & Kline, 2007).

We are interested in what has been happening since the incident. This information gives us clues to the child's coping strategies and their internal and external resources. In this approach, we inquire about how kids have been feeling and if they are having physical experiences that are unusual for them. Refer to Chapter 1 for primary and secondary symptoms that are distinguishing signs that an experience, or experiences, has been greater than could be tolerated. We listen for those signs and work to help kids understand that their reactions are common reactions after a traumatic event. Great care is taken to avoid re-traumatization by refraining from encouraging children to tell the story or probing for a description of the worst thing that happened. Instead, support is given by observing and listening to the child's description of bodily sensations and helping him to move out of possible shock and distress. We are particularly attentive to descriptions of sensations associated with hyperarousal, dissociation, and constriction/freeze. We process arousal and emotion in very small increments, helping kids with "putting on the brakes" as needed.

Remember that as the helper, you should monitor your empathic responses and the sensations in your body so you can re-regulate as needed to take care of yourself and offer interactive affect regulation to the kid. The focus of this work is not on the horror of the event; rather it is on the completion of the body's responses to protect and defend itself and others. Our calm makes it more possible to recognize and continue the strategies that are helpful. Once there is relative calm, solution-focused conversation around the miracle question, exceptions, scaling, and goal setting are useful techniques for crisis relief as well.

Crisis Relief Response With Individuals and Groups

Crisis relief work can be done effectively with individual students, small groups, or an entire class. While some students initially are best served individually, in schools where many students have experienced a catastrophe, providing crisis relief in groups of students is highly effective. The same beneficial reasons we have for implementing SSR groups apply when your work involves helping kids through a crisis. As one student volunteers to process his or her symptoms and get relief, the shyer students gain confidence and ask for their turn. Kids are great sources of support for each other, and they will offer ideas about what works for them. We have all experienced the relief of knowing that others feel the way we do.

At the same time, there are important reasons why we would choose to work with a student individually following a crisis. One of those reasons has to do with the level of trauma exposure. It is essential when working with a group of kids, to group kids with like levels of trauma exposure together. Do not mix kids who have had an intense experience with kids who had less connection to the event. This helps to lessen any chances of one kid's experience traumatizing another.

Adjust language and the activities you choose to the developmental level of the student(s). Guidelines for working either with individual students or with groups of three to five students include the following:

1. **Remember, our calm creates calm.** Take a moment to ground yourself and access your resources for regulation. Do periodic check-ins with yourself, and re-regulate when you need to.

2. **Create a safe container by setting time and confidentiality boundaries.** Do not probe for details of the event. Instead, explain to the student(s) that you will teach skills to help lessen symptoms so they can get some relief and rebalance. If you are working with a student and he or she begins to talk about the details of the experience, listen and then gently bring him or her back to the idea that the skills you are going to teach will help with what has happened.

3. **Normalize responses.** At a developmentally appropriate level, educate the student(s) regarding how the brain responds to emergencies by giving us extra energy. Continue by explaining that if we do not need all that extra energy, it is important to release it. Whether you are working with an individual or a group, explain that they will be learning about inner sensations and how to use them to help release that extra emergency energy and to move stuck feelings, images, and worrisome thoughts out of the body and mind.

4. **Inquire about how the student(s) is feeling in his or her body and normalize any symptoms.** Explain what a *sensation* is (distinguishing it from an *emotion*) and with a group, ask if anyone can identify a sensation they are feeling. Following that, have the group (or individual) brainstorm various sensation words. Write these on the board or a tablet for all to see. Normalize experiencing sensations, such as trembling or shaking, being tearful, jittery, nauseous, warm, cool, numb, or noticing feelings associated with wanting to run, fight, disappear, or hide. Let the group members know that these are sensations that can occur as their bodies are releasing the extra emergency energy that they do not need.

5. **Teach a grounding technique.** You can introduce grounding as a way to re-balance. Ask the student(s) to find a comfortable position in his or her chair or on the floor. Invite the student to feel his or her feet touching the floor, the support of what he or she is sitting on, and the breath as he or she inhales and exhales. Or you may choose a particular grounding activity from Appendix B: Activities, Grounding, to help calm hyperarousal. Make sure the student(s) feels grounded and safe.

6. **Use the experience of grounding to teach the use of mindful awareness to observe tracking sensation.** Have the student(s) describe a sensation of something that brings comfort or pleasure. Have the student(s) describe what he or she feels now as he or she recalls those good feelings. If you are working with a group, do this by going around the group, asking each student for a contribution.

7. **Ask the student(s) what kinds of difficulties he or she is struggling with since the event.** Acknowledge the experience: *Wow, that must have been tough. How have you managed to this point? How have you kept things from getting worse?* Ask him or her to describe what he or she is feeling and noticing in the body when thoughts about the incident arise. The idea is to follow the student's (or group's) lead. Help them to explore, with an attitude of curiosity, what happens next as they notice their internal experiences. Offer them the opportunity to recall positive memories and the experiences to calm themselves.

8. **Discover exceptions to the problem.** Identifying the times when the problem occurs less can identify strategies for lessening the impact of the problem at those times when it reappears. These exceptions may occur in different situations in a person's life, but the skills are useful in all situations. To explore with students to find exceptions, ask the following: *Have there been times when you were involved with a problem similar to this? How did you handle similar situations in a way that seemed to help? In the past, how have you handled other really rough times? When has this problem not occurred?*

9. **Give compliments.** Listen for ways in which the student has improved or kept from getting worse and compliment his or her efforts: *Wow! How have you been able to do that?*

10. **Set goals.** Ask the student what needs to be better for him or her, and help him or her state the goal in specific, behavioral terms. Listen for wishes kids have for possible goals, knowing that students may have a

very different goal in this situation than we would project for them. Their goals drive our work. Ask the students the following: *How do you want things to be? What will you be doing differently when that is occurring? What difference will it make for you when that is happening? Think of a time when you were able to do this, if even for a little while.*

11. **Task development.** Ask the kids the following: *From your descriptions of what has worked before during other tough moments, what would you suggest trying for this afternoon (today, this week)? How will you do that? What can you do (and how can you use what we learned here) to help yourself in the next day (hour, week, etc.)? What will I see you doing when things are just a little better?* Help the student(s) identify what actions he or she will be taking when this different state is occurring and encourage the use of somatic awareness skills to help meet the goal.

12. **Decide if you need another session.** Depending on the situation, you may decide that one meeting is sufficient, or you may decide that you need to meet with the student(s) more than once for follow up and to continue the crisis relief process.

Crisis Relief Response in the Classroom

In the aftermath of a crisis situation that has affected an entire classroom and/or school, the SSR model offers crisis relief following the same principles we use with individuals and small groups. Those principles are (1) calming and grounding ourselves first and re-regulating as necessary, (2) avoiding going over the details of the crisis, (3) teaching students to use somatic skills to discharge any emergency energy and to re-regulate, and (4) helping students to create a goal for themselves of what will make things better for them based on what is working for them already. With a classroom, we do not ask each student for a response, but we do invite students to share their experiences of learning the skills, encouraging full, active participation. The following steps offer a format that you can adapt to respond to a specific crisis:

- **Before entering the classroom, do a body scan.** Check in with yourself and gauge your level of arousal. Use a grounding technique that works for you. Breathe into any areas where there are sensations that are not serving a sense of calm. Remember, your calm alone will be calming. Continue to re-regulate during the time you spend in the classroom when you need to.

- **Match your language to the developmental level of the students.** Tell the students you have come to meet with them because of what has happened. Let them know you are going to teach some skills to use to help them when bad things happen. Explain these skills help to bring us back to a calm place inside. Suggest they can use these skills now and after you leave to help relax. Avoid suggesting they will have any particular problems, while at the same time, presenting the idea when something bad happens, we want to pay attention to how we are affected.

- **Choose a grounding exercise and go through it with the class.** Inquire about how students feel in their bodies, and use the conversation to open a discussion of sensations. Ask students to notice what sensations they might be feeling and to simply watch what happens when we start to notice sensations. Depending on the situation and the students' responses, teach the use of breath to relax. Normalize all responses: Specifically, mention how tears might come to our eyes and/or how we might feel our bodies tremble. As you go through the steps you choose to use, leave time for students to fully experience and consider what you are teaching them.

- **If students begin to describe the details of their experience, calmly and gently bring them back to their somatic experience in the moment.** (Notice the possible need for follow-up with individuals.) End the session with the grounding exercise that was used initially. Check in with the students and inquire again how they are feeling in their bodies. Remind them they can use the skills you have practiced with them to relax anytime they need to. Using solution-focused language, suggest students define a small, specific goal for themselves that will help them in the next days. Decide if a follow up meeting would helpful to these students.

- **Keep an eye out for trauma symptoms.** (See the list of symptoms in Chapter 1.) Consider offering students who are demonstrating these symptoms more individual or small-group time to resolve their response to the crisis.

Classroom and School-Wide Applications of the SSR Model

Even when there is no immediate crisis, there are many things teachers and other professionals can do to help in the classroom and throughout the school with children who have difficulties managing self-regulation. We recommend teaching faculty and staff the SSR somatic awareness skills so they can use them for their self-regulation and teach students to use them. Schools where the faculty and staff have taken specific steps to build supportive school environments for helping kids affected by trauma are sometimes referred to as *trauma-sensitive* (Craig, 2008; Gianesin, Gianesin, & Nau, 2008). A *trauma-sensitive* school climate is one in which caring and calming adults are committed to developing a school culture that can contain, manage, and help transform the life experiences of traumatized children. A trauma-sensitive approach helps educators appreciate that many of the troublesome, seemingly intractable behaviors observed in their students are related to overwhelming experiences of trauma.

These schools serve as protective environments for children, helping them acquire the social, emotional, and physical resources they need to succeed. They are nurturing, developmentally appropriate, and educationally rich environments that advocate for, support, and believe in all children (Garbarino et al., 1992). The following is a list of trauma-sensitive supports that schools can provide:

- **Trauma-specific training for teachers about how to avoid personalization of children's behaviors.** This helps teachers remain emotionally responsive and focused on developing children's competencies rather than engaging in cycles of conflict and trauma re-enactments.

- **A consultation for teachers with a mental-health professional who is knowledgeable about the effects of trauma.** This helps teachers recognize and guard against symptoms of burnout or compassion fatigue.
- **Training for children on how to use mindful awareness to control their emotions and moods and maintain a comfortable level of arousal.** Techniques to include are visualization, deep breathing, grounding, mindful awareness, and tracking sensations.
- **Help for children to identify their window of tolerance for classroom activities.**
- **Teaching children to ask for a break.** Children and adolescents who have experienced trauma do not learn well in highly emotional situations. Teaching children to ask for a break when they have reached their limit helps prevent problems in the classroom. Students can use a signal, a card, or certain words to let the teacher know.
- **Training to help children notice how they feel.** Use some type of rating scale. Ask students to describe the sensations they feel in their bodies. Call attention to the activities that help them feel good.
- **Support for activities or times of day that are particularly difficult for children.** These might include transition times.
- **Providing consistent and predictable activities.** This might include posting the schedule and reviewing it every day. Visual reminders of activities help students know what is coming next.
- **Finding opportunities to check in with students.** The teacher or other adult who is important to the child can smile, shake each student's hand, and ask a scaling question at the beginning of the day to be aware of the emotional states students are experiencing as they arrive.
- **Finding consensus among the adults working with a child about what is expected.**
- **Rehearsing strategies to help children practice the behaviors they will need in a new situation.**
- **Helping kids who are concerned about others intruding in the space around them.** Enlist the help of the students to define boundaries and to tape off the space around each desk on the floor. Have students ask each other's permission to enter the space.
- **Avoiding asking children to explain their behavior.** This can relieve escalation when they appear angry or out of control, providing them with a safe place to cool down before trying to discuss the behavior or to make a plan for avoiding similar occurrences in the future.
- **Providing opportunities for students to use journaling and other writing activities.** This can help them find the words to describe feeling states. Remind students they can include feeling and sensation words.
- **Creating a climate of emotional safety.** You may do this by establishing classroom and school rules that encourage respect for one another.

- **Training for children about the conflict cycle.** Teach the steps to de-escalate conflict. Analyze the behavior of characters who face conflict in favorite stories. Reading stories from multiple perspectives helps children see that the private logic of one character is not the only way of interpreting the events taking place.
- **Giving children experiences being the helper.** Let children be a helper instead of always being the one who is helped.
- **Reminding children frequently you are there to keep them safe.**
- **Creating a crisis-free classroom.** Eliminate terms such as *crisis intervention*. Instead, encourage children to work with you to anticipate problems and create solutions and options for additional support before situations get out of control.
- **Noticing, acknowledging, and actively eliciting acts of kindness.**
- **Following classroom rules such as those described in the book** *You Can't Say You Can't Play* **(Paley, 1992).** The simple rule is this: If a classmate asks to play with you, you can't say that you can't play. Starting with this rule in kindergarten lays a foundation that encourages inclusion and discourages cruelty between children.
- **Actively intervening to stop stereotyping and teasing.**

In Summary

✧ The SSR model combines a relationship with a calming adult using solution-focused approaches with teaching somatic awareness skills to help kids learn to re-regulate, increase adaptive behavior, and improve relationship skills.

✧ The model can be used in individual and group counseling settings, and in the classroom, school-wide, or with crises.

✧ Fundamental to the implementation of the model is the calm perspective of the caring adult with whom the child shares a relationship. The adult's calm state helps the child learn to self-regulate and accept help in regulation from others.

✧ The solution-focused approach brings a perspective that acknowledges the experiences of the child and supports the kid's goals for improvement, using their own resources.

✧ While practicing self-regulation skills, students engage in activities that encourage social–emotional learning, developing their emotional intelligence.

✧ Using the SSR model in a group format allows students to practice self-regulation, generalize the behaviors and skills they've learned, and apply them to everyday use.

✧ Providing crisis relief through the SSR model is different than other crisis intervention models as it does not ask the student to retell the story. Rather, the student is supported in becoming grounded and mindfully aware of his or her sensations; in tracking sensations; and in identifying goals, exceptions, and what he or she is already doing to make things better.

✧ Self-regulation can be encouraged, and kids who have been traumatized can be supported daily in classrooms and throughout the school. Activities that show respect for the individual, take steps to anticipate needs for support, and commit to offering support go a long way toward de-escalating emotional and behavioral problems and help kids learn they are not alone.

References

Agazarian, Y., & Gant, S. (2000). *Autobiography of a theory.* London, England: Jessica Kingsley.

Akin, T., Dunne, G., & Schilling, D. (2000). *Helping kids make wise choices and reduce risky behavior.* Austin, TX: PRO-ED.

Allen, J. (2001). *Traumatic relationships and serious mental disorders.* London, England: Wiley.

Baker, J. (2008). *No more meltdowns.* Arlington, TX: Future Horizons.

Bander, R., & Grinder, J. (1979). *Frogs into princes: Neuro linguistic programming.* Boulder, CO: Real People Press.

Bedi, R. P., Davis, M. D., & Williams, M. (2005). Critical incidents in the formation of the therapeutic alliance from the clients' perspective. *Psychotherapy: Theory, Research, Practice, Training, 42,* 311–323.

Benjo, C., Scotta, C., Letellier, B., & Arnal II, S. (Producers), & Cantet, L. (Director). (2008). *The class* [Motion picture]. France: Haut et Court.

Berg, I. K., & Steiner, T. (2003). *Children's solution work.* New York: Norton.

Bloom, S. (1997). *Creating sanctuary: Toward the evolution of sane societies.* London: Routledge.

Bodrova, E., & Leong, D. J. (1996). *Tools of the mind: The Vygotskian approach to early childhood education.* Englewood Cliffs, NJ: Merrill/Prentice Hall.

Bowlby, J. (1969). *Attachment and loss* (Vol. 1). New York, NY: Basic Books.

Brantbjerg, M. H. (2007) *Resource oriented skill training as a psychotherapeutic method.* Copenhagen: Bodydynamic International.

Campbell, C. A., & Dahir, C. A. (1997). *Sharing the vision: National standards for school counseling programs.* Alexandria, VA: American School Counselor Association.

Carey, B. (2008, July 15). Calm down or else. *The New York Times.* Retrieved from http://www.nytimes.com

Cassidy, J., & Shaver, P. (1999). *Handbook of attachment: Theory, research, and clinical applications.* New York, NY: Guilford Press.

Collaborative for Academic, Social, and Emotional Learning. (2003). *Safe and sound: An educational leader's guide to evidence-based social and emotional learning programs.* Chicago, IL: Author.

Cozolino, L. (2002). *The neuroscience of psychotherapy: Building and rebuilding the human brain.* New York, NY: Norton.

Craig, S. E. (2008). *Reaching and teaching children who hurt: Strategies for your classroom.* Baltimore, MD: Paul H. Brookes.

Damasio, A. (1999). *The feeling of what happens.* New York, NY: Harcourt, Brace.

de Shazer, S. (1985). *Key to solution in brief therapy.* New York, NY: Norton.

de Shazer, S. (1988). *Clues: Investigating solutions in brief therapy.* New York, NY: Norton.

de Shazer, S., Berg, I., Lipchik, E., Nunnally, E., Molnar, A., Gingerick, W., & Weiner-Davis, M. (1986). Brief therapy: Focused solution development. *Family Process, 25,* 207–222.

Downing, K. (2008). *The sensation game.* Austin, TX: Sensation Game.

Erickson, E. (1950). *Identity and the life cycle.* New York, NY: International Universities Press.

Evans, R. I. (1975). *Carl Rogers: The man and his ideas.* New York, NY: Dutton.

Fisher, J. & Ogden, P. (2009). Sensorimotor psychotherapy. In C. Courtois & J. D. Ford (Eds.), *Treating complex traumatic stress disorders: An evidence-based guide* (pp. 312–328). New York, NY: Guilford Press.

Flook, L., Smalley, S. L., Kitil, M. J., Dang, J., Cho, J., Kaiser-Greenland, S., . . . Kasari, C. (2008, April). *A mindful awareness practice improves executive function in preschool children.* Poster presented at the Center for Mindfulness in Medicine, Health Care, and Society 6th Annual Conference, Worcester, MA.

Ford, J. D. (2009). Neurobiological and developmental research. In C. A. Courtois & J. D. Ford (Eds.), *Treating complex traumatic stress disorders: An evidence-based guide* (pp. 31–58). New York, NY: Guilford Press.

Ford, J. D., & Cloitre, M. (2009). Best practices in psychotherapy for children and adolescents. In C. A. Courtois & J. D. Ford (Eds.), *Treating complex traumatic stress disorders: An evidence-based guide* (pp. 59–81). New York, NY: Guilford Press.

Ford, J. D., & Courtois, C. A. (2009). Defining and understanding complex trauma and complex traumatic stress disorders. In C. A. Courtois & J. D. Ford (Eds.), *Treating complex traumatic stress disorders: An evidence-based guide* (pp. 13–30). New York, NY: Guilford Press.

Fosha, D. (2000). *The transforming power of affect: A model for accelerated change.* New York, NY: Basic Books.

Fosha, D. (2003). Dyadic regulation and experiential work with emotion and relatedness in trauma and disorganized attachment. In M. F. Soloman & D. J. Siegel (Eds.), *Healing trauma* (pp. 221–281). New York, NY: Norton.

Fosha, D. (2007, October). *Dyadic affect regulation and the metaprocessing of attachment, emotion, and transformation in the treatment of attachment trauma.* Paper presented at a meeting of the Austin Society for Psychoanalytic Psychology, Austin, TX.

Garbarino, J., Dubrow, N., Kostelny, K., & Pardo, C. (1992). *Children in danger: Coping with the consequences of community violence.* San Francisco, CA: Jossey-Bass.

Gianesin, J., Gianesin, L., & Nau, E. (2008, April). *Creating a trauma sensitive school.* Paper presented at the School Social Workers of America Annual Conference, Denver, CO.

Glading, S. T. (2003) *Group work: A counseling specialty.* Upper Saddle River, NJ: Merrill/ Prentice-Hall.

Goldman, D. (1995). *Emotional intelligence.* New York, NY: Bantam Books.

Goodman, T. (2005). Working with children: Beginner's mind. In C. Germer, R. Siegel, & P. Fulton (Eds.), *Mindfulness and psychotherapy* (pp. 197–219). New York: NY Guilford Press.

Grepmair, L., Mitterlehner, F., Loew, T., Bachler, E., Rother, W., & Nickel, M. (2007). Promoting mindfulness in psychotherapists in training influences the treatment results of their patients: A randomized, double-blind, controlled study. *Psychotherapy and Psychosomatics, 76,* 332–338.

Hanken, D., & Kennedy, J. (1998). *Getting to know you: A social skills curriculum for grades 4 & 5.* Minneapolis, MN: Educational Media.

Heckman, J. (2008). Schools, skills, and synapses. *Western Economic Association International, 45*(3), 289–324.

Homan, K., Logan, G., Meyer, D., & Tsetan, K. R. (2008, March). *Of Buddas and brains: An exploration of contemplative practice and neural integration.* Symposium conducted at the meeting of Austin-In-Connection, Austin, TX.

Hundert, J. (2009). *Inclusion of students with autism: Using ABA-based supports in general education.* Austin, TX: PRO-ED.

Kabat-Zinn, J. (1991). *Full catastrophe living: Using the wisdom of the body and mind to face stress, pain, and mess.* New York, NY: Bantam Books.

Kinsler, P., Courtois, C., & Frankel, A. (2009). Therapeutic alliance and risk management. In C. Courtois & J. D. Ford (Eds.), *Treating complex traumatic stress disorders: An evidence-based guide* (pp. 183–201). New York, NY: Guilford Press.

Lantieri, L. (2008). *Building emotional intelligence.* Boulder, CO: Sounds True.

Lawson, D. M. (2009). Understanding and treating children who experience interpersonal maltreatment: Empirical findings. *Journal of Counseling & Development, 87,* 204–215.

LeDoux, J. (1998). *The emotional brain: The mysterious underpinnings of emotional life.* New York, NY: Simon & Schuster.

Levine, P. A. (1997). *Waking the tiger: Healing trauma.* Berkeley, CA: North Atlantic Books.

Levine, P. A. (2005). *Healing trauma.* Boulder, CO: Sounds True.

Levine, P. A., & Kline, M. (2007). *Trauma through a child's eyes.* Berkeley, CA: North Atlantic Books.

Levine, P. A., & Kline, M. (2008). *Trauma-proofing your kids.* Berkeley, CA: North Atlantic Books.

Linehan, M. M. (1993) *Cognitive-behavioral treatment of borderline personality disorder.* New York, NY: Guilford Press.

Main, M., & Solomon, J. (1990). Procedures for identifying as disorganized/disoriented during the Ainsworth Strange Situation. In M. Greenberg, D. Cichetti, & E. Cummings (Eds.), *Attachment in the Preschool Years: Theory, Research, and Intervention* (pp. 121–166). Chicago, IL: University of Chicago Press.

Malekoff, A. (2004). *Group work with adolescents: Principles and practice* (2nd ed.). New York, NY: Guilford Press.

Martin, D. J., Garske, J. P., & Davis, M. K. (2000). Relation of the therapeutic alliance with outcome and other variables: A meta-analytic review. *Journal of Consulting and Clinical Psychology, 68,* 438–450.

Messina, C. (2003). *Brain friendly guidance activities to build emotional intelligence.* Austin, TX: PRO-ED.

Metcalf, L. (2008). *Counseling towards solutions* (2nd ed.). San Francisco, CA: Wiley.

Miller, A., Rathus. J., & Linehan, M. (2007). *Dialectical behavior therapy with suicidal adolescents.* New York, NY: Guilford Press.

Miller, G. (1997). *Becoming miracle workers: Language and meaning in brief therapy.* New York, NY: Aldine de Gruyter.

Murphy, J. J. (1994). Working with what works: A Solution-focused approach to school behavior problems. *School Counselor, 42,* 59–65.

Murphy, J. J. (2008). *Solution-focused counseling in schools* (2nd ed.). Alexandria, VA: American Counseling Association.

Ogden, P. (2010). Affect regulation, attachment, and trauma: A sensorimotor approach. Austin, TX: Sensorimotor Psychotherapy Institute.

Ogden, P., & Minton, K. (2000). One method for processing traumatic memory. *Traumatology, 6*(3, article 3).

Ogden, P., Minton, K., & Pain, C. (2006). *Trauma and the body.* New York, NY: Norton.

O'Hanlon, B., & Beadle, S. (1997). *A guide to possibility land: Fifty-one methods for doing brief respectful therapy.* New York, NY: Norton.

Paley, V. (1992). *You can't say you can't play.* Cambridge, MA: First Harvard University Press.

Perrin, S., Smith, P., & Yule, W. (2000). The assessment and treatment of post-traumatic stress disorder in children and adolescents. *Journal of Child Psychology and Psychiatry, 41,* 277–289.

Perry, B. D. (2006). Applying principles of neurodevelopment to clinical work with maltreated and traumatized children. In N. Boyd (Ed.), *Working with traumatized youth in child welfare* (pp. 27–52). New York, NY: Guilford Press.

Pichot, T., & Dolan, Y. M. (2003). *Solution-focused brief therapy: Its effective use in agency settings.* Binghamton, NY: Haworth Clinical Press.

Porges, S. (2007). *Being present in body and mind: An integration of clinical treatment and neuroscience research* [CD]. Los Angeles, CA: Lifespan Learning Institute.

Promislow, S. (1999). *Making thet brain/body connection.* West Vancouver, BC, Canada: Kinetic Publishing.

Pynoos, R. S., Frederick, C. J., Nader, K., Arroyo, W., Steinberg, A., Eth, S., . . . Fairbanks, L. (1987). Life threat and posttraumatic stress in school-age children. *Archives of General Psychiatry, 44*(12), 1057–1063.

Rosenthal, N. (2002). *The emotional revolution.* New York, NY: Kensington.

Rothschild, B. (2000). *The body remembers: The psychophysiology of trauma and trauma treatment.* New York, NY: Norton.

Rothschild, B. (2003). *The body remembers casebook.* New York, NY: Norton.

Rothschild, B. (2006). *Help for the helper.* New York, NY: Norton.

Rutan, S., & Stone, W. (2001). *Psychodynamic group psychotherapy* (3rd ed.). New York, NY: Guilford Press.

Saltzman, A., & Goldin, P. (2008). Mindfulness-based stress reduction for school-age children. In Greco, L., & Hayes, S. (Eds.), *Acceptance & mindfulness for children and adolescents* (pp. 139–162). Oakland, CA: New Harbinger.

Sanders, J. (2008, June 11). To protect and serve the most vulnerable. *The Austin American-Statesman,* p. A1.

Saxe, G., Ellis, B., & Kaplow, J. (2007). *Collaborative treatment of traumatized children and teens.* New York, NY: Guildford Press.

Schaefer, C. E. (Ed.). (1999). *Short term psychotherapy groups for children: Adopting group processes for specific problems.* Northdale, NJ: Jason Aronson.

Schechtman, Z. (2006). *Group counseling and psychotherapy with chilren and adolescents: Theory, research, and practice.* Mahwah, NJ: Erlbaum.

Schilling, D., Cowan, D., & Palomares, S. (1994). *Leadership 2000: Preparing students for success and leadership in the workplace.* Austin, TX: PRO-ED.

Schore, A. (1994). *Affect regulation and the origin of the self.* Hillsdale, NJ: Erlbaum.

Schore, A. (2003). *Affect regulation and repair of the self.* New York, NY: Norton.

Schumacher, E. H., Seymour, T. L., Glass, J. M., Fencsik, D. E., Lauber, E. J., Kieras, D. E., . . . Meyer, D. E. (2001). Virtually perfect time sharing in dual-task performance: Uncorking the central cognitive bottleneck. *Psychological Science: Special Issue, 121*(2), 2101–08.

Semple, R. J. (2005). *Mindfulness-based cognitive therapy for children: A randomized group psychotherapy trial developed to enhance attention and reduce anxiety* (Unpublished doctoral dissertation). Columbia University, New York, NY.

Siegel, D. J. (1999). *The developing mind: Toward a neurobiology of interpersonal experience.* New York, NY: Guilford Press.

Siegel, D. J. (2003). An interpersonal neurobiology of psychotherapy: The developing mind and the resolution of trauma. In M. F. Soloman & D. J. Siegel (Eds.), *Healing trauma* (pp. 1–56). New York, NY: Norton.

Siegel, D. J. (2007). *Being present in body and mind: An integration of clinical treatment and neuroscience research* [CD]. Los Angeles, CA: Lifespan Learning Institute.

Siegel, R., Germer, C., & Olendzki, A. (2009). Mindfulness: What is it? Where does it come from? In F. Didonna (Ed.), *Clinical handbook of mindfulness* (pp. 17–36). New York, NY: Springer.

Singh, N., Wahler, R., Adkins, A., & Myers, R. (2003). Soles of the feet: A mindfulness-based self-control intervention for aggression by an individual with mild mental retardation and mental illness. *Research in Developmental Disabilities, 24*(3) 158–169.

Spradlin, S. E. (2003). *Don't let your emotions run your life: How dialectical behavior therapy can put you in control.* Oakland, CA: New Harbinger.

Stern, D. (2002). *Attachment: From early childhood through the lifespan* [CD]. Los Angeles, CA: Lifespan Learning Institute.

Stern, D. (2004). *The present moment in psychotherapy and everyday life.* New York, NY: Norton.

Tatkin, S. (2009). *The psychology of attachment and its application to individual and couples therapy.* Austin, TX: Austin in Connection.

Taylor, S., Klein, L., Lewis, B., Gruenewald, T., Gurung, R., & Updegraff, J. (2008). Behavioral responses to stress: Tend and befriend, not fight or flight. *Psychology Review, 107*(3), 411–429.

Tollison, P. K., & Synatschk, K. O. (2007). *SOS! A practical guide for leading solution-focused groups with kids K–12*. Austin, TX: PRO-ED.

U.S. Department of Health and Human Services. (2004). *Child maltreatment 2004* (NIH NIS-4). Retrieved from http://www.acf.hhs.gov

van der Kolk, B. A. (2006) Clinical implications of neuroscience research in PTSD. *Annals New York Academy of Sciences, 1071,* 277–293.

van der Kolk, B. A. (2007). *New frontiers in trauma treatment.* Portolla Valley, CA: Institute for the Advancement of Human Behavior.

van der Kolk, B. A. (2009). Afterword. In C. A. Courtois & J. D. Ford (Eds.), *Treating complex traumatic stress disorders: An evidence-based guide* (pp. 455–466). New York, NY: Guilford Press.

Whiston, S., & Sexton, T. (1998). A review of school counseling outcome research: Implications for practice. *Journal of Counseling and Development, 76,* 412–426.

Williams, L., & Bargh, J. (2008). Warm drink—warm thoughts. *Science, 322,* 501.

Winnicott, C., Shepherd, R., & Davis, M. (Eds.). (1989). *Psycho-analytic explorations: D. W. Winnicott.* Cambridge, MA: Harvard University Press.

Yalom, I., & Leszcz, M. (2005). *The theory and practice of group psychotherapy* (5th ed.). New York, NY: Basic Books.

Zylowska, L., Ackerman, D. L., Yang, M. H., Futrell, J. L., Horton, N. L., Hale, T. S., . . . & Smalley, S. L. (2008). Mindfulness meditation training in adults and adolescents with ADHD: A feasibility study. *Journal of Attention Disorders, 11*(6), 737–746.

Appendix A: Tools

All items are available in reproducible form on the CD.

A: I. Assessments

Arousal Scale

Using the Arousal Scale

This scale is a useful guide for gauging a student's level of arousal. Through observing breathing and skin tone, the counselor or other mental health practitioner can assess a student's arousal state and make judgments about the pacing of interventions. One purpose of learning to observe the bodily signs of arousal is to become competent in avoiding the highly traumatized (and possibly retraumatizing) state of endangering arousal. We want to slow down the intervention before that state is reached.

Procedure

1. Observe the student's breathing, skin tone, and heart rate.

2. Ask questions like the following:
    *   *What is the temperature in your face right now?*
    *   *Where is your breath mostly? Is your chest moving up and down, or is your stomach moving out and back?*
    *   *What sensations are you feeling right now?*

3. Use the comments column to make notes about the student's needs and what works best for him or her.

4. Contain your curiosity about the trauma. Keep arousal at a low level. Familiarity with the student's resources will help contain arousal.

5. Monitor signs and periodically help to apply the brakes so it is comfortable for the student. Periodic pauses diverting the student to an anchor safe place, or a topic that reminds him or her of resources and strengths can help to keep the session comfortable.

#12873

Student Name _____   Date _____

Counselor _____

State	Description	Indications	Comments
Relaxed system	Breathing is easy and deep. Heart rate is slow. Skin tone is normal.	The client is calm and counseling is progressing comfortably.	
Slight arousal	Breathing or heart rate may quicken while skin color remains normal. Skin may pale and moisten slightly without increases in respiration and pulse.	Excitement and containable discomfort: might include emotions of sadness, anger, or grief. Most can tolerate slight arousal.	
Moderate hyperarousal	Heart beat and respiration are rapid. Skin tone is becoming pale.	The client may be having trouble dealing with what is going on and may be quite anxious. You might want to consider applying the brakes.	
Severe hyperarousal	Heart beat and respiration are accelerated. Skin tone is pale. Client may be cold sweating.	It is time to hit the brakes.	
Endangering hyperarousal	Skin is pale (or reduced color) with slow heart rate. Pupils are widely dilated with flushed color. Slow heart rate with rapid breathing. Very slow respiration with fast heart rate.	These are sign that the client is in a highly traumatized state: The process is speeding out of control. The brakes must be applied, through body awareness and/or strategies such as developing dual awareness and muscle tensing.	

Note. From *The Body Remembers* (pp. 111–112), by B. Rothschild, 2000, New York: Norton. Copyright 2000 by Babette Rothschild. Adapted with permission.

To _____   Date _____

From _____

Please help me by providing information about this student's skills in the following areas.

Student's Name _____

		Never				Always
1.	Describes his/her emotions	1	2	3	4	5
2.	Describes physical sensations separately from description of his/her emotional state	1	2	3	4	5
3.	Displays self-control	1	2	3	4	5
4.	Asks for help before becoming upset	1	2	3	4	5
5.	When upset, calms without assistance	1	2	3	4	5
6.	When upset, calms with assistance from others	1	2	3	4	5
7.	Uses a variety of techniques to manage intense emotions	1	2	3	4	5
8.	Recognizes, accepts, and respects individual differences	1	2	3	4	5
9.	Uses effective communication skills to express him/herself	1	2	3	4	5
10.	Recognizes his/her personal abilities	1	2	3	4	5
11.	Makes and keeps friends	1	2	3	4	5
12.	Uses positive words and actions to solve problems with other students	1	2	3	4	5

Comments: _____

_____

_____

Thank you for your help. Please return to me by _____

Name _____   Date _____

Please circle the number that matches your skill.

		Never	Sometimes	Always
1.	I tell others what I feel.	0	1	2
2.	I know the difference between a feeling in my body and my emotions, and I can tell someone. (Example: I have a pain in my stomach, and I feel sad.)	0	1	2
3.	I calm myself if I get upset, and I think before I act.	0	1	2
4.	If I need help, I ask for help.	0	1	2
5.	If I get upset, I calm myself without help.	0	1	2
6.	If I get upset, I let others help me calm down.	0	1	2
7.	I have lots of ways to help me calm down if I get too upset.	0	1	2
8.	I know everyone is different, and I can stay calm when others do not do what I want them to do.	0	1	2
9.	When I talk to others, they understand what I am saying.	0	1	2
10.	I know the things I do well.	0	1	2
11.	I make friends, and I am a good friend.	0	1	2
12.	When I am upset with someone, I talk to them so we can solve the problem together.	0	1	2

Class _____   Rater _____

Check the rating that matches the class's proficiency in the following skills.

		Definitely	Somewhat	Not at all
Communication skills				
1	Listening to others			
2	Following instructions			
3	Introducing themselves			
Interpersonal skills				
4	Staying out of fights			
5	Handling being corrected			
6	Joining in			
7	Sharing			
8	Complimenting			
9	Helping others			
Coping skills				
10	Relaxing			
11	Problem solving			
12	Expressing anger appropriately			
13	Apologizing			
14	Ignoring distractions			
15	Responding to teasing			
16	Negotiating/compromising			
Classroom skills				
17	Bringing material to class			
18	Completing assignments			
19	Asking for help			
20	Making corrections			
21	Contributing to discussions			
22	Attending to tasks			

Note. From *Inclusion of Students with Autism: Using ABA-Based Supports in General Education* (p. 133), by J. Hundert, 2009, Austin, TX: PRO-ED. Copyright 2009 by PRO-ED, Inc. Reprinted with permission.

A: II. Individual Counseling

Counseling Office Equipment

Elementary

- Sand tray
- Miniatures
- Finger paints
- Chimes
- Fitness ball to sit on
- Biodots
- Clay
- Rubber bands
- Peace or calming corner: photos, elements from nature, calming pictures, quiet instruments, music, chimes, coloring books, drawing paper, pillows, puzzles, stuffed animals
- Distraction-free area or white-noise machine

Middle School

- Sand tray
- Miniatures
- Koosh balls
- Peace corner
- Biodots
- Fitness ball to sit on

High School

- Koosh balls
- Sand tray
- Miniatures
- Biodots

Student Name _____   Grade _____

Referring Person _____   Date _____

1. Describe the behavior of concern with this student.

2. Describe the circumstances surrounding this behavior. (What happens before, during, and after? What is the usual setting? Who is nearby?)

3. What will this student be doing differently (goal) when there is resolution of the problem(s)?

4. What would be evidence of a solid first step toward that goal?

5. Describe times when parts of the goal have already been achieved.

6. How would you account for the student's progress toward the goal at those times?

7. On a scale of 1 to 5, with 5 being the best, circle the number indicating the student's ability to do the following:

Describes his/her emotions	1	2	3	4	5
Describes physical sensations separately from descriptions of his/her emotional states	1	2	3	4	5
Displays self-control	1	2	3	4	5
Asks for help before becoming upset	1	2	3	4	5
When upset, calms without assistance	1	2	3	4	5
When upset, calms with assistance from others	1	2	3	4	5
Uses a variety of techniques to manage intense emotions	1	2	3	4	5
Recognizes, accepts, and respects individual differences	1	2	3	4	5
Uses effective communication skills to express him/herself	1	2	3	4	5
Recognizes his/her personal abilities	1	2	3	4	5
Makes and keeps friends	1	2	3	4	5
Uses positive words and actions to solve problems with other students	1	2	3	4	5

Name _____   Date _____

Step	Sample Language	Notes
Student's goal Find out what needs to happen (kid's goal) in order for counseling to be useful for the kid.	*What needs to happen in our time together to make you feel it has been worthwhile? Or, How do you want things to be?*	
Verify understanding Verify that the counselor's understanding of the goal is accurate by asking difference or scaling questions. If the goal is unclear, repeat step 1.	*What difference will it make when _____ happens? Who else will notice? What difference will that make? On a scale of 1 to 10, with 1 being not at all and 10 being completely achieved, where are you now in the achievement of this goal? (Adjust number scale for younger students.)*	1 2 3 4 5 6 7 8 9 10
Miracle question Ask the miracle question and get as many details of the miracle as possible.	*Suppose tonight while you are asleep a miracle happens and this problem is solved. What will be the first thing you notice when you wake up that will tell you it has happened? What difference will that make for you? Who else will notice? What difference will that make for you?*	
Exceptions Listen for exceptions and follow up on them by getting as many details as possible.	*When is this miracle happening even a little bit? What are you doing to make that happen? How are you managing to keep things from getting worse? When are you able to beat the problem, even a little?*	
Scaling Ask a scaling question to determine the kid's current levels of progress toward his or her goal.	*On a scale of 1 to 10 (10 is that your miracle has come true, and 1 is that your problem is the worst it has been), where are you right now? What lets you know that it is a _____ and not a _____ (lower number)?*	1 2 3 4 5 6 7 8 9 10
Successful efforts Referring to the previous scaling question, find out what the kid has done to reach and maintain the current level of progress.	*Wow! That number is pretty high. How have you been able to do that? Even though it has been tough, you have been able to do that? (Reinforce successful efforts to show it was not just luck.)*	

Others' scales Find out where on the scale the kid thinks others in his or her life would rate him or her.	*Where would your mother (father, coach, teacher, assistant principal) say you are on this scale of 1–10? What will (the referral source) be seeing when you are at a 10? What difference will it make when they are able to see that? What difference will that make?*	1 2 3 4 5 6 7 8 9 10
Others' descriptions Find out what the kid thinks his/her referral source would say about what he or she is doing to deserve that rating.	*If (referral source) was here, what do you think she would tell me about why she rated you a _____ rather than a _____ (lower number)?*	
Differences Ask the kid what significant others would say about what differences the behaviors identified are making.	*What difference would you say those behaviors are having? What else does it tell her to see in you (hanging in there)?*	
Goal scaling Ask the kid where on the scale he/she hopes to be by the next session. Continue to ask questions about how the kid will know he/she is at this specific place on the scale. What will be different then? And so on.	*Where on the scale of 1 to 10 do you hope to be by the next time we get together? How will you know you are a _____? Suppose you are at a _____ (higher number). What do you think would have happened for you to be there? What will be different when you are there? Who else will notice? What difference will that make?*	1 2 3 4 5 6 7 8 9 10
Confidence scaling If high on the scale, use scaling questions for the kid to rate his/her confidence in his or her ability to sustain these changes (or to scale the referral source's confidence that the client can sustain the changes).	*On a scale of 1 to 10, with 10 being that you have complete confidence that you can maintain the changes you have made, and 1 being no confidence at all, where would you put yourself?*	1 2 3 4 5 6 7 8 9 10
Task development Based on responses to the previous questions, invite the kid to assign self-homework.	*I'm wondering as you think about being a _____ (#) on your scale, what is the most important thing you did before coming here today that helped you get there? If it was next week, and you were telling me how you accomplished this, what would you be telling me you did to stay so focused?*	

Note. From *Solution-Focused Brief Therapy* (pp. 30–42), by T. Pichot & Y. M. Dolan, 2003, New York: The Haworth Clinical Practice Press. Copyright 2003 by Haworth Clinical Practice Press.

Tasks for Individual Sessions

- From a calm and regulated state, establish rapport and build a relationship based on secure attachment.
- Teach and practice grounding, mindful awareness, and tracking sensation.
- Establish the kid's goal.
- Gain an understanding of the kid's regulated state (descriptions of sensations, emotions, thoughts, and behaviors).
- Gain an understanding of how the kid manages to keep regulated.
- Build somatic memory of the experience of calmness and self-control.
- Teach the use of somatic memory as an anchor in episodes of dysregulation.
- Identify the factors (either internal or external) that shift the kid from his/her regulated state to a dysregulated state.
- Gain an understanding of the kid's dysregulated state (sensations, emotions, thoughts, and behaviors).
- Practice using self-regulation skills in moments of dysregulation.
- Teach the scaling technique. Have a kid use scaling to describe where on the scale his or her level of regulation is now.
- Establish a task to do between this meeting and the next to increase the scale rating in regulation skills.
- When progress is being made . . .
    - determine suitability for group
    - discuss how group works
    - get informed consent
    - establish group agreements
    - create clear goal(s) for work in the group
    - get parent consent

		Pre rating	Post rating	Change + / -
Student #	Describes his/her emotions			
	Describes physical sensations separately from descriptions of his/her emotional states			
	Displays self-control			
	Asks for help before becoming upset			
	When upset, calms without assistance			
	When upset, calms with assistance from others			
	Uses a variety of techniques to manage intense emotions			
	Recognizes, accepts, and respects individual differences			
	Uses effective communication skills to express him/herself			
	Recognizes his/her personal abilities			
	Makes and keeps friends			
	Uses positive words and actions to solve problems with other students			

			1	2	3	4	5
Student #	Describes his/her emotions	Pre					
		Post					
	Describes physical sensations separately from descriptions of his/her emotional states	Pre					
		Post					
	Displays self-control	Pre					
		Post					
	Asks for help before becoming upset	Pre					
		Post					
	When upset, calms without assistance	Pre					
		Post					
	When upset, calms with assistance from others	Pre					
		Post					
	Uses a variety of techniques to manage intense emotions	Pre					
		Post					
	Recognizes, accepts, and respects individual differences	Pre					
		Post					
	Uses effective communication skills to express him/herself	Pre					
		Post					
	Recognizes his/her personal abilities	Pre					
		Post					
	Makes and keeps friends	Pre					
		Post					
	Uses positive words and actions to solve problems with other students	Pre					
		Post					

A: III. Group Counseling

Strategies for Self-Regulation (SSR) Groups

Focus of the groups

The focus of the group program is achieving positive goals with students. Group leaders use the benefits of the group setting with solution-focused approaches to help students identify their strengths and abilities to solve their concerns. Groups meet at school for ten weeks. During each group session, students will learn important skills to help them be successful. In group, these skills will be tailored to address individual student needs and concerns.

Skills topics

- Self-awareness. Identifying your thoughts, feelings, and strengths, and recognizing how they influence choices and actions

- Social awareness. Identifying and understanding the thoughts and feelings of others, developing empathy, and being able to take the perspective of others

- Self-management. Handling emotions so that they facilitate rather than interfere with the task at hand, setting long-term and short-term goals, and dealing with obstacles that may come your way

- Responsible decision making. Generating, implementing, and evaluating positive and informed solutions to problems, and considering the long-term consequences of your actions for yourself and others

- Relationship skills. Saying no to peer pressure and working to resolve conflicts in order to maintain healthy and rewarding connections with individuals and groups

Dear Parent or Guardian,

Your son/daughter has been invited to participate in the SSR Group at our school. The group will meet

on _____ (day) for _____ minutes. The purpose of the group is to assist

students in identifying their strengths and helping them strengthen their abilities to solve their own concerns.

In addition, students will further their skills in the areas of self-knowledge, social awareness, self-management,

responsible decision making, and relationship skills. Your permission for your son/daughter to participate will

be appreciated.

Please feel to call your son/daughter's teacher, _____ , at _____

with questions about the referral. You may also call the counselor, _____ ,

at _____ with questions about the group. Please return this form to the office by: _____ .

Thanks!

....

By signing below, I give consent for my child to participate in the SSR Group. I understand my child

is responsible for completing any class work that he or she misses while attending group sessions.

Child's Name _____   Date _____

Parent/Guardian's Name _____

Parent/Guardian's Signature _____

Group _____

Session	Competency area	Date	Time	Lesson	Materials
1	Self-awareness-1				
2	Self-awareness-2				
3	Social awareness-1				
4	Social awareness-2				
5	Self-management-1				
6	Self-management-2				
7	Responsible decision making-1				
8	Responsible decision making-2				
9	Relationship skills-1				
10	Relationship skills-2				

Group Sessions Outlines

Session 1

I. Roll Call

Have group members make name tags if they do not already know each others' names.

II. Group Introduction

Say something like, *Welcome to the group! This is a time to come together and work on our concerns. We're going to learn how you've solved problems in the past. Then we'll learn some new skills, and come up with your plan for working on your goals.*

III. Grounding Activity

Choose a grounding activity from Appendix B: Activities, to help the members be in the moment. Return to practice grounding whenever a student needs to within the section.

IV. Group Agreements

You may choose to post on the group room wall your selected group agreements. Say, *There are a few agreements we need to have so that our group will be a good experience for everyone. Let's talk about these agreements for a moment.* (List the agreements.) *How will these agreements help us as a group?* You may direct your question to one member or look to the group as a whole. After one member has answered, compliment the effort and look to other members to extend and amplify the interaction.

V. Individual Goals Discussion

Ask each member to talk briefly about what they want to achieve in the group. Say, *We're interested in each of you. Could you tell us briefly what you would like to achieve in our group? How will you know when things are better for you?* As members describe their goals, watch for opportunities to "connect the dots" or "disconnect the dots" between members. That is, look at where kids are alike and where they are different. Also, watch for opportunities to connect the skills content in the activity to each member's individual goal.

VI. Difference

Ask students to talk about how achieving their goal will effect their lives. Use questions like the following to encourage interaction:

- *What difference will it make for you when you are able to _____ ?*
- *What would _____ say when they notice you managing _____ ?*

- *Suppose I was viewing a videotape of you with this problem much improved. What would I see you doing?*
- *Someday when the problem that brought you here today doesn't bother you as much, what will you get to do more of?*

VII. Exceptions

Ask members to reflect upon times when the problem was not as bad or when it was even a little bit better. Say, *Tell us about a time when you partially completed this goal. When in the past has the problem not interfered for you?*

VIII. Compliment

Identify things members have already been doing to make the situation better. Say, *What have you been doing already to make things better? Wow! How were you able to do that? How have you kept things from getting worse?* Be sure to give students time to think about what they did to make things happen for the better.

IX. Scaling

Discuss how scales will be used each session. Ask members to scale their current level of achievement toward their goals. Say, *Here's how it works. The scale of 1 to 10 shows that 1 is when things were at their worst and 10 is the day after the miracle (or when your goal is achieved). Where are you right now? Wow! How did you manage to do that?* It may be useful when using scaling for the hyperaroused child to consider the scale this way: 10 is calm, regulated, and optimally aroused.

Pass out a folder with the Individual Group Diary for each member of the group. Describe that they can use the diary when they first come to group or during status check-in at the beginning of each group meeting to scale individual progress toward their goals. Ask members to note on the scaling form what number they would give themselves today. Some counselors like to have these folders ready as students arrive. Students pick theirs up, completing the scaling as others arrive. Say, *This will be your goal folder, and we'll work in it each time we have group. In your folder, you can write the goal you are setting for yourself. At the beginning of each meeting, we will check in with one another about the progress we've made toward our goals.*

X. Activity

Select an activity from the Self-Awareness competency area to use with the group.

XI. Apply Lesson to Goals

Say, *What difference will it make that you are able to use these skills?*

 #12873

XII. Task Development

Ask students to commit to a task (of their creation) to work on between now and the next group session.

- *What might you do next week that will help you keep the problem at a distance in your life, so you can do what you really want to do?*
- *What will you do this week to raise your goal rating?*
- *What can you do more of that's already working?*
- *What can you see yourself doing differently to move from a _____(#) to a _____ (#)?*

XIII. Ongoing Evaluation by Group Members

Ask group members to give feedback about how the group is working for them. The following are examples of questions to request feedback:

- *When has group worked well?*
- *When has it worked better?*
- *What were we doing to make that happen?*
- *How would you like the group to be?*
- *What will you be doing differently when the group is working the way it would be most helpful to you?*

XIV. Dismissal

XV. Group Notes and Evaluation

Sessions 2–9

I. Roll call

Have group members fill in their group folder with their current scaling toward their goal. Say, *On a scale of 1 to 10, where are you with your goal?*

II. Grounding, Mindful Awareness, or Tracking Sensation Practice

Choose an activity from Appendix B. As the group leader, you will want to see if any group member needs to practice one of these skills in particular. Focus the practice on one of these, depending on group members' needs. Even though we begin the group session with this self-regulation practice, we continue to come back to it as part of the group intervention whenever a member begins to become dysregulated.

III. Status Check-In

Go around the group, checking in quickly with each student about changes related to their goals. Say the following:

- *What's better or different this week?*
- *What went well for you this week in relation to your goal?*
- *Describe the things you noticed that were better about what you're working on this week.*

Throughout each meeting watch for opportunities to encourage group members to be helpful to one another.

IV. Compliment

While students respond to the status check-in, you and the group can watch for an opportunity to compliment students on what they have done to make things better. If the situation is better, stress the effects of the student's behaviors on others and reinforce what the student did to make it happen: *Wow! What does a _____(#) look like? What did you do to make it better? What else? How were you able to do that?*

If the situation is the same, elicit the details, amplify, and reinforce what the student did to make it happen for the better or to keep things from getting worse. Say, *How did you manage to keep things from getting worse?* (Listen for what is better.)

If nothing is better or it's worse, acknowledge and question for exceptions: *Man, that's tough. Was there a time when it was a little better, say a _____(#)? What will improvement look like? How will you know when things are better for you?*

 #12873

V. Difference

Inquire about the effects of improvement in the students' lives. Say the following:

- *What difference will it make for you when you are able to* _____ *?*
- *What would (an important person to the student) say when they notice you managing* _____ *?*
- *Suppose I was viewing a videotape of you with this problem much improved. What would I see you doing?*
- *Someday when the problem that brought you to group doesn't bother you as much, what will you get to do more of?*

VI. Exceptions

Explore times when the problem is less or nonexistent. Say the following:

- *When in the past has the problem not interfered?*
- *How were you able to do that?*

VII. Activities

Select from the competency areas to use with the group.

Session 2	Self-awareness
Session 3	Social awareness
Session 4	Social awareness
Session 5	Self-management
Session 6	Self-management
Session 7	Responsible decision making
Session 8	Responsible decision making
Session 9	Relationship skills

VIII. Applying Lesson to Goals

Process the skills learned in the activity as they relate to individual member's goals. Say, *What difference will it make when you are able to use these skills?*

IX. Task Development

Ask students to commit to a task (of their creation) to improve their situations between now and the next time the group meets. Say the following:

- *Let's talk now about what you might do next week that will assist you in keeping the problem at a distance in your life, so you can do what you really want to do.*
- *What will you do this week to raise your rating?*
- *What's been working that you could do more of?*
- *What can you see yourself doing differently to move from a _____(#) to a _____(#)?*

X. Evaluation by Group Members

We ask group members to give us feedback as to how the group is working for them. The following are examples of questions to request feedback:

- *What's working well for you in group?*
- *What would you like to be different?*
- *What will you be doing differently when the group is working in the way that it would be most helpful to you?*

XI. Dismissal

XII. Group Notes and Evaluation

Session 10

I. Roll call

Have group members fill in their Individual Group Diary with their current scaling toward their goal. Say, *On a scale of 1 to 10, where are you with your goal?*

II. Grounding, Mindful Awareness, or Tracking Sensations Practice

Select one or several skills to practice.

III. Status Check-In

Go around the group, checking in quickly with each student as to changes related to their goals. Say the following:

- *What's better this week?*
- *What went well for you this week in relation to your goal?*
- *Describe the things you noticed that were better about what you're working on this week.*

Throughout each meeting, watch for opportunities to encourage group members to be helpful to one another.

IV. Compliment

When students respond to the status check-in, you and the group can watch for an opportunity to compliment the student on what he or she has done to make things better.

Better: If the situation is better, stress the effects of the student's behaviors on others and reinforce what the student did to make it happen: *Wow! What does a _____(#) look like? What did you do to make it better? How were you able to do that?*

Same: If the situation is the same, elicit the details, amplify, and reinforce what the student did to make it happen for the better or to keep things from being worse: *How did you manage to keep things from getting worse?* (Listen for what is better.)

Worse: If nothing is better, or it's worse, acknowledge and question for exceptions: *Man, that's tough. Was there a time when it was a little better, say a _____(#)? What will improvement look like? How will you know when things are better for you?*

V. Difference

Ask the following questions:

- *What difference will it make for you when you are able to* _____ ?
- *What would* _____ *say when they notice you managing* _____ ?
- *Suppose I was viewing a videotape of you with this problem much improved. What would I see you doing?*
- *Someday when the problem that brought you to group doesn't bother you as much, what will you get to do more of?*

VI. Exceptions

Ask, *When in the past has the problem not interfered? How were you able to do that?*

VII. Activity

Select an activity from the competency area to use with the group.

Session 10 Relationship Skills

Lesson for Group _____

VIII. Applying the Lesson to Goals

Process the skills learned in the activity as they relate to individual member's goals. Ask, *What difference will it make that you are able to use these skills?*

IX. Celebrating Successes

Talk about the attitudes and behaviors that were present when the group began, the topics that were discussed, the homework assignments, the progress made with respect to their goals, and what still needs to be accomplished. Say, *I am really impressed with the changes you've made. It seems to me you each have a good sense of what you need to do to continue such changes.*

X. Graduation

Ask the students to share with others their plans for continued improvement and how they will face any setbacks that occur. Of course, you can leave the door open for future visits to check in on progress. Tell the group about the planned booster session. Say, *Let's think back to the goals that each of you set for yourself at the beginning of the group. Think of the progress you have made. We learned some skills for staying grounded and for re-regulating when we feel overwhelmed and* _____. *Please tell the group how you plan to continue to make progress toward your goal even when some challenges come along.*

 #12873

Help group members solicit improvements and give compliments to others. For example, *Share, if you will, the improvements you have noticed in others in the group.* _____(name), *please ask* _____ (name) *how he/she has been able to improve things.*

XI.   Evaluation by Group Members

We ask group members to give us feedback as to how the group has worked for them. The following are examples of questions to request feedback: *What worked well for you in group? What would you like to be different? What will you be doing differently because of something helpful from group?*

XII.   Dismissal

XIII.   Group Notes and Evaluation

Name ______________________________ Date ______________

My reason for coming here ______________________________

I will know when things are better for me when I am able to ______________________________

Place an *X* in the square (or color the number of squares in the column) that matches where you are today on the scale toward your goal. (Scale: 1= *The problem is as bad as it can be;* 10 = *The problem is almost nonexistent.*)

Where Are You Today on the Scale?											
Scale	10										
	9										
	8										
	7										
	6										
	5										
	4										
	3										
	2										
	1										
		1	2	3	4	5	6	7	8	9	10
Session											

Group _____   Session _____   Date _____

Activity

Notes

Evaluation

The Students

Initials	Present	Demonstrated self-regulation skills	Met the objective of the lesson	Worked on an identified goal	Scaled current status toward goal	Set a task

The Group Leader

☐ Conveyed to the group that they are trusted to help themselves

☐ Maintained boundaries in the group

☐ Used effective group leadership skills

☐ Other _____

Group Counseling Outcomes

	Change in Self-awareness	Change in Social awareness	Change in Self-management	Change in Responsible decision making	Change in Relationship skills	Average change	Goal completion 1=*yes*, 0=*no*
Student # _____							
Student # _____							
Student # _____							
Student # _____							
Student # _____							
Student # _____							
						% Goal Completion	

Skills Improvement in Group

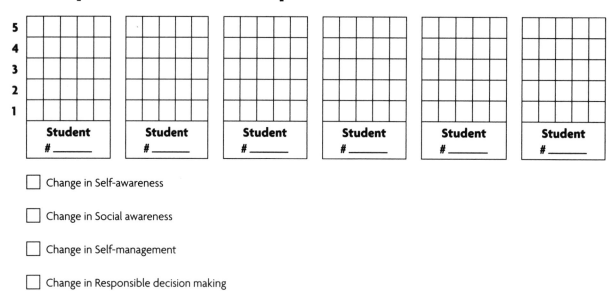

☐ Change in Self-awareness

☐ Change in Social awareness

☐ Change in Self-management

☐ Change in Responsible decision making

☐ Change in Relationship skills

Taking Care of the Helper

- Become calm and self-regulated before beginning to work with the kid.

- Observe the kid's emotional and behavioral self-regulation.

- Notice the effect of that on your state.

- Take steps to again become self-regulated before proceeding.

First Aid for Trauma Prevention

☐ **Check your own body's response first.** Take time to notice your own level of fear or concern. Next, take a full, deep breath, and as you exhale s-l-o-w-l-y, feel the sensations in your own body. Repeat until you feel settled. The time it takes to establish a sense of calm is time well spent. It will increase your capacity to attend fully to the child. Your composure will greatly reduce the likelihood of frightening or confusing the child further.

☐ **Assess the situation.** If the child shows signs of shock, do not allow him or her to jump up and return to activities. You might say something like, "We're going to sit (or lie) still for a while and wait until the shock wears off." Remember, a calm, confident voice communicates to the child that you will help him or her.

☐ **As the shock wears off, guide the child's attention to his or her sensations.** Softly ask the child how he or she feels "in his body." Repeat his answer as a question, "You feel okay in your body?" and wait for a nod or other response. Be more specific in the next question: "How do you feel in your tummy (head, arm, leg, etc.)?" If he or she mentions a distinct sensation, gently ask about its location, size, shape, color, or weight (e.g., heavy or light). Keep guiding the child to stay with the present moment with questions such as, "How does the _____ feel now?"

ficient to facilitate the movement and release of excess energy. Be alert to cues that let you know a cycle has finished. If uncertain whether a cycle has been completed, wait and watch for the child to give you clues. Examples of clues include a deep, relaxed, spontaneous breath; the cessation of crying or trembling; a stretch; a yawn; a smile; or the making or breaking of eye contact. The completion of this cycle may not mean that the recovery process is over. Another cycle may follow. Keep the child focused on sensations for a few more minutes just to make sure the process is complete. Wait to see if another cycle begins or if there is a sense of enough for now.

☐ **Slow down and follow the child's pace by carefully observing any changes.** This may be the hardest part for the adult, but it's the most important part for the child. Allowing a minute or two of silence between questions allows deeply restorative physiological cycles to engage. Too many questions asked too quickly disrupt the natural course. Your calm presence and patience are sufficient

☐ **Keep validating the child's physical responses.** Resist the impulse to stop the child's tears or trembling, while reminding him or her that whatever happened is over and that he or she will be OK. The child's reactions need to continue until they stop on their own. Your task is to

#12873

convey to the child that crying and trembling are normal, healthy reactions. A reassuring hand on the back, shoulder, or arm, along with a few gently spoken words as simple as, "That's OK" or "That's right, just let the scary stuff shake right out of you" will help immensely.

☐ **Trust in the child's innate ability to heal.** As you become increasingly comfortable with your own sensations, it will be easier to relax and follow the child's lead. Your primary function, once the process has begun, is to not disrupt it. Trust the child's innate ability to heal. Trust your own ability to allow this to happen. Your job is to stay with the child, creating a safe container. Use a calm voice and reassuring hand to let the child know that he or she is on the right track. To avoid an unintentional disruption of the process, don't shift the child's position, distract his or her attention, hold him or her too tightly, or position yourself too close

or too far away for comfort. Notice when the child begins to reorient to the environment. Orientation is a sign of completion.

☐ **Encourage the child to rest, even if he or she doesn't want to.** Deep discharges generally continue during rest and sleep. Do not stir up discussion about the mishap by asking questions. Later, the child may want to tell a story about it, draw a picture, or play it through. If a lot of energy was mobilized, the release will continue. The next cycle may be too subtle for you to notice, but the rest promotes a fuller recovery, allowing the body to gently vibrate, give off heat, go through skin color changes, etc., as the nervous system returns to relaxation and equilibrium. These changes happen naturally. All you have to do is provide a calm, quiet environment.

☐ **The final step is to attend to the child's emotional responses and help him or her make sense of what happened.** Later, when the child is rested and calm—even the next day—set aside some time for him or her to talk about the feelings and what he or she experienced. Normalize any feelings expressed and tell the child whatever he or she is feeling is OK and worthy of your time and attention. Drawing, painting, and working with clay can be very helpful in releasing strong emotions. Play works especially well with the preverbal or less verbal child.

Note. Adapted from *Trauma Through A Child's Eyes* (p. 461), by P. A. Levine and M. Kline, 2007, Berkeley, CA: North Atlantic Books. Copyright 2007 by Peter A. Levine and Maggie Kline. Adapted with permission.

_____ School

Confidential Counseling Log

	Student's last name	Student's first name	Seen by	Date	Individual session	Group session	Follow-up status	Follow up by	Parent notified
1									
2									
3									
4									
5									
6									
7									
8									
9									
10									
11									
12									
13									
14									
15									

Follow-Up Status

I Inactive; no follow-up needed

M Maintain periodic contact

P Place in group

A Active; currently being seen

C Community counseling referral

T Teacher alert to observe for difficulties

Crisis Counselors Roster

	Print name	School/Agency	Phone	Email	Assignment	Date	Arrival/Depature time	
1								
2								
3								
4								
5								
6								
7								
8								
9								
10								

Attach to Counseling Log

Appendix B: Activities

 All handouts are available in reproducible form on the CD.

B: Activity Objectives

Activity Objectives

Domain	Title	Objectives
Caregiver Exercise – 1	*Noticing Sensations*	The adult caregivers will observe sensations in the body such as shaky, relaxed, calm, tense, and numb. The caregiver will then focus on particular sensations, change focus, find a comforting resource, and identify a changed sensation based on accessing a comforting resource.
Caregiver Exercise – 2	*Experiencing the Power of Words*	Participants will reflect on personal experiences to acknowledge the power of words on their perceptions. As they discover the connection between the words expressed and their feelings, they will gain insight into using words effectively with students when they are in distress.
Caregiver Exercise – 3	*Identify Internal and External Resources*	Participants will identify their internal and external resources.
Caregiver Exercise – 4	*Tracking Sensation With a Partner*	Participants will concentrate on internal sensations, practice tracking sensation, and practice creating safety and expanded awareness.
Grounding – 1	*Grounding Basics*	The students will experience being grounded and observing their thoughts without judgment or action.
Grounding – 2	*Finding a Still, Quiet Place*	This activity will introduce young students to grounding and mindful awareness and how it feels in their minds and bodies.
Grounding – 3	*Seaweed Practice*	The students will experience the feeling of grounding and mindful awareness. Students will use the awareness of breathing to slow things down in everyday life.
Grounding – 4	*A Simple Centering Exercise*	The students will experience the feeling of grounding and being centered.
Grounding – 5	*Tai Chi Grounding Exercise*	In order to connect with themselves physically, the students will relax and slow down.
Grounding – 6	*Grounding After a Troublesome Interaction*	The students will learn a helpful technique for self-regulation after a difficult interaction with another person.
Mindful Awareness – 1	*Paying Attention Through Mindful Awareness*	The students will strengthen their ability to focus on the present moment by experiencing mindful awareness.
Mindful Awareness – 2	*A Game of I-Spy*	The students will experience noticing objects in the room in great detail.

 #12873

Domain	Title	Objectives
Mindful Awareness – 3	*Being a Noodle*	The students will develop awareness of their bodies using muscle relaxation and visualization.
Mindful Awareness – 4	*Mindfully Eating a Raisin*	The students will experience bringing their full attention to an activity and discover the difference really paying attention makes.
Mindful Awareness – 5	*Paying Attention*	The students will experience bringing their full attention to an activity and discover the difference that really paying attention makes in their ability to notice and remember details.
Mindful Awareness – 6	*What's Different About Me?*	The students will experience bringing their full attention to the features of another person and discover the difference really paying attention makes in the ability to notice and remember details.
Tracking Sensation – 1	*Establish Body Awareness*	The students will develop their own vocabularies to describe sensations and emotions they are experiencing.
Tracking Sensation – 2	*Body Cues Check-In*	The students will learn the signs of stress.
Tracking Sensation – 3	*Sensation Language*	The students will demonstrate sensation language or emotion vocabulary.
Tracking Sensation – 4	*Making a Sensation Treasure Chest*	The students will develop vocabularies to describe sensations they are experiencing.
Tracking Sensation – 5	*Making a Sensation Tasting Tray*	The students will develop their own vocabulary to describe sensations they are experiencing.
Self-Awareness – 1	*Emotion Portfolio*	The students will identify their emotions and learn some additional terms to describe their emotions.
Self-Awareness – 2	*Anchors: Our Favorite Things*	The students will establish at least one anchor to use as a braking tool anytime they encounter difficulties regulating.
Self-Awareness – 3	*Mirroring*	The students will develop body awareness and a sense of control over their bodies. They will use mindful awareness to achieve calming.
Self-Awareness – 4	*Imaginary School Bus*	The students will identify people at home and at school who are resources to them and use that information to internalize a more positive self-image.
Self-Awareness – 5	*Anchoring Yourself in Calm Waters*	The students will learn a method for calming themselves when facing stressful situations.
Self-Awareness – 6	*Sensation Game*	The students will experience a variety of sensations and learn to describe how they experience the sensations in their bodies.

Domain	Title	Objectives
Social Awareness – 1	*Getting Along at School*	The students will identify a number of ways they are getting along successfully at school and use that information to improve interpersonal skills.
Social Awareness – 2	*Anger: Use It and Lose It*	The students will describe the purposes of anger and the feelings underlying anger, such as fear and sadness. Students will demonstrate ways to express anger to avoid violence and resolve it.
Social Awareness – 3	*Nini the Cat Helps With Anger*	The students will learn ways to respond to feelings of anger and frustration in ways that help.
Social Awareness – 4	*Emotional Drama*	The students will be able to identify emotions apparent in others' actions and conversations.
Social Awareness – 5	*Interpersonal Boundaries*	The students will be able to identify their personal boundaries in relation to others.
Social Awareness – 6	*Role Play Activity*	The students will rehearse self-regulation in a variety of situations that involve interaction with others.
Self-Management – 1	*Keep Calm Activity*	The students will learn a method to calm themselves when they face a stressful situation.
Self-Management – 2	*Getting Relaxed: Progressive Muscle Relaxation*	The students will learn a way to relax their bodies.
Self-Management – 3	*Creating a Calming Plan*	The students will identify the strategies for self-calming at home and at school.
Self-Management – 4	*Quick Six*	The students will learn the "Quick Six," six methods to calm themselves when they are facing a stressful situation.
Self-Management – 5	*Calming Supports*	The students will learn about several methods to help calm themselves.
Self-Management – 6	*Affirmations*	The students will identify and practice using affirmations that they can use when they are becoming upset.
Self-Management – 7	*Tensing Peripheral Muscles—Holding Together*	The students will learn how to tense and release specific muscles to help calm anxiety or panic.
Self-Management – 8	*Deep Belly Breathing*	The students will learn to do deep breathing to quiet the mind and relax the body when upset.
Self-Management – 9	*Getting Relaxed: Progressive Muscle Relaxation*	The students will learn a way to relax their bodies and quiet their minds.
Self-Management – 10	*Body Scanning*	The students will learn a way to relax their bodies and quiet their minds.
Self-Management – 11	*The Three Rs for Managing Stress*	The students will learn three strategies for managing stress and create a list of activities they prefer to use when stressed.

Domain	Title	Objectives
Self-Management – 12	*Verbal First Aid*	The students will be reassured that whatever happened is over and will experience a calmer state.
Responsible Decision Making – 1	*Solution-Focused Decision Making*	The students will describe the steps to effective problem solving and decision making. Students will demonstrate applying the solution-focused steps to making a decision or resolving a problem in their lives.
Responsible Decision Making – 2	*Is It My Problem?*	The students will identify the problem and determine ownership.
Responsible Decision Making – 3	*Three-Step Plan for Success: Improving on a Weakness*	The students will identify strengths and weaknesses in academic areas and develop plans for improving in areas of relative weakness.
Responsible Decision Making – 4	*What to Do, What to Do?*	The students will learn and practice a decision-making process.
Responsible Decision Making – 5	*Taking Action to Solve Problems: A Three-Step Problem-Solving Process*	The students will learn a 3-step problem-solving process and practice the process by solving problems of their own.
Responsible Decision Making – 6	*Steps for Solving a Problem Responsibly*	The students will understand and describe how decisions are influenced. The students will develop and practice a process for effective problem solving.
Relationship Skills – 1	*When No One Wants to Play*	The students will learn skills for asking to play and waiting to play with others. Caregivers will learn several techniques to alleviate problems that occur when no one wants to play.
Relationship Skills – 2	*Dealing With Teasing*	The students will learn skills to deal with teasing without becoming upset.
Relationship Skills – 3	*Managing Conflict With I Am Statements*	The students will learn to use I Am statements to manage conflicts.
Relationship Skills – 4	*The Pretend Jump Rope*	The students will notice sensations in their bodies as they become more self-regulated and will learn to assist others in learning self-regulation.
Relationship Skills – 5	*Coyote Chases Rabbit*	The students will notice sensations in their bodies as they become more self-regulated and learn to assist others in learning self-regulation.
Relationship Skills – 6	*Personal Boundaries*	The students will learn what personal boundaries are and how respecting them can be helpful in getting along with others.

B: I. Caregiver

Noticing Sensations

Ages: Adults

Objectives: The adult caregivers will observe sensations in the body such as shaky, relaxed, calm, tense, and numb. The caregiver will then focus on particular sensations, change focus, find a comforting resource, and identify a changed sensation based on accessing a comforting resource.

Materials: None

Procedure

1. Discuss the content by saying: *Through body language, facial expressions, and your tone of voice, your own nervous system communicates with the kids' nervous systems. It's not our words that have the greatest impact; it's the nonverbal cues that create the feelings of safety and trust. Before you can attune to the kids' sensations, rhythms, and emotions, you must first learn to attune to you own. Then your calm can become their calm.*

2. Lead the sensory awareness script.

   - *Let's try this brief experiment to get you started on deepening your awareness. Find a comfortable place to sit. Take some time to notice how you're feeling physically. Pay attention to your breathing. Are you comfortable or uncomfortable? Where in your body do you register your comfort level? What do you notice? Are you aware of your heart beating, or conscious of your breathing? Perhaps you're more aware of muscle tension, relaxation, or the temperature of your skin; perhaps you notice sensations like "tingly." When you feel settled enough to go on, try the simple exercise below.*

   - *Imagine it's a pleasant summer day, and you're driving with your kids to the beach. You are playing a favorite song, and the family is singing along. You're not in a rush, and you love being near the water. The kids will be taking a swimming lesson, and you will be able to do whatever you want: free of responsibilities for an entire hour. Take a minute to notice how you are feeling right now—before you hear anything more. Note the sensations in various parts of your body, such as your belly, limbs, breath, muscles, and skin. Also notice any thoughts or mental pictures you might have as you think about having free time at the beach. (Pause for a minute or two.) Suddenly, from out of nowhere, a hot-rod motorist cuts in front of you, nearly causing a collision. Furthermore, he is rude and shouts profanities at you, right in front of your kids, as if you had done something to cause the mishap.*

   - *What are you noticing in your body and mind right now? Compare these feelings to the ones you had in the first part of the exercise. Pay attention to the changes. What feels different now? Where does it feel different? Are you warm, hot, or chilled? Do you feel tension or constriction anywhere? Notice changes in your heartbeat and breath. Notice if there is anything you feel like doing or saying. Or do you just feel stunned?*

   - *There is no right or wrong answer. Each person has his or her own experience. You may have been scared and felt your shoulders, arms, and hands tightening to turn the steering wheel quickly to swerve. Or you might have blanked out and gone numb. When you imagined the other driver cursing at you, you might have felt irritated. If you did, where*

 #12873

did you sense the irritation, and what did it feel like? You may have noticed the muscles in your upper body tightening as your body prepared to fight. Or you might have noticed a word forming in your vocal cords to shout back, but the sounds never left your lips. When you check your body to feel your reactions and sensations in the present moment, you are experiencing your basic instincts of survival.

- *Now take a little time to let any activation (charged-up feelings) settle down. Think for a moment about a snow globe you shake to make it look like it's snowing. Remember it takes a little time before all the flakes accumulate on the ground and the snowing stops. In order for you to settle, it certainly doesn't help to get all shook up again. Instead, for the settling to occur, it takes a little quiet time of stillness and calm. It can be very helpful to explore the room with your eyes, being aware that you are safe and that the visualization was only an exercise. As you continue to settle, place both feet flat on the floor to help you feel grounded. Next, direct your attention to something in the room that brings comfort, such as a flower, the color of the room, a tree, the sky outside the window, a photo, or a favorite possession. Notice how you are feeling in your body now.*

3. Discuss by saying the following: *This brief exercise was intended to help you see the language of sensation isn't really so foreign after all. Sitting around the dinner table, it's easy to feel a comfortable or overly stuffed stomach after a full meal, or one that feels warm and cozy after sipping hot chocolate. But when people share their feelings, they typically express them as moods or emotions, such as happy, cranky, mad, excited, or sad. Noticing sensations may seem odd at first, but the more you learn about the ups and downs of your own body's "moods," the more intuitive, instinctual, and confident you will become. You may not know this, but your basic sense of well-being is based on your body's ability to regulate itself—rather than to escalate out of control. To be in control this way means to be open to what occurs spontaneously within you. This capacity for self-regulation is enhanced by your ability to be aware of your changing sensations and your ability to know what to do if unpleasant sensations remain stuck over time, thereby causing distress.*

4. Ask the following questions:
   - *What did you experience that was different in this exercise?*
   - *What particular focus seemed to have the effect of calming?*
   - *How can you imagine practicing this in the future?*

Evaluation

The participants notice sensations in their bodies. They then identify something that brings comfort and use it to change the sensations they feel.

Note. From *Trauma-Proofing Your Kids* (pp. 20–22), by P. A. Levine and M. Kline. Copyright 2008 by Peter A. Levine and Maggie Kline. Berkeley, CA: North Atlantic Books. Adapted with permission.

Experiencing the Power of Words

Ages: Adults
Objectives: The participants will reflect on personal experiences to acknowledge the power of words on perceptions. As they discover the connection between the words expressed and their feelings, they will gain insight into using words effectively with students when they are in distress.
Materials: None

Procedure

1. Say: *Not only are words powerful at the time they are spoken, in times of openness and vulnerability, they become etched in the memory. Take a moment now to recall words that have shaped the peaks and valleys of your life; you will have an experiential understanding of just how penetrating they are and how they have textured your life.*

2. Ask participants to do the following for the first part of the exercise:

   - *Write a paragraph or two using all of your senses to describe everything you can remember about a kind person who used words, touch, gestures, and/or actions to comfort and soothe you after something bad happened. Recall in as much detail as possible what it was they said and did that made you feel better and recover.*

   - *Find a comfortable place to rest. Recalling what you just wrote, notice how you are feeling in your body now. Take some time to focus on sensations, emotions, thoughts, and images. Notice what happens to your body's expression and posture as you sink into the experience in this moment. Notice which sensations let you know this memory is a pleasurable one.*

   - *When you did this exercise, an unpleasant experience may have surfaced as well. That's because the amygdala, the part of the brain that imprints emotional memories, stores strong surprise encounters as well. Intense experiences are registered regardless of whether they are pleasant or unpleasant.*

   - *Because of these imprints, it may be that you recalled insensitive treatment, when what you really needed at the time was to be nurtured by an understanding adult. This can be especially hurtful when it was a parent or other close family member who couldn't comprehend what you were going through. If this was the case, you can do the following exercise in order to have a different experience now. As you heal your own wounds, you can better help the students you work with.*

3. Ask participants to do the following for the second part of the exercise:

   - *Write a paragraph or two using all of your senses to describe everything you can remember about an insensitive or unaware person who used words, touch, gestures, and/or actions that made things worse instead of soothing you after something terrible happened.*

   - *Without dwelling on the unpleasant experience you just described, allow an opposite image to help transform any images, words, sensations, and/or feelings you might have recalled. Try not to censure what pops up. Allow the newly formed opposite scene to expand, providing as many healing details as possible. What words, touch, gestures, and*

 #12873

actions are bringing you relief? What in particular is comforting you, making you feel better, and soothing any wounds from the past? Allow yourself to hear the words and see the actions now that you needed back then—replay it in this moment in the same way you would hope to nurture your own child or the students with whom you work.

- *Find a comfortable place to rest. Recalling your new and restorative image, notice how you are feeling in your body. Take some time to focus on sensations, emotions, thoughts, and images. Notice what happens to your body's expression and posture as you sink into the experience now. Note what sensations let you know that this new memory, using your adult resources, is affirming or pleasurable.*

Evaluation

The participants describe a personal experience when they were soothed and comforted by the words of a calm, caring person. They do this by noticing their sensations and feelings. When remembering non-supportive experiences, participants reconstruct a supportive image to use as a future resource. Participants describe the effect of this exercise on their abilities to help students with whom they work.

Note. From *Trauma-Proofing Your Kids* (pp. 86–88), by P. A. Levine and M. Kline, 2008, Berkeley, CA: North Atlantic Books. Copyright 2008 by Peter A. Levine and Maggie Kline. Adapted with permission.

Identify Internal and External Resources

Ages: Adults
Objectives: The participants will identify their internal and external resources.
Materials: None

Procedure

1. Start by saying: *In this exercise, we invite you to experience identifying your internal and external resources.*

2. Using a blank a piece of paper, ask the participants to make two lists vertically down the page. On one side, have them list what they consider to be their external resources and on the other side their internal resources. If something is not clearly one or the other, have them include it in both lists.

3. When their lists feel complete, have the participants look them over and notice which resources stand out as offering them the strongest support in times of stress. Say: *With each of the resources you have listed, take the time to notice what sensations and emotions emerge and where you experience them in your body. You might notice a sense of being held in your back and shoulders, a feeling of strength in your muscles, a smile coming to your face, a feeling of warmth around your heart, or a sense of feeling grounded in your trunk and legs. In some way, note those experiences, either on this page or on another, in an effort to form stronger somatic memories of these resources.*

4. Say: *Going back over your lists, do you notice the need for developing or adding resources? If you do, what might you do to make that happen? For example, it might be in such areas as interpersonal relationships, a meditation practice, or physical activities.*

Evaluation

The participants identify their array of internal and external resources. Once identified, they express appreciation for their resources and a plan to utilize them.

Note. From *Trauma Through a Child's Eyes* (p. 136), by P. A. Levine & M. Kline, 2007, Berkeley, CA: North Atlantic Books. Copyright 2007 by Peter A. Levine and Maggie Kline.

 #12873

Tracking Sensation With a Partner

Ages: Adults

Objectives: Participants will concentrate on internal sensations, practice tracking sensations, and practice creating safety and expanded awareness.

Materials: Language of Sensation Idea Box handout for each participant

Procedure

1. Start by saying:

   - *Often, it is easier to concentrate on internal sensations when you have a partner to help you focus. Choose someone you feel comfortable with and sit across from each other.*

   - *The object of this exercise is to "track" sensation, with your partner being the safe container. Simply put, "tracking" means developing an awareness of your present state with a focus on noticing how sensations change moment by moment.*

   - *As images, thoughts, and feelings come and go, make note of them and what impact they have on your sensations. Your partner follows your lead and helps you to expand the details of your sensations. He or she also keeps you moving forward with a few gentle invitational words that keep pace with your rhythm—just like you would do with your students.*

2. Say: *Switch places. Your partner will practice tracking sensations, and you will practice creating safety, expanded awareness, and movement toward increased fluidity and flexibility. Allow 10–15 minutes each and discuss what you discovered afterward.*

3. Have the pairs read the Language of Sensation Idea Box before getting started. This box serves as a model to ask questions that refrain from analytical thinking. Encourage them to refrain from asking *Why* questions.

Evaluation

The participants notice their internal sensations, track their movements, and describe what happens as they follow the sensations.

Note. From *Trauma Through a Child's Eyes* (p. 108), by P. A. Levine & M. Kline, 2007, Berkeley, CA: North Atlantic Books. Copyright 2007 by Peter A. Levine and Maggie Kline. Adapted with permission.

Language of Sensation Idea Box

Open-Ended

- *What do you notice in your body?* Rather than, *Are you feeling tense?*
- *Where in your body do you feel that?* Rather than, *Do you feel it in your chest?*
- *What are you experiencing now?* Rather than, *Do you still feel shaky?*

Invitational

- *What else are you noticing about your eyes?* Rather than, *Notice your eyes twitching.*
- *Would you be willing to explore how your foot wants to move?* Rather than, *It looks like your foot wants to move.* Or, *Try moving your foot.*
- *Would you be willing to stay with that feeling and see what happens next?* Rather than, *Stay with that feeling.*

Explore Sensation With Details

- *What are the qualities of that sensation?*
- *Does it have a size? Shape? Color? Weight?*
- *Does it spread? Notice the direction as it moves.*
- *Does the (pressure, pain, warmth, etc.) go from inward to outward or vice versa?*
- *Do you notice a center point? An edge? (or where the sensation begins and ends?)*

Broaden Awareness of Sensation

- *When you feel _____, what happens in the rest of your body?*
- *When you feel that _____ in your _____, how does it affect your _____ now?*

Move Through Time

- *What happens next?* (even if the person reports feeling "stuck")
- *As you follow that sensation, where does it go? How does it change?*
- *Where does it move to (or want to move to if it could)?*

B: II. Grounding

Grounding Basics

Ages: All

Objective: The students will experience being grounded and observing their thoughts without judgment or action.

Materials: None

Background Information: Depending on the situation, this exercise can be done sitting, standing, or walking with an individual student or a group.

Procedure

1. Give the following instructions:

   - *Take three deep, slow breaths. Breathe in through your nose and out through your mouth.*
   - *Look down at your feet, and pay attention to the connection of your feet to the floor. Pay special attention to the connection between your heels and the floor.*
   - *Imagine that your feet are growing roots like those of a tree.*
   - *Imagine that these roots are growing deep into the earth to give you a solid connection to the earth.*
   - *Just notice how it feels to be in your body and feel this connection.*
   - *Notice how your feet feel, your legs, and the whole center of your body.*
   - *Take this time to really experience this connection and how it feels throughout your body. We keep this memory with us throughout the day and use it whenever we need to re-connect to ourselves and what is going on inside us.*

2. Talk with the students about how they can use these skills during the day. Have them identify specific situations where they expect to use grounding for self-regulation.

Evaluation

The students will be able to direct their attention to their breathing, and they will experience being centered and grounded.

Finding a Still, Quiet Place

Ages: 5–11

Objective: Young students will be introduced to grounding and mindful awareness and how it feels in their minds and bodies.

Materials: None

Background Information: Children will experience their own Still, Quiet Place and feel it in their body/minds. With older children, the language can be more body focused with less emphasis on the Still, Quiet Place as a location. Children ages 5 to 9 can begin to remember to visit their Still, Quiet Place when they are upset, and some may be able to use the practice to allow them to respond to upsetting circumstances. A general rule of thumb is that children can practice 1 minute for each year of their age.

Procedure

Say the following to the students:

- *I would like to share one of my favorite places with you. I call it my "Still, Quiet Place." It's not a place you travel to in a car, a train, or a plane. It's a place inside you that you can find just by closing your eyes. Let's find it now.*

- *Close your eyes and take some slow, deep breaths. See if you can feel a kind of warm, happy smile in your body. Do you feel it? This is your Still, Quiet Place.*

- *Take some more deep breaths and really snuggle in.*

- *The best thing about your Still, Quiet Place is that it's always inside you. And you can visit it whenever you like. It is nice to visit your Still, Quiet Place and feel the love that is there. It is especially helpful to visit your Still, Quiet Place if you are feeling angry, sad, or afraid. Your Still, Quiet Place is a good place to talk with these feelings and to make friends with them. When you rest in your Still, Quiet Place and talk to your feelings, you may find that your feelings are not as big and powerful as they seem. Remember, you can come here whenever you want and stay as long as you like.*

- *When you are ready, take another slow, deep breath and open your eyes.*

Evaluation

The students will be able to direct their attention to their breathing and experience the image of their Still, Quiet Place.

Note. From *Mindful Awareness-Based Stress Reduction for School-Age Children,* by A. Saltzman & P. Goldin. In *Acceptance & Mindful Awareness for Children & Adolescents* (p. 142), L. Greco & S. Hayes (Eds.), 2008, Oakland, CA: New Harbinger. Copyright 2008 by New Harbinger. Adapted with permission.

Seaweed Practice

Ages: 5–11

Objective: The students will experience the feeling of grounding and mindful awareness. Students will use the awareness of breathing to slow things down in everyday life.

Materials: None

Background Information: If the students in the group are getting wiggly, try this brief movement practice. This practice simultaneously honors the students' natural need for movement and continues to develop their capacity to pay attention. In this exercise, the focus of attention is on the experience of moving.

Procedure

1. Say the following to the students:

   - *Each of us is a strand of seaweed anchored to the floor.*
   - *Initially, we are in a strong current, which gives us big, rapid movements.*
   - *Gradually, the current decreases, and our movements become smaller and smaller until there is very gentle swaying and then stillness.*

2. Throughout the Seaweed Practice, gently remind students to be aware of their physical sensations, thoughts, and feelings.

Evaluation

The students will be able to direct their attention to their breathing and experience gradually slowing movements until they reach stillness.

Note. From *Mindful Awareness-Based Stress Reduction for School-Age Children,* by A. Saltzman & P. Goldin. In *Acceptance & Mindful Awareness for Children & Adolescents* (p. 149), L. Greco & S. Hayes (Eds.), 2008, Oakland, CA: New Harbinger Copyright 2008 by New Harbinger. Adapted with permission.

A Simple Centering Exercise

Ages: 5 and above
Objective: The students will experience the feeling of grounding and being centered.
Materials: None

Procedure

1. Have students stand (with or without music) and feel the connection of their feet to the floor. Ask them to then bend their knees to lower their center of gravity, creating a feeling of greater stability.

2. Next, have them sway, shifting their weight gently from side to side and from foot to foot. Direct their awareness to the sense of going off balance and coming back into balance by finding their center of gravity.

3. After students have explored this movement for a while, have them repeat the exercise and share the sensations they feel in each position. Students can point to the place in their body where they feel "centered." For most, it will be in the area near the navel and about two inches inside the body.

4. Next, students can repeat the above, this time moving forward and backward instead of from side to side. Young children can pretend to be a toy top moving about in a circle with hands on hips. As the "top" slows down, it wobbles until it finally rests, stopping completely.

Evaluation

The students will experience becoming centered and be able to describe the sensation as it is in their bodies.

Note. From *Trauma Through a Child's Eyes* (p. 336), by P. A. Levine & M. Kline, 2007. Berkeley, CA: North Atlantic Books. Copyright 2007 by Peter A. Levine and Maggie Kline. Adapted with permission.

Tai Chi Grounding Exercise

Ages: 5 and above

Objective: In order to connect with themselves physically, the students will relax and slow down.

Materials: None

Background Information: *Tai Chi* originated in China thousands of years ago. It is a system of slow, meditative physical movement. The following simple exercise can help students. Interestingly, this exercise can also be used with students who need to feel more energized.

Procedure

1. Using language that matches the students' developmental levels: Introduce the exercise with the name *Tai Chi* if you feel it will raise the students' interests. Depending on your goal for the exercise, describe the exercise as grounding and/or energizing. Suggest that it can be used any time the students feel it would be helpful to them.

2. Ask the students to stand with their feet at a distance of about shoulder width apart, so that the sides of their feet are approximately even with the ends of their shoulders. Their arms should be at their sides with an open space under their arms as if they have a Ping-Pong ball under there. Their palms should be turned toward the back.

3. Ask the students to bend their knees slightly and to notice their feet's connection to the ground as they take a slow inhale and exhale. Ask them to slowly bend their knees just a little more. Sometimes, the direction, "soft knees" can be helpful.

4. Now, ask the students to simultaneously and slowly (1) take an inhale breath, (2) raise their arms up in front of them until they are about mid-chest height, and (3) straighten their legs slightly. Suggest "soft arms, hands, or knees."

5. Next, ask the students to simultaneously and slowly (1) exhale, (2) return their knees to the less slightly bent position, and (3) return their arms back to their sides.

6. Repeat Steps 4 and 5, two more times.

7. After the third set of movements, have the students place their hands on their stomachs to experience the feelings of relaxation and connection.

8. If you are working with students who need to experience more energy in their bodies, after the third set of movements, ask them to notice any feelings in their stomach area. Identify sensations as energy for them and ask them to let it spread throughout their bodies.

9. All students may need some practice with this exercise to experience its benefits. It might be one you will choose to start each session.

 #12873

Evaluation

The students will experience gradually becoming centered and be able to describe the sensation in their bodies.

Grounding After a Troublesome Interaction

Ages: 5 and above

Objective: The students will learn a helpful technique for self-regulation after a difficult interaction with another person.

Materials: None

Background Information: This grounding activity is especially helpful with self-regulation after a difficult interaction with another person.

Procedure

1. Using language that matches the students' developmental levels, give the following directions:

   - *From either a standing or sitting position, breathe in through your nose for a long, slow inhale, and then slowly exhale through your mouth. Let's do this three times.*

   - *If standing, notice the connection of your feet to the ground. If sitting, notice your body's connection to the chair and your feet to the ground. Continue with nice, slow inhales and exhales.*

   - *Now bring your thoughts to the person you had trouble with. Scanning your body from head to toe, say to yourself: Let any energy that (the person's name) may have left with me, go back to them.*

   - *Take a long, slow inhale and exhale. Now say to yourself: Let any energy I may have left with (name the person) come back to me.*

   - *Take another long, slow inhale and exhale as you notice that you feel more comfortable knowing that this troublesome interaction is over. Notice again your connection to the ground.*

   - *If you feel you need to, you can repeat one or both sentences to yourself.*

2. Give the following directions:

   - *Take another cleansing breath and think about other situations where this technique may be helpful.*

   - *What difference will it make for you when you are able to do this?*

Evaluation

The students will experience gradually becoming grounded and calmer following a troublesome interaction with another person.

#12873

B: III. Mindful Awareness

Paying Attention Through Mindful Awareness

Ages: 5–7

Objective: The students will strengthen their ability to focus on the present moment by experiencing mindful awareness.

Materials: None

Background Information: This exercise helps children experience mindful awareness as a way of improving their ability to pay attention to the present moment without judgment. It is a capacity that everyone has, and it can be nurtured through practice and integrated into everyday life. Mindful awareness as a calming tool teaches us to bring our full attention to what we are doing, when we are doing it. Mindful awareness can be practiced as a kind of meditation or used as a way of bringing our full attention to everyday activities, such as taking a walk. During a mindful awareness exercise, we welcome wherever the mind goes by simply noting and labeling where our thoughts have drifted and then returning our attention to our breath as an anchor. The main task of mindful awareness is to strengthen our ability to pay attention. We do not judge ourselves when our minds wander, since it's only natural. We simply return to our breath as the anchor of our experience.

Procedure

1. Say the following to the students:

   - *Sit comfortably in your chair with your feet on the floor and your hands resting comfortably in your lap.*

   - *Let's take a deep breath so your breath fills up your belly. Slowly let the air out as you relax.*

   - *Take another deep breath into your belly and slowly let the air out. In . . . and out . . . in . . . out.*

2. Have the students become aware of their breathing. Say the following:

   - *Now close your eyes. As you breathe in, notice where your breath comes from. Notice where it goes. In . . . out . . . in . . . out.*

   - *As you are focusing on your breath, notice if your mind has any other thoughts. Ask yourself, how am I feeling right now? Am I noticing a certain part of my body? Can I notice my thoughts coming and going? Name what's going on, like daydreaming or thinking. Then come back to your breath as it goes in and out, in and out.*

   - *Now notice the chair you are sitting on. How does it feel? How do your feet feel on the floor? Notice your breathing one more time and then open your eyes.*

3. Ask the students to talk about what it was like to just notice their breathing. Ask: *What did you notice happening as you paid attention to your breathing? Were there times when you started to think about other things? What was going on then? How was it to go back to noticing your breathing?*

 #12873

4. Suggest to the students that they try noticing their breathing at different times during the day, for instance, when they are in their classes or on the bus. Say: *This noticing our breath is called* mindful awareness. *It can be very helpful to you when you want to relax or focus on an activity.*

Evaluation

The students will be able to direct their attention to their breathing and redirect their attention to their breathing when their minds wander.

Note. From *Building Emotional Intelligence* (pp. 36–37), by L. Lantieri, 2008, Boulder, CO: Sounds True, Inc. Copyright 2008 by L. Lantieri. Adapted with permission.

A Game of I-Spy

Ages: 5 and above

Objective: The students will experience noticing objects in the room in great detail.

Materials: None

Background Information: I-Spy is a guessing game where you describe something you see in the general vicinity and the child tries to guess what you are looking at. For groups, have a student spy an object while the rest of the group guesses.

Procedure

1. Say: *Let's try a game called I-Spy. Have you ever played it before? It's a way to start noticing what it is like to see mindfully. In I-Spy, I'll tell you something I see or "spy with my little eye," and you'll try to guess what it is. I'll start.*

2. Begin with an example. Pick an object in plain sight, such as a toy ball, and describe it: *I spy with my little eye . . . something round and blue.*

3. Add more description if the student(s) needs it until he or she can guess what the object is. For instance, *It's about as big as your fist, and it bounces.*

4. Explain that the object of this game is not to win or lose, but to notice what is in the room and really, really look closely at everything around us. Try a few rounds of I-Spy, with you first describing the object and the students guessing. Then have the student describe an object, and you guess what it is.

5. Ask the students what they thought of the game of I-Spy: *How was that game for you? Did you notice anything in the room that you hadn't noticed before? What?*

6. Explain that what you were doing in this game was seeing mindfully.

Evaluation

The students are able to recognize and describe physical objects in the room with increased detail.

Note. From *Building Emotional Intelligence* (p. 56), by L. Lantieri, 2008, Boulder, CO: Sounds True, Inc. Copyright 2008 by L. Lantieri. Adapted with permission.

Being a Noodle

Ages: 5–11

Objective: The students will develop awareness of their bodies using muscle relaxation and visualization.

Materials: Paper and crayons, markers, or pencils

Procedure

1. Ask the students: *Have you ever seen a spaghetti noodle before and after it's been cooked?*

2. Talk about how stiff and rigid it is before, and how floppy and flexible it becomes after it is cooked.

3. Have the students act like an uncooked noodle by guiding them verbally to tighten different muscles, stand stiff, and be as tight and rigid as possible. Talk the students through the cooking process, relaxing them as you go: OK, *the noodle is being put in a big pot of hot water! It's in there, and oh, it's starting to get sort of soft in the middle! It's bending a little bit at the middle. . . . Now up top it's getting a little floppy. Relax your neck a little bit. . . . Now the arms are beginning to wiggle around a little bit. . . . Uh oh, the legs are getting so soft I'm not sure they'll be able to hold the noodle straight anymore!*

4. Continue in this fashion until the students are totally relaxed. Then let the students take turns "cooking" you.

5. Explore with the students the times and places where "being a noodle" could help.

Evaluation

The students will be able to demonstrate the difference between being stiff and being relaxed throughout their bodies by responding to visualization cues.

Note. From *Collaborative Treatment of Traumatized Children and Teens* (p. 241), by G. N. Saxe, B. H. Ellis, and J. B. Kaplow, 2007, New York: Guilford. Copyright 2007 by Guilford. Adapted with permission.

Mindfully Eating a Raisin

Ages: 8–11

Objective: The students will experience bringing their full attention to an activity and discover the difference really paying attention makes.

Materials: Raisins

Background Information: This is an activity that requires really paying attention. The student will be eating a raisin in a very different way than either of you have experienced before. The student will do it very slowly—as if he or she was eating it in slow motion—in order to explore what it's like to be mindfully aware while we eat.

Procedure

1. Give the student and yourself two raisins each on a paper plate or napkin. You might want to give the student a chance to eat one raisin before continuing. You could say: *I've got these raisins. I'm wondering if you'd like to taste one before we begin this activity.*

2. Now ask the student to bring all of his or her attention to the second raisin: *First, look at the raisin carefully, and then touch it, but don't put it in your mouth yet.*

3. After a few minutes of looking and touching silently, ask him or her for words that describe the raisin: *What are some words to describe your raisin? What color is it? How big is it? Is it soft or hard? What does it smell like? What else do you notice about it? Describe it as if you were talking to a Martian who has never seen one before.*

4. Have the student pick up the raisin and eventually put it into his or her mouth and eat it. You could say:

   • *Now, in slow motion, bring your hand with the raisin in it to your mouth and slowly put the raisin into your mouth. Let it stay in your mouth without biting it yet. Perhaps you can close your eyes and just feel it with your tongue as you move it around in your mouth.* (Pause for 10 seconds.)

   • *Next, slowly take one bite and start to really taste the raisin, noticing your tongue and teeth as you continue to chew it slowly. Notice what is happening to the raisin. What side of your mouth are you chewing on? Now slowly swallow it.*

5. Ask: *So what was that like? What did you notice? Any surprises? Was that hard or easy to do? Why?*

Evaluation

The students will describe noticing different sensations when they experience doing an everyday activity in a mindfully aware way.

Note. From *Mindful Awareness-based Cognitive Therapy for Children: A Randomized Group Psychotherapy Trial Developed to Enhance Attention and Reduce Anxiety,* by R. J. Semple, 2005, Unpublished doctoral dissertation, New York: Columbia University. Copyright 2005 by R. J. Semple. Adapted with permission.

 #12873

Paying Attention

Ages: 12 and above

Objective: The students will experience bringing their full attention to an activity and discover the difference that really paying attention makes in their ability to notice and remember details.

Materials: 15 everyday objects, such as a bell, paper, pens, a timer, a peeled and sectioned orange, and so on.

Background Information: This is an activity that explores the concept of mindful awareness through two challenge games that require the students to be fully aware. These games will help the students to quiet their minds and strengthen their abilities to pay attention. You may decide to do the object activity twice: giving the students another look and asking for a second list while you hold the first one. You could have a discussion first to see whether the students tried to remember the objects by working out a system. Usually, the students will do a lot better with the second list.

Procedure

1. Introduce the activity by saying: *Today, I'd like to try a calming technique that will help quiet our minds and improve our concentration. In fact, it helps us do a lot of things better, and it's called* mindful awareness. *'Mindful awareness' simply means being aware of what you are feeling or thinking in the present moment, paying attention on purpose to what you are feeling or thinking right now, and paying attention to what you are doing as you are doing it. On any day in our lives, we do a lot of things without really noticing what we are doing—especially if we do them everyday—like brushing our teeth or eating. Our minds are not really focused on what we are doing a lot of the time. For example (look at the clock), it is about ___ o'clock right now. Let's see if we can remember what we were doing yesterday at this time. What about a week ago?*

2. Pause for a few minutes to discuss. You may make the point that we often think we remember everything, but don't. Increased focus on paying attention to the present moment can help us do that. Explain: *When we are mindfully aware, we bring our full selves and whole heart to any daily activity. Learning how to quiet our minds helps us to focus our attention better, and that improves our concentration and the ability to learn new things. I'd like to try out a fun activity with you now to explore what it feels like to be mindfully aware and really concentrate on what you are seeing. It's a memory game.*

3. Have the tray of 15 everyday objects available, but covered. Explain the game: *In a moment, I am going to show you a tray that has several objects on it, and I am going to give you 1 minute to look at the objects. You can't touch them or write down anything during this minute. Remember, this is just a fun game. It is meant to give you some practice in really concentrating. After the first minute, I will ring the bell and cover the objects. You will have a few minutes to write down as many objects as you can remember. Then we will take a look and see what happens.*

4. Give each student a pen and paper. Take the cover off the tray and begin!

---

5. Have a discussion afterward about how difficult it is to stay focused and train our minds to pay attention. However, with practice, we can train our minds to concentrate better, and that is what the concept of mindful awareness helps us with. *Now I want to try one more experience of mindful awareness with you. I am going to set the timer for 3 minutes. During this time, without speaking, we will each eat an orange in slow motion, taking only a couple of bites from it. As you taste your orange, stay in the present moment, touching the orange, smelling it, slowly peeling it, and finally taking a couple of bites. Notice the taste in your mouth and how it feels on your tongue. Then swallow it and take another. Remember, we are doing this whole experience in slow motion and want to let it last the full 3 minutes.*

6. Afterward, ask: *So what was that like? What did you notice? Any surprises? Was that hard or easy to do? Why?*

Evaluation

The students will describe noticing different sensations when they experience doing an everyday activity in a mindfully aware way.

Note. From *Building Emotional Intelligence* (pp. 124–125), by L. Lantieri, 2008, Boulder, CO: Sounds True, Inc. Copyright 2008 by L. Lantieri. Adapted with permission.

What's Different About Me?

Ages: 12 and above

Objective: The students will experience bringing their full attention to the features of another person and discover the difference really paying attention makes in the ability to notice and remember details.

Materials: None

Procedure

1. Have two group members pair off and mindfully observe each other. Suggest they observe as many details about each other as possible.

2. Have students turn their backs, change three things (e.g., glasses, watch, hair), and turn back toward each other. Ask each member of the pair to notice the changes.

3. For a variation, try "Whose Penny?" Have every group member take a penny from a bowl, hold it for a moment, and put it back in the bowl. Then, each member takes one again and really studies it. Then he or she puts it back in the bowl. Finally, each member tries to pick out his or her own penny. Discuss whether they could have identified their pennies the first time. Why not?

Evaluation

The students will experience noticing more details when they are mindfully aware and focused in their attention.

B: IV. Tracking Sensation

Establish Body Awareness

Ages: 5 and above

Objective: The students will develop their own vocabularies to describe the sensations they are experiencing.

Materials: (Optional) Cards or poster of sensation words; puppets or dolls

Background Information: Establishing body awareness helps us identify and name sensations. For younger students, use a few basic terms until the students become adept at describing sensations with them, then expand their sensation vocabulary. Once students can describe sensations, work with them to identify the first sensation they feel as they are beginning to be upset. Help them to become calm. Then students can practice activation and de-activation. Take time with students to reflect on their sensations. Consider repeating this activity frequently.

Procedure

1. Ask the students to describe what these terms feel like in their bodies: *tired, alert, hungry, full, thirsty, sated, cold, warm, comfortable,* and *uncomfortable* or other sensation words they suggest.

2. Ask the students to remember a time when they felt calm, at ease, or comfortable. Have them notice the sensations in their bodies.

3. To help students identify bodily sensations that accompany being upset, ask them, *What are you aware of in your body when you are upset? Did you notice that your breathing changed? Or how the heat rose in your face? Or how hard it was to swallow just then? What is the very first sensation you notice when you are upset?*

4. Say: *As you remember being upset, go back to the memory of a time you were calm and comfortable. Notice the effect of that memory on your feeling upset.*

5. Process with the students how they will use the calm memory when they are upset.

Evaluation

The students are able to recognize and describe physical sensations in their bodies and practice de-activating when they are upset.

 #12873

Body Cues Check-In

Ages: 8–11

Objectives: The students will learn the signs of stress.

Materials: How Do I Feel When I Am Stressed? handout

Background Information: Before you can release stress, you first need to be aware that you are stressed. This activity will help students learn the signs of stress through the use of a checklist. As the leader, you can model this awareness by making a note of times when your heart was beating fast, your breathing was shallow, or you noticed other signs of stress.

Procedure

1. Ask the student to think about a time within the past few days when he or she felt very upset, stressed, frightened, or nervous: *Now, I would like you to think about a time in the last several days when you felt very stressed. You were really upset. You might have been worried, angry, or frightened. It might have been a person who upset you, a place—maybe you were at recess—or a situation—like taking a test. Where were you? Who were you with? What was happening?*

2. Have a discussion about the physical symptoms of stress, using the handout How Do I Feel When I Am Stressed? Say, *Now, thinking about that stressful time, let's give some thought to how our bodies feel when we are stressed. Let's take a look at this list and check off everything we remember feeling when we were in that stressed situation.*

3. Acknowledge that our minds and bodies react very differently when we are feeling stressed, and that sometimes we are able to notice those differences, but not always. Also, what bothers one person might be different from what bothers someone else.

4. As an optional extension activity, introduce biodots as a way to help the students become more aware of their physiological responses to different levels of stress. The biodot is a reasonably accurate, temperature-sensitive instrument. It changes color when subjected to variations in skin temperature. It works because blood flow to the extremities, such as the hands, is greatly reduced when we are in a stressed condition, and the biodot responds to such a change. Say:

   - *Sometimes we know when we are feeling calm or upset, but sometimes we cannot tell clearly how we feel. Let me show you something called a biodot.* (Put one on the web of your hand between the thumb and index finger.)

   - *This little dot changes colors depending on how stressed or calm we feel inside. When we are experiencing stress, our hands feel cold because our tiny blood vessels called capillaries close down; when we are relaxed, our blood flow increases, and our hands get warmer. This little dot can read those kinds of changes in our bodies and change color to match.*

5. Tell students to notice what colors their dots are and compare them to the chart on the biodot card. You may need to substitute some different words in order for the student to understand the meaning of each color: purple is very calm; blue is tranquil (relaxed and peaceful); green is calm (but not as calm as blue); beige is involved (doing an activity like working or playing, and feeling relaxed while doing it); brown is stressed; and black is very stressed (maybe very worried, anxious, or angry).

Evaluation

The students are able to recognize and describe at least one episode of having felt stressed and the bodily sensations that accompanied that feeling.

Note. From *Building Emotional Intelligence* (p. 72), by L. Lantieri, 2008, Boulder, CO: Sounds True, Inc. Copyright 2008 by L. Lantieri. Adapted with permission.

 #12873

Name _____ Date _____

How Do I Feel When I Am Stressed?

☐ Jumpy

☐ Can't sit still

☐ Fast breathing

☐ Shaky hands

☐ Cold hands

☐ Shaky legs

☐ Cold feet

☐ Heart pounding and beating fast

☐ Tight feelings in chest

☐ Get angry easily

☐ Worried or afraid over little things

☐ Feel like crying

☐ Dry mouth

☐ Muscles feel tense

☐ Upset stomach

☐ Sweating

☐ Hard time falling asleep

☐ Other _____

_____

_____

Sensation Language

Ages: 12 and above

Objectives: The students will demonstrate sensation language.

Materials: An object that is special or comforting and a Sensation Language handout for each student

Background Information: The way you distinguish a sensation from an emotion and from a thought is by being able to locate it in your body and experience it in a directly physical way. A sensation has a location, size, shape, and specific quality. Establishing body awareness helps us to identify and name emotions. The better acquainted students are with sensations, the less scary sensations become. With younger students, try using a very reduced list of basic terms until the students become adept at describing sensations with them, then expand their sensation vocabulary. Young students may enjoy drawing the place in their bodies where a sensation occurs or pointing to a puppet or doll to show a location.

Procedure

1. Begin by saying: *When someone asks you how you're doing, you may answer with, "OK" or "Not so good." But try asking yourself, "What sensation in my body tells me I'm feeling OK?" You may well get some more information: "My head feels heavy; my left shoulder is tingly; and my hand is warm." Fear might be experienced as a rapid heartbeat or a knot in the gut. You see how much more specific that description is— how much more connected to your body it is. This may feel like a different language to you at first, but with practice, it will become easier.*

2. Direct the students to find a comfortable place to sit, either in a chair or on the floor. Have the students begin by identifying something that gives them comfort or is special to them: *Think of an object that gives you comfort or is special to you. It could be a stone, a crystal, a flower, a stuffed animal, or a favorite picture or photograph.*

3. Say the following:

   • *Now tune in to the sensations your body is experiencing. . . . Feel how the chair or floor holds your weight. . . . Notice your clothing on your skin, and begin to place your awareness on the muscles underneath your skin as well. . . . Notice how your feet are grounded through the floor and the foundation and down into the earth. . . . Try to feel this sense of grounding with your whole body.*

   • *Now gaze at your comforting object, and slowly move your attention back and forth between your body and the object in front of you. If, for example, you have a stone in front of you, look at the stone with a sense of your bodily experiences in the background. Then, shift your awareness so that the image in front of you recedes and you become more aware of your bodily experience.*

   • *You might ask yourself if your object makes you feel more grounded. . . . Where in your body do you feel that sense, and what is the physical sensation? Continue for several minutes to shift back and forth, at your own rhythm, between the object and the sensations in your body.*

 #12873

- *Now allow your focus to shift to an inner sense of where the comfort is experienced in your body, and take some time to explore the nuances of this sensation. . . . Where does the sense of comfort begin? Perhaps you sense tense muscles beginning to let go, or a sense of spaciousness around your heart, or warmth in your belly. . . . Perhaps you were feeling anxious initially, and this feeling has changed in some small way.*

- *Observe the sensations and follow these changes. . . . It might not feel like much is happening at first. Or it might feel like too much is happening. . . . You can adjust your experience to fit your need by shifting focus between your sensations and the comfortable object or image that you chose as a resource. . . . Remember that you are in control.*

- *Let's choose some words that describe the sensation you noticed in your body. Here are some terms that might fit for you. . . .* (Refer to the Sensation Language handout.)

4. Have the students try on new terms to describe the sensations they were feeling in their bodies. Ask: *Describe how you know it is a sensation rather than an emotion. What new words seem to match your sensation?*

Evaluation

The students are able to recognize and describe at least two physical sensations in their bodies.

Note. From *Healing Trauma* (pp. 50–53), by P. A. Levine, 2005, Boulder, CO: Sounds True. Copyright 2005 Peter A. Levine. Adapted with permission.

Sensation Language

dense	dizzy	tremulous	expanded	breathless
spacey	knotted	tingly	queasy	tight
blocked	numb	heavy	achy	thick
full	fluid	suffocating	fluttery	trembly
hot	wobbly	buzzy	constricted	icy
hollow	sweaty	flowing	nervous	floating
electric	wooden	congested	twitchy	bubbly
calm	energized	warm	light	cold

Making a Sensation Treasure Chest

Ages: 5 and above

Objective: The students will develop their own vocabulary to describe sensations they are experiencing.

Materials: A container such as a box, can, or bag large enough for all objects; 10 to 12 objects with distinctly different textures, including a feather; a piece of sandpaper; a variety of rocks of different shapes, sizes, and textures; a cotton ball; a slimy toy; a piece of satin or silk fabric; steel wool; paper and pencil to list descriptors

Background Information: Sensory awareness is a very important part of childhood development. It not only promotes cognitive growth and self-awareness, it is fun for children to explore taste, smell, sight, sound, and touch.

Procedure

1. Hide the objects in the container.

2. Have the child close his or her eyes (or use a blindfold), pick an object, and try to guess what it is by the way it feels.

3. Once all of the items have been identified, have the child touch each object and then tell you how it feels on his or her skin (*tickly, prickly, cool, heavy*, etc.)

4. Next, have the child compare the rocks of different weights by holding them in his or her hands and noticing how his or her muscles feel when rocks are different weights.

5. Ask the child to notice the difference he or she feels in the body when he or she touches something slimy as compared to something soft, etc. Have him or her point to the place in the body where he or she notices the difference. Is it in the arms, the tummy, on the skin, or in the throat?

6. Have the child make up some questions for you, and take turns continuing to compare and contrast sensations.

7. Make a list of the sensations that were discovered.

Evaluation

The students are able to describe various physical sensations related to the objects and then identify where in their bodies they felt the sensations.

Note. From *Trauma Through a Child's Eyes* (pp. 91–92), by P. A. Levine and M. Kline, 2007, Berkley, CA: North Atlantic Books. Copyright 2007 Peter A. Levine and Maggie Kline. Adapted with permission.

Making a Sensation Tasting Tray

Ages: 5 and above

Objective: The students will develop vocabularies to describe sensations they are experiencing.

Materials: Cups; edibles with different tastes and textures (e.g., sweet, salty, bitter, spicy, tart, crunchy, soft, etc.); blindfold; paper and pencil

Procedure

1. Place the edible items in small cups on a tray.

2. Using a blindfold to avoid visual clues, have the child taste and identify the various foods. You can give a cracker between each taste test to clear the palate.

3. As the child tastes each sample, have him or her tell you how the texture felt (*creamy, hard, slippery, gooey,* etc.) and then how it tasted.

4. Now ask how each sample made his or her tongue feel (*tingly, prickly, cold, slippery, dry, relaxed, curled, numb, hot,* etc.).

5. Ask the child to notice the difference he or she felt in his or her body when tasting something slimy as compared to something crunchy, etc. Have the child point to the place in the body where he or she notices the difference. Is it in the arms, the tummy, or on the skin, or in the throat?

6. Have the child make up some questions for you, and take turns continuing to compare and contrast sensations.

7. Make a list of the sensations that were discovered.

Evaluation

The students are able to describe various physical sensations related to the objects and then identify where in their bodies they felt the sensations.

Note. From *Trauma Through a Child's Eyes* (p. 92), by P. A. Levine and M. Kline, 2007, Berkley, CA: North Atlantic Books. Copyright 2007 by Peter A. Levine and Maggie Kline. Adapted with permission.

 #12873

B: V. Self-Awareness

Emotion Portfolio

Ages: 5 and above

Objective: The students will identify their emotions and learn some additional terms to describe their emotions.

Materials: Paper and crayons, markers, or pencils

Background Information: The emotion portfolio can be adapted for different ages. Older students may choose to do more abstract representations of feelings within the circle on the page. Younger students may need to see pre-drawn faces and then can participate by trying to guess the feeling depicted. As a group application, the students could work on their own portfolio and then share with the members of the group. The portfolio is a good activity for students to begin as soon as they enter the group room, and while they are waiting for other members to arrive. The emotion portfolio can be worked on and developed over time. New experiences or words can be added to the face sheets as you go. The students may wish to collect the different emotion face sheets and make them into a book. Students enjoy creating decorative covers for their portfolios; for instance, using collages that depict their range of emotions.

Procedure

1. Draw a large circle on a piece of paper. Ask the student to name an emotion and draw a corresponding face. Have the student write the name of the emotion on top. Do this for as many emotions as the student can think of (or until you have a range of basic emotions), each on a different sheet of paper. If there are any critical emotions missing (e.g., anger, fear), prompt the child by thinking of scenarios in which that feeling is likely to occur. If the child is having difficulty thinking of what the facial expression looks like for a particular emotion, take turns trying to act out that feeling and showing it on your faces. You can also take this time to talk about how different people show emotions in different ways.

2. On the bottom of each emotion face page, write "I feel (whichever emotion) when . . . ." Help the student brainstorm different activities or events that make him or her feel a certain way, and write these on the bottom of the face page. Some items may show up on more than one emotion face page. Point this out and talk about how you can have more than one feeling about the same thing.

3. On the back of each emotion face page, brainstorm a list of related words with the student. In this way, you can introduce the student to words he or she may not know. Spend some time thinking together about how the different words might provide different information (e.g., *glad* vs. *joyful* vs. *content*) and making up scenarios in which you (or a puppet or friend) might feel the different ways.

4. As an advanced alternative, students can draw two side-by-side circles and depict an emotion as reflected on the outside in one and as reflected on the inside in the other. Have the students discuss the differences and the effects on others' understanding.

 #12873

Evaluation

The students will be able to match facial expressions to the labels for basic emotions.

Note. From *Collaborative Treatment of Traumatized Children and Teens* (p. 247), by G. N. Saxe, B. H. Ellis, and J. B. Kaplow, 2007, New York: Guilford. Copyright 2007 by Guilford. Adapted with permission.

Anchors: Our Favorite Things

Ages: 5 and above

Objective: The students will establish at least one anchor to use as a braking tool anytime they encounter difficulties regulating.

Materials: None

Background Information: The concept of anchors sprang from neuro-linguistic programming (NLP) (Bander & Grinder, 1979), but has been adapted for use with people who have experienced trauma. An *anchor* is a concrete, observable resource (as opposed to an internalized resource like self-confidence). It is preferable that the anchor be chosen from the student's life, so that the positive memories in both body and mind can be utilized. Examples include a person (grandmother, special teacher, friend), animal (favorite pet), place (home, a place in nature), object (tree, boat, stone), activity (swimming, hiking, biking). A suitable anchor is one that gives the student a feeling (in body and emotion) of relief and well-being.

Procedure

1. Notice when students are talking about things that have pleasant memories associated with them. As they talk, perhaps their breathing slows, the color rises in their cheeks, and they seem less agitated.

2. Ask the students to think about something that for them is relaxing, calming, or helps them feel better when they are upset. Say: *When you think of the times you are calm and feeling really good, what's happening then? Is somebody or something special there with you? Tell us about that special time. What do you call this special thing?*

3. Lead the students in remembering as many details as they can about the special person, place, or object. Say: *Tell us about the special thing (place, person). Make it seem as if we are watching a video.*

4. Listen for details about resources and exceptions to the problem to use later with the students as they create solutions.

5. Have the students hold the memory of the special thing in mind and say: *When you remember _____ now and imagine _____ here, how do you feel in your body?*

6. Have the students describe in as much detail as possible the sensations they feel, where they feel them, and how the sensations change. Have them notice how their emotions change as their sensations change. Say: *Notice those sensations and tell me about them. Are they cool, hot, tingly? How is your breathing? Does your mind seem calm?*

7. Ask the students to think now of the situation where they have been experiencing some dysregulation. Maybe for some students it is the time of the day when they have to transition from one activity to another. For other students, maybe it is when classmates are in their space or "bugging" them.

 #12873

Evaluation

The students will demonstrate the use of at least one anchor they have developed to help themselves feel relieved and calm.

Mirroring

Ages: 5–8
Objective: The students will develop body awareness and a sense of control over their bodies. They will use mindful awareness to achieve calming.
Materials: None

Procedure

1. Stand facing the student. Tell him or her that you are looking into a magical mirror, where each person is the other's reflection. Start by having the student make slow movements and mirror his or her body movements with your body.

2. After a few minutes, switch, so that the student follows your movements.

3. Then change again, with neither person identified as the lead. This time, either person can make movements, and you can both take turns without verbally telling the other when you are changing. Try to make different emotional expressions and move very slowly. Rules: Do not touch the mirror (the other person), use slow movements only, and make no sound.

4. Discuss with the students the experience of being mirrored and of mirroring someone else. Ask them to talk about any new information they learned about themselves. Have the students reflect on the effect on their bodies of focusing on their slow movements. Have the students plan how to use this mindful focus in upsetting situations.

Evaluation

The students will demonstrate the ability to mirror another's expressions and body movements. The students will identify at least one new awareness they have about themselves.

Note. From *Collaborative Treatment of Traumatized Children and Teens* (p. 240), by G. N. Saxe, B. H. Ellis, and J. B. Kaplow, 2007, New York: Guilford. Copyright 2007 by Guilford. Adapted with permission.

Imaginary School Bus

Ages: 5 and above

Objective: The students will identify people at home and at school who are resources to them and use that information to internalize a more positive self-image.

Materials: None

Procedure

1. Work with the students to generate a list of people who are supportive of the student or who the student thinks would support him or her (e.g., superheroes or celebrity figures). Feel free to put yourself on the list, teachers, or anyone else the student might not think of, whom you suspect could be a supportive person.

2. Ask the student to visualize getting on a school bus and seeing each of those people in a seat. Help the student visualize this in a way that is easiest for him or her: drawing a picture of the bus, putting names of people on seats (Who would sit next to whom?), or closing his or her eyes while you describe all the people on the bus. Ask:

   - *Which seat would you pick?*
   - *Who would you sit near?*

3. Have the student imagine everyone on the bus wants the student to sit next to him or her. If the student is having a specific problem, ask the student to imagine that all the people in the bus are generating ideas about what the student could do in the situation. For example, *What would your best friend say?*

Evaluation

The students will identify at least three persons who are resources to them and describe possible solutions these supporters would suggest.

Note. From *Collaborative Treatment of Traumatized Children and Teens* (p. 244), by G. N. Saxe, B. H. Ellis, and J. B. Kaplow, 2007, New York: Guilford. Copyright 2007 by Guilford. Adapted with permission.

Anchoring Yourself in Calm Waters

Ages: 8–11
Objective: The students will learn a method for calming themselves when facing stressful situations.
Materials: None

Procedure

1. Help students to think of a favorite place or their happiest time. Help them to vividly recreate it in their mind. If you are in an individual session, you may want the student to describe it to you. If you are in a group setting, ask the students to think about what they see, smell, hear, touch, and taste in their special places. Ask them what other sensations they feel in their bodies

2. Help the students anchor the sensations in their bodies. Tell them they can do this by:

   • Deciding on an inconspicuous trigger point they can press in public without calling attention to themselves (e.g., pressing into a thigh or the palm of a hand)

   • Thinking of their favorite place or happiest time: vividly recreating it in their minds so they can see it, smell it, hear it, touch it, and taste it

3. Have the students firmly push on their anchor points to reinforce noticing their positive feelings.

4. Encourage the students that when they are under stress and starting to "lose it," to press on their anchor points. They will be reminded of their way of averting stress.

Evaluation

The students will demonstrate the ability to follow the steps: achieving a happy memory and then anchoring it to a trigger point to achieve a calmer state. Students will make a plan to use this or other techniques in specific situations during the following week.

Note. From *Making the Brain/Body Connection* (p. 88), by S. Promislow, 1999, West Vancouver, BC, Canada: Kinetic Publishing. Copyright 1999 by Sharon Promislow. Adapted with permission.

Sensation Game

Ages: 5 and above

Objective: The students will experience a variety of sensations and learn to describe how they experience the sensations in their bodies.

Materials: Sensation Cards handout

Background Information: The activities that follow are recommended as a helpful way to teach kids the language of sensations, how to ground, and track physical sensations. For full-color activity cards and a manual, see *The Sensation Game* by Kris Downing.

Procedure

1. Explain to the group that each student will take turns picking a card from the pile. Have the student read the card and respond.

2. Go around the group with each student responding to the card.

3. Have the second student select a card from the pile and repeat the process.

Evaluation

The students will demonstrate the ability to experience various sensations and describe how they feel in their bodies.

Note. From *The Sensation Game,* by Kris Downing. Copyright 2008 by Kris Downing. The Sensation Game is available at www.sensationgame.com.

Choose an object that feels like you feel right now.

Talk about it.

Point to where you feel that in your body.

Raise your arms very slowly as you breathe in. Then slowly lower them as you breathe out.

What do you notice?

Stand and face a partner. Repeat this activity.

Place your hands on your face and take a slow, deep breath.

Move your hands to a different part of your body and keep breathing.

What do you notice?

Stand or sit quietly.

Move as if the wind is blowing you.

What sensations do you feel inside your body?

Share something that makes you feel good inside.

Draw a picture of it on a piece of paper.

Close your eyes and imagine that you are full of color.

What colors do you have inside of you?

Where are the colors in your body?

Think of a time when you felt peaceful, calm, or content.

Choose an object that feels or looks like you felt inside.

Where did you feel that in your body?

Pretend you are blowing up a balloon.

Now pretend you are blowing a big bubble.

What was different about your breathing?

Open your eyes and mouth as big as you can; stick out your tongue and make some kind of noise.

Then relax.

What do you feel in your face right now?

Find the most relaxed or rested place inside of you right now.

Describe it. Where is it? What color is it? How do you know it is relaxed?

Show how big it is with your hands.

Note. From *The Sensation Game,* by Kris Downing. Copyright 2008 by Kris Downing. The Sensation Game is available at www.sensationgame.com.

Sit back in your chair (or lie on the floor).

Feel all of the places where the chair (or floor) is touching and supporting your body.

Shift any way that is more comfortable.

Pick up your favorite object and talk about why it is your favorite.

Hold it. Close your eyes and breathe for a while.

What did you notice?

Cross your arms. Gently tap your arms or shoulders and breathe.

Keep tapping and breathing for 30 seconds.

Notice how your body is feeling and share what you notice.

Pick your favorite shape (triangle, circle, square).

Find that shape in three places around you.

Draw the shape in the palm of your hand.

Breathe in.

Put your hand on the place where your breath goes.

Follow your breath in and out with your fingertips three times.

Lightly put your hand on your throat while you hum.

What do you feel?

Now try holding a note with a partner for as long as you can. What did you feel inside?

Share something you do with your body to help yourself feel better (breathe, stretch, hug, dance, jump, etc.).

Lead other players in doing it, too

Shake and jiggle yourself out, from your nose to your toes.

Then be still. Breathe and rest. Notice what sensations you feel inside.

What did you notice?

Pick up two different objects and notice how they feel. Which one feels better?

Notice how you feel holding each one.

Find two places in your body that feel different (tight/loose, cool/warm).

Tap your fingers all over the top of your head, neck, and shoulders.

Tap from temples across eyebrows, back to temples, across cheek, back to temples, across jaws and chin and back.

What do you notice?

B: VI. Social Awareness

Getting Along at School

Ages: 5–11

Objective: The students will identify a number of ways they are getting along successfully at school and use that information to improve their interpersonal skills.

Materials: Notebook paper and pencils or pens

Procedure

1. Have each student write at the top of a page of notebook paper, *20 Ways List*, and number the lines from 1 to 20.

2. Say the following: *Even when we are having some troubles at school, there are often lots of things we are doing to help us get along at school. Today we want to see how many ways you can think of that you've been getting along at school.*

3. Write one list for the group of students or have them make their own lists.

4. Have the students rate the top three ways they use to get along at school. Ask: *What are you doing in these situations that could help you in other situations?*

5. Suggest other times in our lives when we act out on our feelings of anger or frustration.

6. Have the students identify other actions people could take to help the situation.

7. Ask the students to identify one possible situation they may encounter in the next week that might lead to them feeling upset (angry or frustrated).

8. Ask the following:

   - *On a scale of 1 to 10, with 10 being the best, how do you handle acting on your anger or frustration?*
   - *What would have to happen for that number to improve by one point?*
   - *When are you already doing that a little bit?*
   - *How can you do more of that in the next week?*
   - *What would _____ (e.g., your teacher) notice you doing when things are better?*

Evaluation

The students will be able to list coping strategies they are using successfully and make a plan to use one or more the next time they have difficulty with others.

 #12873

Anger: Use It and Lose It

Ages: 5–11
Objective: The students will describe the purposes of anger and the feelings underlying anger, such as fear and sadness. Students will demonstrate ways to express anger to avoid violence and resolve it.
Materials: What's Beneath the Anger? handout, craft sticks, and glue

Procedure

1. Give each student a copy of What's Beneath the Anger? Have students cut out the dog puppet and the two cat puppets. Then have them glue each puppet to a craft stick.

2. Have the students choose a partner to role-play with. One student takes the cat puppets; the other student takes the dog puppet.

3. Lead the students through the role play by asking the following questions:

    • *How many of you have a cat?*

    • *What do cats look like when they are happy and contented?*

    • *Show with the docile puppet how cats act when they feel happy. What do they sound like?*

4. Now ask: *Have you ever seen cats change their behavior very quickly? What would happen if the dog puppet came bouncing into the room and up to the cat?*

5. Ask the students with the angry dog puppets to charge toward their partner's docile cat. Ask them to use sounds and actions. Tell the partners to show their aggressive cat puppets and vividly demonstrate how the cat would change its behavior and react angrily toward the dog.

6. Have the students set the puppets aside and begin the discussion. Ask the students the following questions:

    • *Why did the cat become aggressive?*

    • *Although the cat became angry and aggressive, what was he feeling?*

    • *Can fear also make people angry?*

    • *How does anger lead to violent behavior?*

7. Explain to the students that anger is a signal that something is wrong. We may be angry because of fear, but we may also get angry because we are sad about something. For this reason, anger is a useful emotion. It can tell us that something is wrong, and then we can choose how to respond to it. Say: *Here are some steps we can take to resolve the anger. This means we should get help for the underlying problem rather than just trying to control the angry feelings.*

---

8. Explain to students the following steps for resolving anger:

- *Stop and take a deep breath. Ground yourself.*
- *Ask, "What am I feeling right now?"*
- *Ask, "What seems to be making me angry?"*
- *Ask, "What do I need?"*
- *Get what you need by helping yourself or by asking someone else to help you.*

9. Ask the students how they can help other people who seem angry. (We might ask them what is bothering them and encourage them to talk about their feelings or go to an adult for help.)

10. The students list at least three ways to express anger without hurting themselves or anyone else. Lists may include some of these items:

- Talking to a counselor, teacher, parent, or friend
- Writing down the angry thoughts
- Writing down what I need
- Expressing my feelings through art
- Exercising
- Drinking water to reduce my stress
- Talking directly to the person I am angry with

Evaluation

The students will demonstrate the steps for resolving anger.

Note. From *Brain Friendly Guidance Activities to Build Emotional Intelligence* (pp. 46–48), by C. Messina, 2003, Austin, TX: PRO-ED. Copyright 2003 by PRO-ED, Inc. Adapted with permission.

 #12873

What's Beneath the Anger?

Nini the Cat Helps With Anger

Ages: 5–11

Objective: The students will learn ways to respond to feelings of anger and frustration in ways that help.

Materials: Nini the Cat handout and a cat puppet or stuffed toy

Procedure

1. Give each student a copy of the Nini the Cat handout and have them fold it into a small book.

2. Read the story to the group or ask students to take turns reading paragraphs aloud.

3. Afterward, ask:
   - *What did the boy seem to be feeling?*
   - *Why was he hurting cats?*
   - *What was making him angry?*
   - *What else was he probably feeling?*
   - *How was he expressing his anger and frustration?*
   - *How did the boy change the way he expressed his anger and frustration?*
   - *What was the important lesson the boy learned from Nini?*

4. Suggest other times in our lives when we act out on our feelings of anger or frustration. Have the students identify other actions people could take to help the situation.

5. Ask the students to identify one possible situation they may encounter in the next week that could make them upset (angry or frustrated).

6. Ask the following:
   - *On a scale of 1 to 10, with 10 being the best, how do you handle acting on your anger or frustration?*
   - *What would have to happen for that number to improve by one point?*
   - *When are you already doing that a little bit?*
   - *How can you do more of that in the next week?*
   - *What would _____ (e.g., your teacher) notice you doing when things are better?*

Evaluation

The students will demonstrate awareness of their responses to anger and frustration and plan to use strategies in future situations.

Note. From *Brain Friendly Guidance Activities to Build Emotional Intelligence* (pp. 46–48), by C. Messina, 2003, Austin, TX: PRO-ED. Copyright 2003 by PRO-ED, Inc. Adapted with permission.

Nini the Cat

Once there was a boy who liked to do mean things to the helpless cats in the neighborhood. He threw rocks at them, pulled their tails, and even threw them against walls. Then he would laugh and run away as if he felt better after these cruel acts.

One day, the boy was in an alley looking for a cat to tease. He saw a black furry cat a few feet away. He decided to pick up a rock and throw it to frighten the cat. But this time, as he picked up the rock, a very strange thing happened. He heard a voice say, "Why are you so angry?"

"Who said that?" the boy asked.

"I did," the cat said as he walked up to the boy and looked him in the eye.

"Why are you so angry? The cats around here certainly have not hurt you. So, why are you trying to hurt us?"

The boy was amazed. He didn't know what to do, so he just stood there looking at the talking cat. Then the cat spoke again, "Why don't you pick me up. I'm very soft and cuddly, and I think you could use a gentle touch. My name is Nini."

At first, the boy was afraid. But slowly, he bent down and picked up the cat. The cat nuzzled the boy and purred in his arms. The boy felt the cat's heart beating and began to stroke him. Suddenly, large tears began to run down the boy's face.

"Why are you crying?" asked Nini.

"I don't know," said the boy. "Not many people are as nice to me as you are. I can't read very well, and the kids at school tease me."

"I don't know why kids would tease you just because you need help with your reading," said Nini.

"Well, I haven't really asked anybody for help. When the teacher wants me to read, I just act silly and pick on other kids. I pretend to be mean so they won't bother me."

Nini purred and said, "Gee, it sounds like you should tell your mom and dad what is going on, because you are taking your anger and frustration out on others who have nothing to do with your problem."

The boy quietly told Nini more about himself. "My father is always busy working, and so is my mother. When they come home, they are so tired that I don't want to bother them. And, most of all, I don't want them to know they have a stupid son."

"My, my," said Nini, "I think we had better have a long talk." Nini and the boy sat for hours while Nini told the boy how special he was. Nini explained that the boy's mother and father were indeed busy, but they loved him very much and would certainly help him if he would only tell them about his anger and frustration. Nini also told the boy his parents were working hard to buy things for him, but they would really want to know how they could help him in other ways, too. Nini convinced the boy that he must give it a try and talk to his parents.

"Thanks you so much," said the boy to Nini. "I will talk to my parents. Won't you come home with me and be my cat?"

"Thank you for the offer, but I am used to roaming around freely," said Nini. "I think it would be nice if you went to the animal shelter and adopted a cat who needs a home."

Well, this story has a happy ending. The boy's parents were so glad that he told them about his anger and frustration and inability to read well. They immediately went to the school, and with the help of his teacher, got tutoring and extra help for the boy.

After that, the boy's reading and behavior improved in school. He started making friends, and his parents promised to slow down and communicate with him and with each other on a regular basis. However, the best thing that happened for the boy was that he and his parents went to the local animal shelter and adopted a beautiful little kitten. You guessed it. Now the boy has his own Nini."

He never again wanted to hurt an animal. The boy even spoke to his classmates about being kind to animals and to one another. He taught his friends to ask for help just as Nini had taught him.

As for the original Nini, that cat is still prowling the alleys and teaching humans how to be more humane!

Emotional Drama

Ages: 8 and above
Objective: The students will be able to identify emotions apparent in others' actions and conversations.
Materials: The Boring Script handout and slips of paper with emotion words written on them
Background Information: This activity uses The Boring Script handout, but you might consider using your own or one written with the student. The idea is to have a script of a brief, neutral dialogue that two people can act out.

Procedure

1. Write a variety of emotion words on slips of paper and put them into a container. Give a copy of The Boring Script handout to each student. Ask students to form pairs and read through the script together once, with each of them taking a role.

2. After they have read through the script, students draw an emotion slip from the container, without showing the other person. They then reread the script, but this time each person enacts his or her role as if he or she were experiencing the emotion from the emotion slip.

3. Discuss the differences in the portrayal when various emotions were included. Have the students guess each other's emotions and give feedback about why they identified those emotions. Have students continue drawing emotions and reenacting the script, or have other members of the group choose emotion strips and reenact the script. Discuss the following questions:

   - *What indicators did you pay attention to as you decided which emotion the actors portrayed?*
   - *What other words could you use to describe the emotions others showed?*

Evaluation

The students will be able to use verbal and nonverbal cues to identify the emotional states of others.

Note. From *Collaborative Treatment of Traumatized Children and Teens* (p. 248), by G. N. Saxe, B. H. Ellis, and J. B. Kaplow, 2007, New York: Guilford. Copyright 2007 by Guilford. Adapted with permission.

 #12873

The Boring Script

Scene: A donut shop

Customer: Hello, I'd like to have a coffee, with milk and a donut.

Salesclerk: We're out of coffee.

Customer: Oh. Out of coffee? I'll just have tea, then.

Salesclerk: We're out of tea.

Customer: Oh. Well, could I just have the milk then?

Salesclerk: Nope, no milk either.

Customer: What? No milk?

Salesclerk: No milk. None at all.

Customer: Well, I guess I will just have the frosted donut.

Salesclerk: We're out of donuts.

Customer: You are out of donuts?

Salesclerk: Yup. Out.

Customer: Well, OK. I guess I'll have to go somewhere else. Is there anywhere else I can go around here for a cup of coffee and some donuts?

Salesclerk: Out the door and to the left. Third door down.

Customer: Thanks. Goodbye.

Salesclerk: Have a nice day.

Interpersonal Boundaries

Ages: 8 and above

Objective: The students will be able to identify their personal boundaries in relation to others.

Materials: Yarn or rope

Background Information: This activity illustrates the difficulty many people have feeling their boundaries and being able to say "No" or "Stop." In this exercise, sometimes the stationary student's sensation and emotional state won't change, so he or she never says "stop" and the moving student ends up walking into him or her. When this happens, it is usually because the starting distance was already inside of the stationary student's interpersonal boundary. It is not possible for the stationary partner to feel his or her boundary when the moving student is already past it at the start point. In this situation, try repeating the exercise from a greater start distance. Point out to students that this is also true of people in their daily lives. It is not possible to feel where your "stop" or "no" point is if someone has already crossed it. When in doubt, have either student move a little and note what happens.

Procedure

1. Have the students divide into pairs. One partner slowly walks toward the other. The stationary partner keeps track of his or her own body sensations and says, "stop" when he or she begins to feel uncomfortable.

2. Repeat this exercise several times with the stationary partner standing at different angles to the moving partner—face, right and left shoulder, back toward the walking partner. It is important that the stationary partner talks about sensations and emotions. Ask these questions:

    - *What sensations and emotions did you notice as the other person moved closer to you?*
    - For the moving partner: *What sensations and emotions did you experience as you moved closer to the stationary partner?*
    - *What emotions did you notice in the other's face and body language as you tried to find the boundary?*
    - *What difference did the various stances make in defining the boundary?*
    - *How can we watch others and gauge their comfort level with our closeness or let others know when we are uncomfortable with how close they are?*

3. A second interpersonal boundary exercise involves the use of yarn (or rope) to help visualize one's boundary. A student takes a length of yarn and uses it to draw a circle around himself or herself, indicating his or her comfort distance. Have the student talk about the experience as he or she is doing it, including how if feels in his or her body to make this boundary concrete.

4. Then, with the student's permission, have the leader or another group member roam about the room, moving in and out of the student's boundary (as we actually do with others all the time). Ask the student to track his or her sensations and emotions, expressing what is happening as the other person walks. The student should notice when he or she feels an unmolested space and when he or she feels intruded upon. The student should also feel free to adjust his or her boundary at

 #12873

any time. Note that the wider the radius of the boundary, the more easily it is invaded and the more frequent and intense the student's feelings of intrusion.

5. When the student is ready, an additional intervention can be useful. With the student's permission, the leader pauses just inside the student's yarn and does not move. The student will usually feel uncomfortable, sometimes angry. The leader then helps the student to figure out that if he or she draws the boundary in a tighter circle, the leader will no longer be intruding inside of the boundary. Often, this gives the student a feeling of mastery over his or her personal space, which the student can carry into daily life at school, on the bus, at home, etc.

Evaluation

The students will be able to identify their comfortable physical boundary and experience others' boundaries.

Note. From *The Body Remembers: The Psychophysiology of Trauma and Trauma Treatment* (pp. 142–143), by B. Rothschild, 2000, New York: Norton. Copyright 2000 by B. Rothschild. Adapted with permission.

Role Play Activity

Ages: 5 and above

Objective: Students will rehearse self-regulation in a variety of situations that involve interactions with others.

Materials: Role Play Situation Cards cut into individual cards

Background Information: Whether you are working with kids individually or in a group, role play can be used to develop and rehearse self-regulation in a variety of situations that involve interaction with others. Role-play activities help kids internalize new behaviors more effectively than just talking about a change. Role plays are particularly useful for helping students take another person's perspective in situations that involve conflict. Role plays also give students the opportunity to rehearse better ways to handle situations. In addition, having kids take positive adult roles in imaginary play has been shown to improve the kids' self-regulation (Bodrova & Leong, 1996). Children and adolescents can practice how it feels to have responsibility and to make good choices in daily life. Adding adult roles to any of the suggested activities below, or to those you create, offers such opportunities.

Procedure

1. Have the students divide into pairs. One partner draws a card from the stack and shares it with his or her partner. Together, they plan their roles in the role play.

2. Give the students several minutes to discuss their scenario.

3. Have the pairs role-play their scenarios for the next few minutes.

4. Ask the pairs to talk about their role play by asking questions such as:

   - *What's the conflict?*
   - *What did you notice about how you managed to stay calm?*
   - *What do you think the other person was thinking?*
   - *What helped you manage the situation?*

5. Ask for volunteers to role-play their scenario for the group. Ask the group for feedback on questions like those above.

Evaluation

The students will be able to identify behaviors that can help them stay regulated in situations that involve conflict with others.

 #12873

Difficult interactions in the hallway	Any transition time in class
Standing in line and someone cuts in front of you or bumps into you	Planning a meal with others
Going shopping for clothes	A disagreement with a friend
Telling someone you like them	Believing you are being wrongly accused by a teacher, friend, or parent
Making a mistake and having to deal with the problems it causes	Losing your wallet or other valuable

Taking care of someone who is sick or injured	Meeting a new person and making a friend
Dealing with a bully	Needing help with a problem
Being surprised with a test you didn't expect	Having to wait to go to the water fountain
Being line leader when others don't follow the rules	Waiting to be picked for teams in PE
Being unsure of when an important assignment is due	Riding the bus when some kids are misbehaving

B: VII. Self-Management

Keep Calm Activity

Ages: 5–7
Objective: The students will learn a method to calm themselves when they face a stressful situation.
Materials: None

Procedure

1. Tell students when they are facing a stressful situation, they can do the following:

   - *Tell yourself to stop and take a look around.*
   - *Tell yourself to keep calm.*
   - *Take a deep breath through your nose while you count to five: 1, 2, 3, 4, 5.*
   - *Hold it in while you count to two: 1, 2.*
   - *Then breathe out through your mouth while you count to five: 1, 2, 3, 4, 5.*
   - *Repeat these steps until you feel calm.*

2. Have the students suggest a possible stressful situation. Practice following the steps. Ask the students to reflect on which steps seem to help and describe how they help.

Evaluation

The students will demonstrate the ability to follow the steps and achieve a calmer state. Have the students make a plan for using this technique, or others, in specific situations during the following week.

Note. From *Building Emotional Intelligence* (p. 26), by L. Lantieri, 2008, Boulder, CO: Sounds True, Inc. Copyright 2008 by Linda Lantieri. Adapted with permission.

Getting Relaxed:
Progressive Muscle Relaxation

Ages: 5–7
Objective: The students will learn a way to relax their bodies.
Materials: None

Procedure

1. Say to the students: *Welcome to this special quiet time together. We're going to learn how to relax ourselves and notice how different parts of our bodies feel when we're relaxed—our heads, our shoulders, our arms and hands, our bellies, our legs, and all the way down to the tips of our toes.*

2. Say:

   - *Lie down comfortably on the floor on your back with your arms at your sides, and place your breathing buddy—any soft toy the size of your fist—on your belly. This is to help remind you to breathe so your belly gets bigger.*

   - *Take a little stretch or wiggle if you need to and get really comfortable. Let yourself begin to get really relaxed . . . and now close your eyes.*

   - *Take a big belly breath and feel your belly getting big like a balloon. Breathe in . . . in . . . in . . . in . . . and now slowly let the air out: 1, 2, 3, 4. Take another belly breath in and feel your belly getting bigger and your breathing buddy rising: 1, 2, 3, 4 . . . and out: 1, 2, 3, 4.*

   - *Now imagine you have a ball of clay in each hand. . . . Squeeze the clay with your hands. . . . Make your fists tight. . . . Squeeze . . . squeeze . . . squeeze . . . as tightly as you can. And now let go. . . . Let the clay just drop to the floor. . . . Feel your arms relaxing. . . . Let your hands relax. . . . Let your fingers relax. . . . Let your arms relax . . . completely . . . while I count to 5: 1, 2, 3, 4, 5.*

   - *Good. . . . Your hands and arms are relaxed.*

   - *Now lift your shoulders up toward your ears. . . . Keep squeezing them up there . . . as tightly as you can. . . . Keep squeezing them up a little more. . . . Now, let go and let your shoulders relax. . . . Let them drop back down. . . . Let your shoulders relax completely . . . while I count to 5: 1, 2, 3, 4, 5. . . . Great. . . . Your shoulders are relaxed.*

   - *Squeeze your eyes tight. . . . Squint like you do when the sunlight is too bright. . . . Open your mouth as wide as you can . . . like you're going to take a giant bite, and stick out your tongue. . . . Hold . . . hold . . . hold. . . . Now let go and let your whole face relax. . . . Let your face relax and rest while I count to 5: 1, 2, 3, 4, . . . 5. Your face is relaxed.*

   - *Now try to pull in your belly as much as you can toward your back . . . and give yourself a great big hug. . . . Keep hugging the whole middle of your body as tightly as you can. . . . Hug . . . hug . . . hug. . . . Now relax. . . . Let your belly be soft. . . . Let your chest relax and let your arms fall to the floor as I count to 5: 1, 2, 3, 4, 5. . . . Good. . . . Your belly and chest are relaxed.*

- *Now tighten your legs and feet, making them stiff, and curl all 10 toes . . . keep holding your legs and squeezing. . . . And now let go and relax. . . . Feel your legs and feet resting on the floor . . . as I count to 5: 1, 2, 3, 4, 5. Your feet and legs are relaxed.*

- *And now one last time. . . . Tighten up your whole body. . . . Tighten your hands . . . arms . . . shoulders . . . face . . . belly . . . chest . . . legs . . . feet. . . . Tighten everything, and make your body as stiff as you can. . . . And now . . . let go. Let your whole body relax as you lie down and feel like you are melting into the floor.*

- *Take a belly breath in . . . and let it out. . . . Again, in . . . and out . . . One more time on your own. . . . You can hear your breath relaxing you. Now take a little time to notice if any part of your body might still feel tense or uncomfortable. . . . Check in with your body and ask yourself, Are my feet relaxed? Do my legs feel relaxed? How do my arms feel? Take a little time to see how your whole body is feeling . . . from your toes all the way to the top of your head. Notice how your body is feeling right now.*

- *Now gently open your eyes and begin to wiggle your toes and your fingers, and let your body take a nice big stretch. Slowly begin to sit up and feel how relaxed your body feels. That's wonderful. You just learned how to help your body feel calm and relaxed—and you can do this anytime you want. Thanks for trying this out with me.*

Evaluation

The students will demonstrate the ability to tense and relax muscles in their bodies. Give the students an opportunity to talk about how this technique could work for them. Have them identify what aspects seem to help them. The students will make a plan for using this technique, or others, in the following week.

Note. From *Building Emotional Intelligence* (pp. 47–49), by L. Lantieri, 2008, Boulder, CO: Sounds True, Inc. Copyright 2008 by Linda Lantieri. Adapted with permission.

 #12873

Creating a Calming Plan

Ages: 5 and above

Objective: The students will identify strategies for self-calming at home and at school.

Materials: Creating a Calming Plan handout

Background Information: Children learn general calming strategies to help them think before they act. Some of the research supporting this idea is based on studies looking at the effects of social and emotional learning programs (SEL) in schools, where children are taught about their emotions, how to calm themselves, and learn ways to solve interpersonal problems. The first step of many SEL programs is to help children develop ways to stop and calm down before deciding how to solve a problem. The best calming strategies come from talking with children to find out what works for them. This discussion should take place during calm moments.

Procedure

1. To help students identify their calming strategies, give each student the Creating a Calming Plan handout. Ask them to answer all of the questions on the handout. Younger students may wish to dictate their answers or draw an illustration of their response.

2. Then ask students to talk about their plans for using the strategies they wrote about.

Evaluation

The students will identify what triggers their periods of being upset, and strategies for calming themselves. They will also identify their supports in school and at home.

Note. From *No More Meltdowns* (p. 44), by J. Baker, 2008, Arlington, TX: Future Horizons. Copyright 2008 by Future Horizons. Adapted with permission.

Creating a Calming Plan

Feeling Upset

How do I know when I am upset? ————————————————————

Home Plan

What calms me down at home? ————————————————————

Who can I talk to at home to help solve the problem? ————————————————————

School Plan

What calms me down at school? ————————————————————

Who can I talk to at school to help solve the problem? ————————————————————

"Quick Six®"

Ages: 5 and above

Objective: The students will learn the "Quick Six" (Promislow, 1999), six methods to calm themselves when they are facing a stressful situation.

Materials: None

Background Information: The "Quick Six" create a calm, balanced energy state. Students can think "Quick Six" as a fast fix whenever they feel themselves slipping into non-serving behavior patterns.

Procedure

1. Tell the students that when they are faced with a stressful situation they might want to try drinking water. Say:

   - *Water is an instant brain boost. Drinking lots of water heightens energy, improves concentration, mental and physical coordination, and academic skills.*

   - *Sipping water throughout the day helps to correct body stress created by dehydration.*

2. Encourage students to "plug in" for balanced energy. Explain that this simple activity can help make us feel more alert, clearer, and centered. It's great when your thinking gets fuzzy, or you feel confused. Tell students to:

   - *Make a claw with one hand, and point your five fingertips in a circle around your navel, with your thumb pointing up toward your head. Continue to point inward for the next two steps:*

   - *With your other hand, massage in the hollows just below the collarbone, on either side of the breastbone—between the first and second ribs.*

   - *Or massage above and below the lips.*

3. Cross patterning is simple to learn and activates communication between the two brain hemispheres and the whole body. Explain to students that they can use it whenever it is hard to "do" and "think" at the same time. While alternating between the cross march and the one-sided march, ask students if they can think of any stressful situation, then use positive affirmations to further aid stress management. Say:

   - *Do a set of cross-marches: Cross the right arm to touch the raised left leg. Release, and cross the left arm to touch the raised right leg. Do 6 or 7 pairs of the cross march with deliberate, controlled movements and relaxed shoulders.*

   - *Switch to a one-sided march: Raise the same hand and leg together, then lower them. Now raise the other side's arm and leg together, and lower. Do 6 or 7 pairs.*

   - *Alternate between a set of cross marching and a set of one-sided marching, 6 or 7 times or until the shift is smooth. Always end on cross march.*

4. "Cook's Hook Up" is an activity students can use anytime they are upset, sad, or confused. Tell students to begin by sitting in a comfortable chair with feet flat on the floor. For Position 1, tell students to:

- *Put one ankle over the other knee.*
- *Use the opposite arm to grasp the bent leg's ankle.*
- *Bend the other arm, and reach over to grasp the ball of the bent leg's foot.*
- *Put your tongue on the roof of your mouth and breathe deeply.*
- *Hold this position for a minute or two, or until you feel calm. If you feel like it, reverse the posture. When you feel relaxed, move to Position 2, keeping your tongue on the roof of your mouth.*

5. Explain Position 2:

- *Uncross your legs and place your feet flat on the floor. Let your tongue remain on the roof of your mouth.*
- *Put the tips of your fingertips together gently and breathe deeply.*
- *Hold Position 2, thinking of your stressor, for a minute or two or until you sigh, yawn, or feel even more relaxed.* "Cook's Hook Up" was developed by Wayne Cook.

6. Offer students this variation for standing up:

- *Cross your right wrist over your left wrist and your right ankle over your left ankle (or vice versa). Turn the palms of your hands to face each other and interlace your fingers. Turn your hands in toward your body and up. Put the tip of your tongue on the roof of your mouth, breathe deeply, and when you feel relaxed, move to Position 2, as described above.* This variation, called "Hook Ups," was developed by Paul and Gail Dennison for Brain Gym.

7. Whenever students feel under pressure, hurt, or shocked, they can take the emotional edge off by holding their Emotional Stress Release Points. Say:

- *Put your fingertips gently on your forehead, above your eyebrows.*
- *Tug up slightly on the skin, while you think through your problem, pre-rehearse a successful outcome, or talk it out.*

8. Explain to students how to pinpoint the Be Sense-able Eye Points:

- *For a quick "pick-me-up," massage your "eye points" at the back of your head, in the hollows above the bony ridge of the lowest turn of your skull.*
- *Look in all directions as you rub these hollows on the left and right.*
- *Also focus on something close and then on something distant, to activate near/far accommodation.*

9. This is a good exercise to do when students feel their attention wandering:

- *Gently unroll your ear edges a few times, from top to bottom.*
- *Give your ears a gentle tug to the side.*
- *You will notice your attention sharpens and you can both hear and think better. Massage your ears before you have to speak, write, receive instructions, or just because you like to!*

Evaluation

The students will demonstrate the ability to follow the steps of each of the "Quick Six," achieve a greater sense of calm, and make a plan to use one or several of these techniques when upset.

Note. From *Making the Brain/Body Connection* (pp. 58–60, 85, 103, 121, 125), by S. Promislow, 1999, West Vancouver, BC, Canada: Kinetic Publishing Corp. Copyright 1999 by Sharon Promislow. Used with permission.

 #12873

Calming Supports

Ages: 5 and above
Objective: The students will learn about several methods to help calm themselves.
Materials: None

Procedure

1. Talk with students about the times when they were able to calm themselves, and then explore the techniques they used and their relative effectiveness. Have the students share their best techniques with the rest of the group.

2. Tell the students you have a variety of things others have found helpful to calm themselves when they are upset. Add any of the methods the students have mentioned. Tell them: *Today, we are going to run an experiment to try some calming supports. First, let's explore each one.*

3. Ask students to explore the following methods and any others that students brought up:

   - *Take small drinks of water*
   - *Squeeze a Koosh ball or a balloon filled with flour or salt*
   - *Wear a rubber band on the wrist and pop or stretch it*
   - *Have someone else sit next to you, helping you to feel the ground and to inhale and exhale more slowly*
   - *Have someone else place a firm hand on your shoulder or back as you ground yourself, communicating calmness through contact*

4. Tell the students: *Think for a minute of the last time you were upset in your class. As you remember how you felt in that situation, let's choose one of these methods to try.*

5. Have each student pick a method, and take a few minutes to try it.

6. Give the students an opportunity to talk about which technique seemed to be the best fit. Have them identify what aspects seemed to help them. Have the students make a plan for using one or more techniques in the following week.

Evaluation

The students will demonstrate at least one method to calm themselves. The students will be able to name one situation in which they plan to use the technique.

Affirmations

Ages: 8 and above

Objective: The students will identify and practice using calming affirmations that they can use when they are becoming upset.

Materials: None

Procedure

1. Collaborate with the students to find an affirming slogan or phrase they can repeat to themselves or visualize when they are having a hard time. For instance, "I am lovable," "I am here to learn; I don't have to get it right the first time—just try," "I know people who believe in me."

2. When a booster message has been selected, you can reinforce it by making banners, using puffy-paint on a T-shirt, or making a poster.

3. Have the students practice saying the statements aloud as well as to themselves. Work with each student to imagine scenarios in which he or she would typically become upset. Practice visualizing the phrase and/or the poster/banner/T-shirt with each of these. When the students are facing situations that are likely to make them upset, encourage them to visualize the poster, banner, or T-shirt and repeat the phrase in their mind 10 times.

Evaluation

The students will identify at least one affirmative phrase they can use when they are likely to become upset and practice using their phrase(s) in several situations.

Note. From *Collaborative Treatment of Traumatized Children and Teens* (p. 244), by G. N. Saxe, B. H. Ellis, and J. B. Kaplow, 2007, New York: Guilford. Copyright 2007 by Guilford. Adapted with permission.

 #12873

Tensing Peripheral Muscles—
Holding Together

Ages: 8 and above

Objective: The students will learn how to tense and release specific muscles to help calm anxiety or panic.

Materials: None

Background Information: In addition to increasing general emotional stability, muscle tensing is used by some people as an emergency measure when anxiety threatens to escalate into overwhelming anxiety or panic. This activity demonstrates several postures that can be used to tense specific muscles. Most people will find at least one of them as an aid to on-the-spot containment. Of course, any postures that increase anxiety should not be used. Any tensing should be done only until the muscle feels slightly tired. Release of the tensing must be done slowly. This is not progressive muscle relaxation. The idea here is to maintain a little of the contraction/tension. If tensing causes any adverse reaction (nausea, a spacey feeling, anxiety, etc.), neutralize that reaction by gently stretching the same muscle—making an opposite movement.

Procedure

1. Explain the following muscle tensing exercises to students:

   - *Side of Legs: Stand with feet a little less than shoulder-width apart and knees relaxed (neither locked nor bent). Press knees out directly to the side so that you can feel tension along the sides of the legs from knee to hip.*

   - *Left Arm: Sit or stand with arms crossed right over left. The right hand should be covering the left elbow. First, the right hand provides resistance as the left arm lifts directly away from the body. You should feel tension in the forward-directed part of the upper arm from shoulder to elbow. Next, the right hand provides resistance to the back of the elbow as the left arm pushes directly left. You should feel tension in the left-directed part of the upper arm from shoulder to elbow.*

   - *Right Arm: Sit or stand with arms crossed left over right. The left hand should be covering the right elbow. First, the left hand provides resistance as the right arm lifts directly away from the body. You should feel tension in the forward-directed part of the upper arm from shoulder to elbow. Next, the left hand provides resistance to the back of the elbow as the right arm pushes directly right. You should feel tension in the right-directed part of the upper arm from shoulder to elbow.*

   - *Thighs: Sitting in a chair, place both feet flat on the floor. Press weight onto your feet just until you feel tension build in your thighs.*

2. Give the students an opportunity to talk about which technique seems to be the best for them. Have them identify what aspects seem to help them. Have students practice by calling to mind typically upsetting scenarios while using one of the muscle tensing techniques. Ask students to make a plan for using at least one technique in the following week.

Evaluation

The students will demonstrate at least one favorite muscle tensing technique fluidly and without prompting. The students will be able to name one situation in which they plan to use the technique.

Note. From *The Body Remembers: The Psychophysiology of Trauma and Trauma Treatment* (pp. 138–139), by B. Rothschild, 2000, New York: Norton. Copyright 2000 by Barbara Rothschild. Adapted with permission.

 #12873

Deep Belly Breathing

Ages: 8–11

Objective: The students will learn to do deep breathing to quiet the mind and relax the body when upset.

Materials: One balloon

Procedure

1. Say to the students: *One of the ways we can relax is by breathing really deeply. However, since breathing is something we do without thinking, we don't usually pay much attention to it, and we may not know if we are breathing deeply or not. We'll take a few moments now to notice how we breathe.*

2. Start the relaxation exercise by saying:

   - *Let's get comfortable where we are sitting. You might want to gently close your eyes and relax. Now begin to notice your breath going in and out.* (Pause while the students breathe in and out a few times.)

   - *As you take in a breath, notice if you are taking it in through your nose . . . or your mouth. . . . Notice if your chest is getting bigger as you breathe in. Is there any other part of your body rising? As you let out your breath, notice what part of your body is moving.*

3. Ask the students to open their eyes and together reflect on what they noticed. Mention that one of the ways we know we are taking a deep breath is when we see our bellies going up and down, rather than just our chests. Say: *We might not always be taking deep breaths when we breathe. I want to try something right now: an experiment. Stretch your arm out in front of you, higher than your shoulder, with your pointer finger up as if you are pointing up. Now move your finger back and forth like a windshield wiper. Do this about five times.* (Demonstrate with your finger and pause to give the students time to try it.)

4. Now ask the students about what happened to their breathing during the experiment. You might say:

   - *What did you notice about your breathing while you were doing this experiment?*

   - *Were you breathing, or holding your breath?*

   - *Was your belly moving, or just your chest?*

5. Since it is common to hold the breath while doing this experiment or to not breathe very deeply, this is an opportunity to point out to students that we often go through our day without breathing as deeply as we need to in order to relax our bodies and focus our minds.

   - *Lots of things in our day might interfere with how we breathe. These things can make us not breathe deeply enough.*

   - *When we are distracted, or stressed, or even upset, we should fully fill up our lungs and take in the oxygen we need for our bodies to stay healthy.*

6. Inflate a balloon about one-quarter full, and tell students you are going to show them what you mean with the help of the balloon.

   - *When we don't breathe deeply—when only our chests move, and not our bellies— then we are filling our lungs only one-quarter of how full they can be, like this balloon is now. But when we breathe deeply, we fill up our lungs completely* (blow up the balloon to capacity) *and that makes our bellies rise and move in all directions, expanding like this balloon.*

   - *When our lungs are full of air, we have all the oxygen we need for our bodies to do the work they need to do. It's important to let all the air out of our lungs as well. This breathing in and out deeply keeps us healthy, and it also relaxes us.*

7. Have students give deep breathing a try. Say:

   - *Let's take in a breath right now and put both our hands on our bellies. Let's see if our bellies can get bigger when we take in a breath. And when we let out the air, let's see if our bellies can go down. Ready? In, 1, 2, 3, 4, 5, and out, 1, 2, 3, 4, 5.*

   - *When we take a really deep breath, not only do our chests go up, but our bellies do, too. This kind of breathing is called* abdominal *or diaphragmatic* breathing. *Our diaphragm is a muscle that divides our lungs from our lower organs, such as our stomach. When we belly breathe, we use our diaphragm to make more room for our lungs, so they can hold more air.*

8. Now have students try it again. Say: *Let's try it again. Breathe in to a count of 5: 1, 2, 3, 4, 5. Breathe out: 1, 2, 3, 4, 5.*

9. Repeat a few more times until students have made their bellies rise on the in-breath and fall on the out-breath. If students are still not breathing deeply enough for their bellies to rise, ask them to place their hands gently on their bellies to help.

Evaluation

The students demonstrate deep belly breathing and name situations where they will use it to reduce stress.

Note. From *Building Emotional Intelligence* (pp. 74–76), by L. Lantieri, 2008, Boulder, CO: Sounds True, Inc. Copyright 2008 by Linda Lantieri. Adapted with permission.

 #12873

Getting Relaxed:
Progressive Muscle Relaxation

Ages: 8–11
Objective: The students will learn a way to relax their bodies and quiet their minds.
Materials: None

Procedure

1. Say to the students: *We are going to spend a little time together learning how to release stress from the body by focusing on different parts of the body—one part at a time. We'll practice tensing different muscles and then notice how it feels to relax each part as well. This helps to release some of the tension that may be in your body, so you can feel even healthier and happier.*

2. Say:

   - *So let's get ready to begin. . . . Lie down comfortably on the floor on your back. You may want to loosen any clothing you feel is too tight; maybe take off your shoes; and just begin to relax with your arms at your sides and your legs straight out in front of you. Now, gently close your eyes.*

   - *Begin to take some slow, deep breaths, and remember, as you breathe in, feel your belly and chest rising. As you breathe out, say to yourself, "Relax," as your belly goes down.*

   - *Breathe in 1, 2, 3, 4, 5 . . . and out. Relax 1, 2, 3, 4, 5. . . . And again, in 1, 2, 3, 4, 5 . . . and relax, and you let air out 1, 2, 3, 4, 5.*

   - *Try to listen to my voice as best you can and focus on what I am saying as you become more and more relaxed.*

   - *Imagine you have a soft piece of clay in your right hand. Now squeeze the clay in your right hand and make as tight a fist as you can, and make your whole right arm tense as well. Squeeze . . . squeeze . . . squeeze. . . . Feel the tension in your right hand and arm.*

   - *Now, quickly let your right hand go limp and let the imaginary clay drop to the floor. Let your right hand and arm completely let go and relax as I count to 10: 1, 2, 3, 4, 5, 6, 7, 8, 9, 10. Feel your right hand and arm very warm and relaxed.*

   - *Now we are going to concentrate on your left hand and your left arm and do the same thing. So imagine you have a soft piece of clay in your left hand. Squeeze the piece of clay in your left had and make as tight a fist as you can as your whole left arm tenses up as well. Squeeze . . . squeeze . . . squeeze. . . . Feel the tension in your left hand and arm.*

   - *Now quickly let your left hand go limp and let the imaginary clay drop to the floor. Let your left hand and arm completely let go and relax as I count to 10: 1, 2, 3, 4, 5, 6, 7, 8, 9, 10. Feel your left hand and arm very warm and relaxed. Good job. Your hands and arms are relaxed.*

- *Now we are going to focus on relaxing your neck and your shoulders. Tense your shoulders by raising your shoulders up to your ears and tighten your shoulders and neck. Hold it as I count to 5: 1, 2, 3, 4, 5, . . . and relax. Let your shoulders drop away from your ears. Let your neck and shoulders relax as I count to 10: 1, 2, 3, 4, 5, 6, 7, 8, 9, 10. Just feel how relaxed your shoulders and neck are. Good job. Your shoulders and neck are relaxed.*

- *Now turn your attention to your had and your face. See if you can tighten all the muscles in your face. Squeeze your eyes closed as tightly as you can and wrinkle your nose and your forehead. Bite down hard and hold that tension as I count to 5: 1, 2, 3, 4, 5 . . . and let go and relax. Let your whole face and head be relaxed and soft. Keep your eyes gently closed and relax your forehead, nose, and mouth as I slowly count to 10: 1, 2, 3, 4, 5, 6, 7, 8, 9, 10. . . . Feel how relaxed your head and face are. Excellent. Your head and face are relaxed.*

- Tell students they will be relaxing the chest area. *Take a deep breath in and fill your lungs up completely. Hold your breath for a moment . . . and let go. . . . Let out the air and let your chest become relaxed as you continue to breathe in and out, deeply and slowly.*

- *Next we will focus on your belly and the lower part of your body. Try to pull your belly in and bring it as close to your back as you can. As you're doing this, make the whole lower part of your body tense. Make your belly as tight as you can and hold it until I count to 5: 1, 2, 3, 4, 5 . . . and relax and let go. Let your belly and all the muscles around it be soft and relaxed. Just continue to relax as I count to 10: 1, 2, 3, 4, 5, 6, 7, 8, 9, 10. . . . Feel how relaxed your stomach area is. Good job. The lower part of your body is relaxed.*

- *Now we will relax the legs and feet and even your toes. Begin by tensing your right leg and foot and making them as stiff as you can—even curl up your toes on your right foot. Keep tensing your right leg and foot . . . and now let them go. Relax them as I count to 10: 1, 2, 3, 4, 5, 6, 7, 8, 9, 10. . . . Feel how relaxed your right leg and foot feel.*

- *Now let's do the same thing with your left leg and foot. Tighten your left leg and foot, making them as stiff as you can—even curl up your toes on your left foot. Keep tensing your left leg and foot . . . and now let go. Relax your left leg and foot as I count to 10: 1, 2, 3, 4, 5, 6, 7, 8, 9, 10. . . . Feel how relaxed both your legs and feet feel. Feel the relaxation to the tips of your toes. Good job. Both your legs and feet are relaxed.*

- *Now one last time: At the count of 3, try to tighten up your whole body all at once. Ready? 1, 2, 3. . . . Tighten and tense your whole body. . . . Hold it. . . . Squeeze . . . squeeze . . . squeeze. And let go. Let your whole body relax as you lie down and feel like you are melting into the floor. Feel the wave of warmth and relaxation throughout your whole body and let go of any last bit of tension.*

- *Take a little time and notice if any part of your body might still feel tense or uncomfortable. Check in with each part of your body and ask yourself, "Are my face and head relaxed?" "How about my chest area and my belly area?" "Are both my arms to the tips of my fingers relaxed?" "Are my legs and feet relaxed?" Just notice how relaxed your body is feeling right now.*

- *Now gently begin to wiggle your toes and move your fingers and start to notice the sounds around you. Open your eyes and let your body take a nice big stretch. Then slowly begin to sit up and feel how relaxed you are.*

- *Thanks for trying this out with me.*

#12873

Evaluation

The students will demonstrate the ability to tense and relax muscles in their bodies. Give the students an opportunity to talk about how this technique will work for them. Have them identify what aspects seem to help them. Have the students make a plan for using this or other techniques in the following week.

Note. From *Building Emotional Intelligence* (pp. 77–80), by L. Lantieri, 2008, Boulder, CO: Sounds True, Inc. Copyright 2008 by Linda Lantieri. Adapted with permission.

Body Scanning

Ages: 12 and above
Objective: The students will learn a way to relax their bodies and quiet their minds.
Materials: None

Procedure

Say to the students:

- *Today, we are going to learn to relax our bodies and quiet our minds. The calming activity we will practice involves tensing and relaxing the different muscle groups in our bodies. We are also going to begin to notice a little more deeply what parts of our bodies feel more relaxed and where we hold most of the tension in our bodies. This exercise will help us learn how to relax different parts of our bodies, so we can ease tense muscles whenever we feel the need to. It's called* progressive muscle relaxation, *or* body scanning. *By 'progressive,' we mean that we are going to progress or move through the whole body, paying attention to different parts of the body, moving from one part to the next, and tensing and relaxing each different muscle group.*

- *After going through the tensing and relaxing exercises, we'll go through our bodies one more time—becoming aware of how each part of the body feels, what parts of the body feel more relaxed, and what parts of the body still need to relax. That's the part where we'll scan our bodies. That's why it is also called 'a body scan.'*

Part A

Say:

- *So let's get ready to begin. . . . Lie down comfortably on the floor on your back. You may want to loosen any clothing you feel is too tight; maybe take off your shoes; and just begin to relax with your arms at your sides and your legs straight out in front of you. Now, gently close your eyes.*

- *Begin to take some slow, deep breaths and remember as you breathe in to feel your belly and chest rising. As you breathe out, say to yourself, "Relax," as your belly goes down.*

- *Breathe in 1, 2, 3, 4, 5 . . . and out. Relax 1, 2, 3, 4, 5. . . . And again, in 1, 2, 3, 4, 5 . . . and relax, and you let air out 1, 2, 3, 4, 5.*

- *Try to listen to my voice as best you can and focus on what I am saying as you become more and more relaxed.*

- *Imagine you have a soft piece of clay in your right hand. Now squeeze the clay in your right hand and make as tight a fist as you can, and make your whole right arm tense as well. Squeeze . . . squeeze . . . squeeze. . . . Feel the tension in your right hand and arm.*

- *Now, quickly let your right hand go limp and let the imaginary clay drop to the floor. Let your right hand and arm completely let go and relax as I count to 10: 1, 2, 3, 4, 5, 6, 7, 8, 9, 10. Feel your right hand and arm very warm and relaxed.*

 #12873

- *Now we are going to concentrate on your left hand and your left arm and do the same thing. So imagine you have a soft piece of clay in your left hand. Squeeze the piece of clay in your left had and make as tight a fist as you can as your whole left arm tenses up as well. Squeeze . . . squeeze . . . squeeze. . . . Feel the tension in your left hand and arm.*

- *Now quickly let your left hand go limp and let the imaginary clay drop to the floor. Let your left hand and arm completely let go and relax as I count to 10: 1, 2, 3, 4, 5, 6, 7, 8, 9, 10. Feel your left hand and arm very warm and relaxed. Good job. Your hands and arms are relaxed.*

- *Now we are going to focus on relaxing your neck and your shoulders. Tense your shoulders by raising your shoulders up to your ears and tighten your shoulders and neck. Hold it as I count to 5: 1, 2, 3, 4, 5, . . . and relax. Let your shoulders drop away from your ears. Let your neck and shoulders relax as I count to 10: 1, 2, 3, 4, 5, 6, 7, 8, 9, 10. Just feel how relaxed your shoulders and neck are. Good job. Your shoulders and neck are relaxed.*

- *Now turn your attention to your head and your face. See if you can tighten all the muscles in your face. Squeeze your eyes closed as tightly as you can and wrinkle your nose and your forehead. Bite down hard and hold that tension as I count to 5: 1, 2, 3, 4, 5 . . . and let go and relax. Let your whole face and head be relaxed and soft. Keep your eyes gently closed and relax your forehead, nose, and mouth as I slowly count to 10: 1, 2, 3, 4, 5, 6, 7, 8, 9, 10. . . . Feel how relaxed your head and face are. Excellent. Your head and face are relaxed.*

- Tell students they will be relaxing the chest area. *Take a deep breath in and fill your lungs up completely. Hold your breath for a moment . . . and let go. . . . Let out the air and let your chest become relaxed as you continue to breathe in and out, deeply and slowly.*

- *Next we will focus on your belly and the lower part of your body. Try to pull your belly in and bring it as close to your back as you can. As you're doing this, make the whole lower part of your body tense. Make your belly as tight as you can and hold it until I count to 5: 1, 2, 3, 4, 5 . . . and relax and let go. Let your belly and all the muscles around it be soft and relaxed. Just continue to relax as I count to 10: 1, 2, 3, 4, 5, 6, 7, 8, 9, 10. . . . Feel how relaxed your stomach area is. Good job. The lower part of your body is relaxed.*

- *Now we will relax the legs and feet and even your toes. Begin by tensing your right leg and foot and making them as stiff as you can—even curl up your toes on your right foot. Keep tensing your right leg and foot . . . and now let them go. Relax them as I count to 10: 1, 2, 3, 4, 5, 6, 7, 8, 9, 10. . . . Feel how relaxed your right leg and foot feel.*

- *Now let's do the same thing with your left leg and foot. Tighten your left leg and foot, making them as stiff as you can—even curl up your toes on your left foot. Keep tensing your left leg and foot . . . and now let go. Relax your left leg and foot as I count to 10: 1, 2, 3, 4, 5, 6, 7, 8, 9, 10. . . . Feel how relaxed both your legs and feet feel. Feel the relaxation to the tips of your toes. Good job. Both your legs and feet are relaxed.*

- *Now one last time: At the count of 3, try to tighten up your whole body all at once. Ready? 1, 2, 3 . . . tighten and tense your whole body . . . hold it . . . squeeze . . . squeeze . . . squeeze. And let go. Let your whole body relax as you lie down and feel like you are melting into the floor. Feel the wave of warmth and relaxation throughout your whole body and let go of any last bit of tension.*

Part B

Tell students they will now do a body scan.

- *We're going to use the body scan to go through our body one more time and become aware of how relaxed or tense we may still feel. Make yourself as comfortable as you can. I am going to ask you to take a moment to notice any part of your body that might still be holding any tension. As you begin to scan your body, notice first how you are breathing. Make sure your breathing is deep belly breathing, the kind you practiced at the beginning of this session.*

- *Now start with your feet. Notice what's happening with your feet. Is there any tension in your feet? If you find any pockets of tension, silently and gently ask your feet to relax and let go.*

- *Now take a moment to tune into your legs. What's happening in your legs? Are you feeling any tension? And again, just gently ask your legs to relax and let go.*

- *Now notice your belly. Are you holding tension in your belly? If so, relax and let go.*

- *Bring your attention to your chest. Are you holding tension in your chest? What about your back and shoulders? Just ask these parts of your body to relax and let them go.*

- *Now notice any sensation you might have in your back and shoulders. Relax and let go.*

- *How about your neck? Are you holding tension in your neck? If so, relax and let go.*

- *What about your face? Is there tension in your face? If so, relax and let go.*

- *Notice your whole head. Are you holding any tension anywhere in your head? If so, relax and let go.*

- *Take a moment to scan your entire body, from the tips of your toes all the way up to the top of your head . . . noticing any tension you might have anywhere in your body. Then, just take a moment to bring your attention to that part of the body and gently ask it to relax. See if there is any other part of your body that feels some tension. Again, focus there and gently allow it to relax. And now, in your mind, scan your body beginning with your head. Move all the way to your toes, noticing how you feel. And now slowly begin to take in the sounds of this room. Notice the floor you are lying on. Slowly open your eyes and take a nice big stretch. Whenever you feel upset and sense your muscles getting tense, you can scan them, and then tell yourself, "Relax and let go."*

- *Thanks for trying this out with me.*

Part C

Give the students an opportunity to talk about how this technique will work for them. Have them identify what aspects seem to help them. Have the students make a plan for using this technique, or others, in the following week.

Evaluation

The students will demonstrate the ability to tense and relax muscles in their bodies and plan for specific situations in which they will practice these skills.

Note. From *Building Emotional Intelligence* (pp. 112–115), by L. Lantieri, 2008, Boulder, CO: Sounds True, Inc. Copyright 2008 by Linda Lantieri. Adapted with permission.

The Three Rs for Managing Stress

Ages: 12 and above
Objective: The students will learn three strategies for managing stress and create a list of activities they prefer to use when stressed.
Materials: Strategies to Reduce Stress handout for each student

Procedure

1. Say to the students: *Today, we are going to learn three different ways to approach reducing our stress. I'll call them the three Rs. The Rs stand for:*

   Remove (1) the stressor and (2) yourself from the stressor

   Reduce the stressor

   Re-educate your brain/body response (so your buttons aren't pushed every time you encounter the stressor.)

2. Ask the students to think of a type of situation that is particularly stressful for them. Maybe it causes them frustration or keeps them in a high state of arousal so they are not functioning well.

3. Using that situation, talk with the students about the feasibility of using each of the three Rs. Generate ideas from the students and ask for help from the other group members for creative ways of looking at the students' stressors.

4. Tell the students: *More often than we realize, we can take steps to remove the stressor or remove ourselves from the stressor, but sometimes we can't do that. In those situations, we can try some things to reduce the stress.*

5. Using the handout, Strategies to Reduce Stress, have the students circle the ideas they have used. Have the students compare notes from their lists.

6. Then have the students indicate the top three ideas they plan to use in the future by placing a *1, 2,* and *3* beside them.

Evaluation

The students will indicate their top three choices for reducing stress and make a plan to use those strategies the next time they are under stress.

Note. From *Building Emotional Intelligence* (p. 120), by L. Lantieri, 2008, Boulder, CO: Sounds True, Inc. Copyright 2008 by Linda Lantieri. Adapted with permission.

Name _____ Date _____

Strategies to Reduce Stress

Circle the star by the ideas you have used to reduce stress. Place a 1, 2, and 3 by the top three ideas you will use the next time you're under stress.

_____ ★ Use positive self-talk. When you want to calm down, remind yourself that whatever is happening is not really an emergency. You might say to yourself, "Breathe. This is not a real emergency, and I can deal with this."

_____ ★ Take a bubble bath or a warm shower.

_____ ★ Read a small portion of a good book every day at the same time.

_____ ★ Listen to a piece of your favorite music.

_____ ★ Draw, paint, or make a collage.

_____ ★ Take a walk.

_____ ★ Exercise, do some yoga, or dance.

_____ ★ Take time in nature to look at the clouds, smell the flowers, or listen to the birds.

_____ ★ Cook or bake something you love to eat.

_____ ★ Watch an inspirational or funny movie.

_____ ★ Cuddle with a pet and/or walk the dog.

_____ ★ Say "no" to some things so your plate doesn't get so full that there is not enough free time for things you like to do.

_____ ★ Do something that has repetitive movement, such as jumping rope, knitting, or chopping vegetables.

_____ ★ Do some gardening.

_____ ★ Work on a puzzle that has lots of pieces—how about 1,000?

_____ ★ Sing out loud.

_____ ★ Use earplugs when you want to cut down the noise.

#12873

_____ ★ Visualize a quiet, peaceful place, like a beach, and go there in your imagination.

_____ ★ Write in a journal or write yourself an email or text encouraging yourself about something that concerns you. Send it to yourself.

_____ ★ Do some deep breathing, counting slowly to five on the in breath and backward on the out breath. Repeat at least seven times to feel yourself relaxing.

_____ ★ Start counting backward from 100 by threes.

_____ ★ Go swimming.

_____ ★ Ride a bike.

_____ ★ Have a joke book handy that you can read when you need a good laugh.

_____ ★ Spend quality time with a good friend.

_____ ★ Play a sport.

_____ ★ Have a hobby and make time to do it regularly.

_____ ★ Spend quality time with an adult you can trust and talk to.

_____ ★ Play with a young child.

_____ ★ Do a crossword puzzle.

_____ ★ Build something.

_____ ★ Make a list of the things in your life for which you are grateful.

_____ ★ Volunteer or do something positive to address a concern you have.

_____ ★ Your ideas:

_____

_____

_____

Verbal First Aid

Ages: All

Objective: The students will be reassured that whatever happened is over and will be guided to a calmer state.

Materials: None

Background Information: When students experience a frightening event, it can put them in an altered state. Skillfully selected words and the timing and tone of your voice can help students cope with an event that is potentially traumatizing.

Procedure

1. Use your tone of voice to convey to the student that you understand what it must be like to be in his/her shoes. Say something that accomplishes the following:

   - Show the student that you compassionately accept what happened.

   - Ensure that the student feels safe and connected, rather than alone.

   - Reassure him or her that whatever happened is over (if it is).

   - Help move time ahead from the past to the present by guiding him or her to notice sensations until there is a discharge and shift.

   - Remind the student of his or her resources for coping.

2. Immediately after the incident, look for bodily clues such as pale skin, cold sweaty palms, shallow breathing, and wide eyes. If the student is still somewhat stunned, it is probably best for him or her to be sitting or lying down. Then you might say something like, *The hard part is over, but you're still a little bit shook up. . . . I'll stay with you until the (shaky or numb, etc.) feeling wears off. You might get a little shivery or jittery or wiggly . . . or maybe even a little giggly. It could be that some tears will come. I'll stay with you until the last tear (or jitter or shiver) is gone.*

Evaluation

The student will be in a calmer state, and he or she will indicate feeling comforted.

Note. From *Trauma-Proofing Your Kids* (pp. 85–86), by P. A. Levine and M. Kline, 2008, Berkeley, CA: North Atlantic Books. Copyright 2008 by Peter A. Levine and Maggie Kline. Adapted with permission.

B: VIII. Responsible Decision Making

Solution-Focused Decision Making

Ages: All
Objective: The students will describe the steps to effective problem solving and decision making. Students will demonstrate applying the solution-focused steps to making a decision or resolving a problem in their lives.
Materials: The Solution Six handout

Procedure

1. Talk with students about the difficulties we can face when we become so focused on a problem that it seems there are no ways to solve it. Say something like: *Have you ever had the experience of being so worried (or upset) about a problem that even though you tried and tried, you couldn't think of a way to solve it? Getting stuck like that happens to everyone. Today, we are going to talk about some steps we can take to manage that. It's called focusing on solutions, not problems.*

2. Have students choose a partner and talk about a situation that is problematic for them. Ask for volunteers to briefly share what their partner said.

3. Distribute the handout to each student and review the steps. Practice questions the students might ask themselves to guide their problem solving. Check students' breathing.

4. Have each student choose one situation and apply the steps.

5. Ask the students to reflect on the process and the effects of breathing and relaxing as they contemplate their solutions.

Evaluation

The students will identify steps they can use when trying to solve a problem. They will also learn the value of generating multiple options.

Note. From *Brain Friendly Guidance Activities to Build Emotional Intelligence* (p. 101), by C. Messina, 2003, Austin, TX: PRO-ED. Copyright 2003 by PRO-ED, Inc. Adapted with permission.

The Solution Six

The step	What you might say to yourself
1. Identify the decision to be made or problem to solve.	*What is going on that is a problem for me?*
2. Consider your choices or options.	*When is the problem not so bad or not a problem?*
3. Take three deep breaths. Relax and think about what you want and need.	*How do I want things to be?*
4. Focus on solutions. Be open to the possibility of multiple solutions.	*What is already happening to help the situation? How can I do more of that? What else?*
5. Choose the solution that feels, seems, and looks right for you.	*Which solution do I think is most likely to work?*
6. If that solution was not the best for you, return to Step 1, ask for help, or just choose again.	*What has worked in the past? What have others suggested I do to make the problem better? What else?*

Is It My Problem?

Ages: 8 and above

Objective: The students will identify the problem and determine ownership.

Materials: Is It My Problem? poster

Background Information: The purpose of this lesson is to help students decide which problems they are responsible for and which they are not. They need to see that some problems are beyond their control, but to accept responsibility for problems they create.

Procedure

1. Read this story aloud: *Beth is upset. She learned just last night that her family is moving to Toronto. When Mary invites Beth to play soccer at recess, Beth snaps at Mary and stomps away in tears.*

2. Ask: *What is the problem? What might Mary do?*

3. Model the skill using think-aloud strategies. For example, *Is your problem that the secretary yelled at you, or is the problem that you were late to school?* Discuss the following steps:

    1. *What is the problem?*

    2. *Did I cause it?*

    3. *Can I solve it?*

    4. *Do I want to?*

4. Model for students by discussing a problem that you (or someone you know) are responsible for and a problem that you (or someone you know) are *not* responsible for.

5. Ask students to role-play in pairs. Have them brainstorm problems. Students might also try role-playing about causing a problem (e.g., stealing) and then denying it. After students perform their role plays, discuss as a group.

6. Ask students to role-play the following situations: 1) School: All the equipment is gone in PE, and you are left without any; 2) Home/Community: Your mom burns the toast and yells at you; 3) Peers: Steve is angry that he didn't get invited to a neighborhood party.

Evaluation

The students will determine ownership of problems and make plans to address them based on this determination.

Note. From *Getting To Know You! A Social Skills Curriculum for Grades 4 & 5* (p. 119), by D. Hanken and J. Kennedy, 1998, Minneapolis, MN: Educational Media Corporation. Copyright 1998 by Dennis Hanken and Judith Kennedy. Adapted with permission.

Is It My Problem?

1. What is the problem?

2. Did I cause it?

3. Can I solve it?

4. Do I want to?

Three-Step Plan for Success: Improving on a Weakness

Ages: 5 and above

Objective: The students will identify strengths and weaknesses in academic areas and develop plans for improving in areas of relative weakness.

Materials: Three-Step Plan for Success handout, pencils, and notebook paper

Procedure

1. Distribute pencils and notebook paper. Have students write the heading, "Things I Am Good at in School," at the top of their papers and list three specific things under the heading. Suggest that they avoid naming general subjects. Explain: *Rather than write that you are good at math and English, for example, you might specify that you are very good at recalling the multiplication tables and writing poems. Or you might say that you are good at conducting science experiments, naming the characteristics of mammals, estimating, counting money, giving oral reports, and reading mysteries.*

2. Below the first list, have the students write a second heading, "Things I Need to Improve on in School." Again, suggest to students that they list three specific items.

3. Distribute the Three-Step Plan for Success handout. Tell students you want them to write an "action plan" for one of the items on their improvement list. Have them complete the heading "My plan for improving in . . . " by filling in exactly what they plan to work on.

4. Have the students form dyads and brainstorm specific ways each partner can obtain help in his or her area of improvement. Say: *If you need to work on punctuation, maybe you can ask a student who is good at punctuation to work with you twice a week. If you need to improve your spelling, maybe you can ask a parent or an older brother or sister to quiz you at home. Write down all the alternatives you come up with under the subheading, "How I can get help."*

5. Point out that to improve their skills, students will have to practice. Instruct the partners to plan practice schedules and list them under the subheading "Where and when I will practice my new skill."

6. Ask the students to list the names of people to whom they might demonstrate their improved skill.

7. Ask volunteers to share their completed plans with the class. Pause at each step of a given action plan and invite the group to make additional suggestions. In this way, students will be sure to have several alternatives to choose from. Even those who prefer not to share will benefit from listening to suggestions and will obtain new ideas for their plans.

 #12873

8. Challenge the students to put their improvement plans into action and report in a week on any progress made or obstacles encountered. Conclude the activity with a group discussion. Ask:

- *How do you feel when you perform well in an area of study at school?*
- *How do you feel when you improve in an area of weakness?*
- *How do you feel about getting help?*
- *Why is it important to make a plan of action when you want to improve in an area that is difficult?*

Evaluation

The students will determine their strengths and weaknesses and make an action plan to use their strengths to address their weaknesses.

Note. From *Helping Kids Make Wise Choices and Reduce Risky Behavior* (p. 45), by T. Akin, G. Dunne, & D. Schilling, 2000, Austin, TX: PRO-ED, Inc. Copyright 2000 by PRO-ED, Inc. Adapted with permission.

Name _____   Date _____

Three-Step Plan for Success

1. My plan for improving in _____

   _____

   _____

2. How I can get help _____

   _____

   _____

   _____

3. Where and when I will practice my new skill_____

   _____

   _____

   _____

4. To whom I will show off my new skill _____

   _____

   _____

   _____

What to Do? What to Do?

Ages: 8 and above
Objective: The students will learn and practice a decision-making process.
Materials: The IDEAL Decision-Making Process handout, pencils, and Decision Situation cards

Procedure

1. Begin by asking the students to make some quick decisions:

   - *Would you rather have a hamburger or a hot dog?*
   - *Would you rather go to the beach or an amusement park?*
   - *Do you want to wear a red shirt or a blue shirt?*
   - *Would you rather do math or reading?*

2. Explain that these are examples of simple, quick decisions that we all make daily.

3. Next, ask the students to think about decisions they have made so far today. These might include what clothes to wear, food to eat, or route to take to school; what games to play, whom to play them with, what book to read at school, etc.

4. Point out that the more important a decision is, the more care is required in making a final choice. Introduce and explain the IDEAL decision-making process. Illustrate the process using a familiar example, such as deciding what gift to buy for a friend. Write thoughts and alternatives on the board adjacent to these steps:

   > Identify the problem or issue to be decided.
   >
   > Describe the possibilities.
   >
   > Evaluate your ideas.
   >
   > Act.
   >
   > Learn from the decision.

5. Next, give the students a chance to practice this concrete, easy-to-remember model. Have them form pairs. Distribute the IDEAL Decision Making Process handout.

6. Give two Decision Situation Cards to each pair. Give the pairs 10 minutes to make both decisions, following the IDEAL process. Tell them to complete their experience sheets in the process. Since students cannot actually evaluate their decisions (final step), they should describe how they would evaluate them if the situations were real.

7. Have the pairs explain their decisions to the group. After each report, ask several open-ended questions to stimulate discussion:

   - *How did the IDEAL process help you in making a decision?*
   - *What was the hardest part about using it?*
   - *How well did you work together as partners?*
   - *What can you do when you find that a decision isn't working?*

Evaluation

Have the students write a simple play to dramatize their decisions, illustrating their knowledge of the process.

Note. From *Helping Kids Make Wise Choices and Reduce Risky Behavior* (pp. 57–58), by T. Akin, G. Dunne, & D. Schilling, 2000, Austin, TX: PRO-ED, Inc. Copyright 2000 by PRO-ED, Inc. Adapted with permission.

 #12873

The IDEAL Decision-Making Process

Decision-making step	Situation 1	Situation 2
Identify the issue to be decided or problem to be solved.		
Describe all choices, possibilities, and alternatives.		
Evaluate the choices by considering the consequences of each.		
Act on the alternative that has the best chance of succeeding.		
Learn from the decision by evaluating the results.		

You received incorrect change while shopping. Decide what to do.

Several of your friends have gotten trendy haircuts recently. You want one, too, and have the money, but your parents don't like the haircuts at all. What do you do?

Your older brother wants to borrow your new T-shirt, but the last time he borrowed a shirt, he returned it stained. What is your decision?

You love chocolate, but frequently get a headache when you eat it. Your friend offers you a brownie with fudge icing. What do you do?

You want to be in the band, but it would conflict with participating in sports during part of the year. What do you do?

Your friend's parents are not home. The friend gets into the liquor cabinet, opens a bottle of wine, and offers you some. What do you do?

You invite a friend to go with you to the movies. In the afternoon, the friend calls and says he or she was invited to spend the night at another friend's house. What do you do?

You are scheduled to take a difficult math test at third period today. A friend who has the class at first period offers to tell you the problems and the answers beforehand. What do you do?

Your friend's bicycle was stolen from school. Later, you see another friend riding the bicycle in the neighborhood. What do you do?

You are in a group of four students working on a class project. One of the students refuses to do any of the work, making it difficult for the group to get the project completed. How do you handle this situation?

Taking Action to Solve Problems: A Three-Step Problem-Solving Process

Ages: 8 and above

Objective: The students will learn a three-step problem-solving process and practice the process by solving problems of their own.

Materials: Action Plan for Solving Problems handout, chalkboard, and chalk

Background Information: Students experience problems every day. A good time to lead this activity is when a student in the group has asked for help with a problem that could be solved independently by going through this problem-solving process.

Procedure

1. To teach the process, first describe a simple problem that you have, such as "My houseplants are turning yellow and dying." Then go through the steps, making notes on the board and involving the students in the brainstorming and decision-making portions of the process.

2. Describe the problem in as much detail as possible: *The leaves on my houseplants started to turn yellow a month ago when we had a spell of hot, humid weather. I watered the plants every day, but the leaves turned more and more yellow; until the plants began to die.*

3. List possible ways to solve the problem:

   - *Read a book on houseplants to learn about plant care and diseases.*
   - *Look on the Internet for a site that describes taking care of houseplants.*
   - *Look in the index of a book under "leaves, yellow," or "yellowing."*
   - *Ask a friend who is good with houseplants for advice.*
   - *Call a nursery and describe the problem.*
   - *Throw the plants away and start over.*

4. Ask students for their opinion about the best solution. Then describe what "you did" to solve the problem: *I looked in a plant book and checked several sites on the Internet. I decided from what I learned that I probably gave my plants too much water during the hot spell. So I removed the yellow leaves and cut back on the water. Now they're doing much better.*

5. Distribute the Action Plan for Solving Problems handout and go over the directions. Take a couple of minutes to help the students identify problems they are currently experiencing. Elicit several examples from the group. Then give the students about 10 minutes to complete the sheet. Allow them to work alone or in pairs.

6. Conclude the activity with a brief discussion:

- *Why is it important to know how to solve problems?*
- *How do you think this skill will help you in school and at home?*
- *If you try all of your solutions and none of them work, what can you do next?*
- *What kinds of problems should always be solved with the help of a parent or other adult?*

Evaluation

Have the students write a simple play to dramatize their solutions.

Note. From *Helping Kids Make Wise Choices and Reduce Risky Behavior* (pp. 60–61), by T. Akin, G. Dunne, & D. Schilling, 2000, Austin, TX: PRO-ED, Inc. Copyright 2000 by PRO-ED, Inc. Adapted with permission.

#12873

Name _____   Date _____

Action Plan for Solving Problems

Do you have a problem? Do you want to solve it? Follow the steps below. See if you can come up with a good solution. Happy thinking!

STEP 1: Describe the problem. What are the parts of the problem? What is, or is not, happening? How do you feel about the problem? List all of the details.

_____

_____

_____

_____

_____

STEP 2: List possible ways of solving the problem. Write down as many as you can think of—even those that seem silly. Remember, one of the solutions may be to ask for help.

_____

_____

_____

_____

STEP 3: Choose the best solution and write it below. Then try it. If it works, congratulations! If it doesn't, try the next-best solution. Keep trying your solutions until you find one that works.

_____

_____

_____

_____

_____

Steps for Solving a Problem Responsibly

Ages: 11 and above

Objective: The students will understand and describe how decisions are influenced. The students will develop and practice a process for effective problem solving.

Materials: Steps for Solving a Problem Responsibly handout, chalkboard, and chalk

Procedure

1. Distribute the Steps for Solving a Problem Responsibly handout. Have the students read each step in the problem-solving process. Generate discussion after each step by asking open-ended questions. Introduce a personal example (a problem you need to solve) and take it through the process as part of the discussion. If time permits, go through the process a second time, using as an example a problem described by one of the students.

2. Ask the following questions for discussion:

   Stop all blaming.

   - *What happens when you get bogged down in the blaming game?*
   - *What are people who constantly blame others for their problems trying to avoid?*
   - *How is blaming others the same as giving away your power?*

   Define the problem.

   - *Why is it so important to know what the problem is?*
   - *Why does it matter whether it's your problem or someone else's?*
   - *When should people not be left to solve their own problems?*
   - *What can happen when people get all worked up about a problem that isn't even theirs?*

   Consider asking for help.

   - *When is it wise to ask for help?*
   - *Who gets to decide what kind of help you need?*
   - *If what you want is information or advice, and instead the person tries to solve the problem for you, what can you do?*

   Think of alternative solutions.

   - *What is the advantage of thinking of alternative solutions?*
   - *If you can't think of more than one or two alternatives, what should you definitely do before making a decision?*
   - *How does collecting information expand your alternatives?*

   Evaluate the alternative solutions.

   - *What are some of the ways of collecting information?*
   - *Why not just do the first thing that comes to mind?*
   - *Why is it important to imagine what will happen as a result of trying each alternative?*

 #12873

Make a decision.

- *If you still can't make a decision, which steps in the process could you return to? (2, 4, 5, and 3, in that order. The problem may be incorrectly defined; you may need to gather additional information; the consequences may need further consideration; or help may be called for.)*

Follow through.

- *Why stick to a decision?*
- *What can you do if the solution doesn't work or more problems come up?*
- *How can you evaluate your decision?*
- *What's an example of a big problem in our society that used to be a much smaller problem with a relatively easy solution?*

Evaluation

The students will be able to apply the process to a real-life problem.

Note. From *Leadership 2000: Preparing Students for Success and Leadership in the Workplace* (pp. 78–79, 215–216), by D. Schilling, D. Cowan, & S. Palomares, 1994, Austin, TX: PRO-ED, Inc. Copyright 1994 by PRO-ED, Inc. Adapted with permission.

Steps for Solving a Problem Responsibly

What is a problem?

A problem can be a complicated issue or a question that you have to answer. Or it can be something in your life that is causing you frustration, worry, anger, or some other kind of distress. In order to answer the question or get rid of the distress, you must "solve" the problem. Problems often have several parts. Solving the whole problem involves making a series of decisions: at least one decision for each part of the problem.

Next time you are faced with a problem, follow these steps to a solution.

1. **Stop all blaming.**
   It will help me to understand that blaming someone (including myself) for the problem will not solve it. If I really want to solve the problem, I need to put my energy into working out a solution. Blaming myself and others is a waste of time.

2. **Define the problem.**
   Next, I need to ask myself two questions to get started. "What exactly is the problem?" and "Whose problem is it?" If I find out that it's not my problem, the best thing I can do is to let the people who "own" the problem solve it themselves. Or I can ask them, "How can I help you?"

3. **Consider asking for help.**
   Once I'm sure I "own" the problem and know what it is, I may choose to ask someone for help. For example, I may decide to talk over the problem with someone.

4. **Think of alternative solutions.**
   I need to ask myself, "What are some of the things I could do about this?" I need to think of as many reasonable ideas for solving the problem as I can. To do this, I will probably need to collect some information.

5. **Evaluate the alternative solutions.**
   Next, for each idea I come up with, I need to ask myself, "What will happen to me and the other people involved if I try this one?" I need to be very honest with myself. If I don't know how someone else will be affected, I need to ask that person, "How would you feel if I . . .".

6. **Make a decision.**
   I need to choose the alternative that appears to have the best chance of succeeding. If my solution is a responsible one, it will not hurt anyone unnecessarily—and it will probably work.

7. **Follow through.**
   After I've made the decision, I'll stick to it for a reasonable length of time. If the decision doesn't work, I'll try another alternative. If the decision works but causes more problems in the process, I'll start over again to solve them. And I'll try not to blame myself or anybody else for those problems.

B: IX. Relationship Skills

When No One Wants to Play

Ages: 5–7 and adult caregivers
Objective: The students will learn skills for asking to play and waiting to play with others. Caregivers will learn several techniques to alleviate problems that occur when no one wants to play with a child.
Materials: Getting Others to Play poster

Procedure

1. Have the students think about the times when playing with others has gone really well for them. Ask: *How did that happen? What did you do to start playing and get along? How do you like to be asked to play with someone else? How can you remember to do that each time you want to play with others?*

2. Teach the students how to ask and wait to play. Sometimes children forget to ask to play, and instead engage in self-defeating, irritating behaviors to try to engage others. Show students the poster and discuss the following steps:

   - "Choose people who like to play with me." Ask: *How do we know when someone likes to play with us? What tells us? What do we notice about people when they like to play with us?*

   - "Ask the person to play." Say: *What are some ways we can ask others to play with us?*

   - "If they are not ready, ask when they can play." Say: *Show us how we can do that.*

   - "Find another activity to do while I am waiting for others to play with me." Say: *Tell us two things you can do by yourself when you are waiting for others to be ready to play.*

   - "Choose activities that we both like." Ask: *How can you figure out what others like to do? What do you do if the other person wants to do an activity you don't like or don't know you like?*

For Caregivers

Make available engaging activities for children to do while waiting to play with others. Examples might include the following:

1. A "to do" box that has several activities from which to choose

2. Access to favorite games or activities, such as books, puzzles, or handheld video games

3. Encouraging them to help with a job, such as preparing materials, setting the table, etc.

 #12873

Evaluation

The students demonstrate asking others to play, waiting to play, and choosing activities for play. They then make a plan to use those skills in the next week.

Note. From *No More Meltdowns* (pp. 128–129) by J. Baker, 2008, Arlington, TX: Future Horizons. Copyright 2008 by Future Horizons. Adapted with permission.

Getting Others to Play

1. Choose people who like to play with me.

2. Ask the person to play.

3. If they are not ready, ask when they can play.

4. Find another activity to do while I am waiting for others to play with me.

5. Choose activities that we both like.

Dealing With Teasing

Ages: 5–7

Objective: The students will learn skills to deal with teasing without becoming upset.

Background Information: The most important thing a school can do to ease the burden of teasing is to prevent it and help develop peer support to establish a safe and friendly environment.

1. Establish and enforce clear rules about abusive teasing. In school or at home, this means confronting accused bullies and letting them know there will be consequences for continued aggression.

2. Protect the confidentiality of those students who report teasing. In schools, it is important that staff not reveal the names of students who report bullying behavior so that students feel it is safe to tell adults.

3. Provide empathy and conflict management training to students, especially to bullies, who may not have these skills.

4. Create a peer buddy program for students who are isolated. This involves sensitizing peers to the needs of isolated children and training them to engage with and protect these students.

5. Provide ongoing counseling to students who have been chronically teased to check whether the teasing continues and to teach ways to handle peer problems.

Materials: Dealing With Teasing poster

Procedure

1. The main thrust here is to help students maintain self-esteem and not let the teasing control how they feel. The steps for dealing with teasing are outlined below. The first two steps emphasize that what the teaser says is not necessarily true: This takes some of the power out of the words. Have the students think about the times when they have successfully handled teasing. Ask: *How did that happen? What did you do to make that happen? How can you remember to do that each time you face teasing?*

2. Show the students the poster and discuss the following steps:
   - "Ask if the person was serious or just kidding." Say: *Let's practice some different ways to ask this question.*
   - "Consider that the person who teases has the problem, not you." Ask: *What thoughts do you have as you consider this?*
   - "Calmly tell the other person to stop." Ask: *What calming techniques work best for you? How do you use them in this moment? How do you say this?*
   - "If the person continues, walk away."
   - "If the person still teases or threatens harm, tell an adult." Ask: *Who will you tell? How will you tell them?*

Evaluation

The students demonstrate dealing with teasing by showing the language they will use and the actions they will take. Students will make a plan to use those skills in the next week.

Note. From *No More Meltdowns* (p. 123), by J. Baker, 2008, Arlington, TX: Future Horizons. Copyright 2008 by Future Horizons. Adapted with permission.

 #12873

Dealing With Teasing

1. Ask if the person was serious or just kidding.

2. Consider that the person who teases has the problem, not you.

3. Calmly tell the other person to stop.

4. If the person continues, walk away.

5. If the person still teases or threatens harm, tell an adult.

Managing Conflict With
I Am Statements

Ages: All

Objective: The students will learn to use *I am* statements to manage conflicts.

Materials: *I Am* Statement poster

Background Information: This skill is best suited for situations in which a close friend or family member said or did something that upset the student. Presumably, close friends and family members care about the student's feelings, so the student should feel safe telling them how he or she feels. This is not the skill to use with a bully or a stranger. When it comes to strangers or bullies, it is best to use the skill "dealing with teasing" in activity RS-1.

Procedure

1. Show the poster to the students and discuss each item.

2. Have students construct practice *I am* statements. Invite several students to read their statements to the group. Get the students to think of typical situations and together develop *I am* statements for each one.

Evaluation

The students demonstrate using *I am* statements for managing conflict by showing the language they will use and the actions they will take. Students will make a plan to use those skills in the next week.

Note. From *No More Meltdowns* (p. 124), by J. Baker, 2008, Arlington, TX: Future Horizons. Copyright 2008 by Future Horizons. Adapted with permission.

I Am Statement

1. Schedule a time to talk.

2. Tell the other person what you want without insulting him or her. Use an "*I Am* Statement."

   I FEEL _____
   (feeling word)

   WHEN YOU _____
   (what they said or did)

   BECAUSE _____
   (the reason it upsets you)

   WHAT I WANT OR NEED IS _____ .

3. Listen to the other person's side so you can offer solutions that work for both of you.

The Pretend Jump Rope

Ages: 5–11

Objective: The students will notice sensations in their bodies as they become more self-regulated. They will also learn to assist others in learning self-regulation.

Materials: None

Background Information: This game gives students an opportunity to run toward (rather than away from) something that creates activation and to experience a successful escape. No jump rope is needed. The reason for not using an actual rope is that the lack of a real one engages the imagination and reduces the likelihood of falling. The imaginary jump rope symbolizes a manageable threat coming toward them. This elicits spontaneous movements and gives the students the satisfaction of a successful escape.

Procedure

1. This game is done in pantomime. Two students or adults hold a pretend jump rope while the others line up for a turn, just like in regular jump rope. First, the rope is swung back and forth at a low level near the ground. You can increase the imaginary height if the student seems to desire more of a challenge. One by one the students jump over the "rope" to safety.

2. Check in with the students, asking for a show of hands to identify the various sensations they may be feeling.

3. After playing this game for a while, have the group participants stand up and feel their legs and their connection to the ground so that they can discharge activated energy through their bodies.

4. Model for the group how to support another who needs extra help to feel self-regulated. A child complaining of fatigue might lie down or rest his or her head on the shoulder of another student or adult. A child who is hyperactive and/or who might need help to settle down can be seated by an adult or a more regulated student. These mentors can help the child to feel the ground and to inhale and exhale more slowly.

Evaluation

The students will experience shifts in their self-regulation, identify changes in their bodily sensations, and note ways to assist others in becoming more self-regulated.

Note. From *Trauma-Proofing Your Kids* (p. 210), by P. A. Levine and M. Kline, 2008, Berkeley, CA: North Atlantic Books. Copyright 2008 by Peter A. Levine and Maggie Kline. Adapted with permission.

#12873

Coyote Chases Rabbit

Ages: 5–11
Objective: The students will notice sensations in their bodies as they become more self-regulated and will learn to assist others in learning self-regulation.
Materials: Two balls of different colors and sizes
Background Information: This game is designed to simulate the flight response.

Procedure

1. To start, adults and students form a standing circle and then sit on the floor in that arrangement. The leader holds up one ball and says, *This is the rabbit.* Then the rabbit gets passed around the circle very slowly from hand to hand. The adults encourage the students to gradually increase the pace. Soon, participants begin to feel their sensations of anticipation grow as the rabbit "runs" from student to student.

2. An adult then introduces a second ball and says, *This is the coyote,* and starts the second ball chasing the "rabbit." The pace increases naturally as the students identify with the strength of the coyote and the speed of the rabbit, and as the excitement of the chase escalates. The complexity of the game can be increased for older students by calling out a change in direction. The idea is not to win or lose but to feel the excitement of the chase and the power of the team effort to pass the balls quickly so as not to get "caught."

3. Next, the students rest. As they settle, check in with the students. Ask for a show of hands to identify the various sensations they may be feeling. After playing this game for a while, have the group participants stand up and feel their legs and their connection to the ground so that they can discharge activated energy through their bodies.

4. Model for the group how to support another who needs extra help to feel self-regulated. A child complaining of fatigue might lie down or rest his or her head on the shoulder of another student or adult. A child who is hyperactive and/or who might need help to settle down can be seated by an adult or a more regulated student. These mentors can help the child to feel the ground and to inhale and exhale more slowly.

Evaluation

The students will experience shifts in their self-regulation, identifying changes in their bodily sensations, and noting ways to assist others in becoming more self-regulated.

Note. From *Trauma-Proofing Your Kids* (p. 209) by P. A. Levine and M. Kline, 2008, Berkeley, CA: North Atlantic Books. Copyright 2008 by Peter A. Levine and Maggie Kline. Adapted with permission.

Personal Boundaries

Ages: 5–11

Objective: The students will learn what personal boundaries are and how respecting them can be helpful in getting along with others.

Materials: A hula hoop for each person

Procedure

1. Give the students hula hoops and let them exercise with the hoops for a few minutes while playing music.

2. Stop the music after a few minutes and take one hula hoop. Demonstrate how the hula hoop creates a circle around your body. Take the hula hoops away and ask students if they can still imagine the circle around you.

3. Ask the students to give you a definition of the word *boundary* (a line showing an area or a territory). Use features of the room or areas on a map to illustrate the concept.

4. Explain that we all have personal boundaries or a space around us we are most comfortable keeping between us and others. Say something like: *We all have a right to our personal boundaries. This means it is not OK for someone to grab you, hit you, or otherwise invade your personal boundary space. We call not doing these things "respecting others' space or boundaries." People can come within your personal boundary space if you choose to let them, but we also have a responsibility to respect the personal boundary space of others. This means using self-control to avoid hurting someone else by inappropriately intruding on their personal boundary space. This could be by touching, hitting, taking something from someone else, etc.*

5. Explain that boundaries are also fluid and can change. Say something like: *When the hula hoop is circling around us, it is sometimes close to us and sometimes farther away. In this same way, we have the right to choose when to let someone come close to us or when we prefer that they stay farther away. Acceptable boundaries can also vary among cultures. It is important to let people know when they are violating our personal boundaries.*

6. Have the students suggest a list of ways to show respect for personal boundaries. Here are some possible examples:

   - *Keep hands and feet to ourselves.*
   - *Stay a comfortable distance from people when talking with them.*
   - *Respect the property of others.*

7. In partners, ask the students to role-play some typical situations where peoples' boundaries may be affected. Have them show a variety of verbal and nonverbal ways to respect others' boundaries and have others respect theirs. Ask the members to talk about which methods worked the best for them.

Evaluation

The students will demonstrate awareness of their personal boundaries in a variety of situations. They will identify ways to assist others in knowing their boundaries and demonstrate ways to show respect for others' boundaries.

Note. From *Brain Friendly Guidance Activities to Build Emotional Intelligence* (pp. 81–82), by C. Messina, 2003, Austin, TX: PRO-ED. Copyright 2003 by PRO-ED, Inc. Adapted with permission.

Glossary

Acknowledge means to notice and allow whatever is there to be there. We accept what is happening for the student at this time.

Action talk means a behavioral description of the complaint or presenting problem.

Affect regulation refers to the control of one's emotions.

Amygdala is a structure in the midbrain that initiates emergency response. With unresolved stress, it can take charge and respond as if there is a threat even when there is none.

Anchor is a positive image or experience that can be called upon by an individual to assist with calming. Breath can be used effectively as an anchor.

Arousal is physiological activation that is experienced as sensations in the body.

Arousal energy is an increase in physiological and mental activity. It is an automatic response to a threat to survival.

Attachment figures are individuals in the environment on whom the child can depend for safety and emotional connection.

Attachment stance refers to an approach to working with kids that offers them a relationally corrective experience: one that provides reliable, responsive interaction and promotes secure attachment.

Basic trust is a stage of psychological development in which a child internalizes the sense that he or she can depend on caregivers for reliability, support, and protection.

Body scan is a simple technique we can use to check in with our physical states—going from head to toe and noticing places of relaxation and/or tension.

Calming breaks are moments to re-regulate. Students and adults can learn quick techniques to use before they become severely dysregulated.

Compassion fatigue is characterized by feelings of incompetence and difficulty maintaining the level of emotional detachment needed to manage feelings toward children whose behavior is repeatedly out of control. Professionals also can experience symptoms commonly seen in traumatized children: hyperarousal, nightmares, anxiety, and depression.

Complex trauma is a response to the experience of both chronic and developmentally adverse events, most often within a child's caregiving system, including disrupted attachment.

Constriction is a physiological and psychological response to extreme stress. Breathing, blood flow, muscle tone, and posture constrict. Our attention also constricts in a form of hypervigilance with our full attention focused on the perceived threat.

Containment describes an environment that offers relational attunement: a calming presence that reflects competency.

Corrective relational experience refers to the potentially transformative experience of a positive relationship when past relational experiences were less than optimal.

Difference question refers to a solution-focused question that goes like this: "What difference will it make for you when that (the preferred state) is happening?"

Disrupted attachment refers to the impact on children of home environments in which primary caregivers have not been able to provide consistent enough care, thus depriving children of a secure bond with their caregivers and hampering the development of self-regulation.

Dissociation is a psychological response to extreme physical and emotional stress in which there is a disconnect between an individual's present awareness and his or her present physical and emotional experience. It is effective when it is brief and there is a reconnect once the stressor has passed.

Dose refers to the amount of time, detail, frequency, and/or intensity offered to a student or group of students in SSR sessions.

Down-regulate refers to the brain function that is facilitated by the hippocampus in which there is re-absorption of stress hormones. This makes it possible for the body to calm down and move out of hyperarousal once a threat has passed.

Dysregulation of emotion and behavior is the experience of feeling out of control and without the ability to calm oneself.

Emotion refers to the awareness of a feeling state of the body.

Emotional regulation refers to the ability to self-regulate emotional responses.

Emotional states are relatively stable, repeated patterns of specific activity, cognition, affect, and relatedness.

Exception is a term used in solution-focused work to identify times when a problem was perceived to be of little consequence or not present.

Executive function refers to adaptive decision making, including planning for the future, anticipating consequences, and inhibiting inappropriate responses.

Explicit memory system (working memory) provides the information we use in the here and now, informing the choices we make about what action to take.

External resource is a relationship, an object, or service outside of oneself that can be used for personal benefit, including self-regulation.

Fear and stress circuitry is a network of neural connections activated by the perception of threat. In kids with complex trauma, this circuitry is too easily activated.

Freeze is the brain–body automatic response that occurs when we are threatened and neither fight nor flight is possible. There is constriction, and the emergency energy that would have been discharged gets bound up and amplified in the mind–body.

Gauge refers to using your somatic awareness to get information about your level of physical and emotional arousal.

Ground (grounding) is the technique and practice of purposely connecting to the ground beneath us and to our somatic experience in the moment. It is the active practice of creating a physical and emotional inner experience of calm connection to our own body and our surroundings. Grounding facilitates interactive affect regulation.

High road survival circuit is a brain circuit that is immediately available when there is a threat to survival-in-the-moment, but unlike the low road survival circuit, it is organized for finding adaptive responses and for regulating emotion.

Hippocampus is a brain structure that categorizes experience, connecting available information and memory to contextualize threat in terms of the present time and place. It has the function as part of the high road to down-regulate the amygdala.

Hyperarousal is a physiological and mental response to a perceived threat. Physical symptoms include an increase in heart rate, difficulty breathing, cold sweats, and tingling muscle tension. Mental symptoms include an increase in thoughts, mind racing, and worrying.

Hypoarousal is a physiological and psychological response to stress in which there is a physical appearance of slowed response, lack of muscle tension, and slowed cognitive and emotional responses.

Implicit memory system is part of the brain's survival plan. It stores what is perceived as life-threatening in such a way that it is immediately available anytime the perception of that threat appears.

Interactive affect regulation is the emotional regulatory activity of one persons' nervous system affecting the emotional regulatory activity of another.

Interactive regulation is the ability to self-regulate using help from another person.

Interactive repair is the process of acknowledging a disruption in our relationship with a student with the goal of reconnecting and strengthening the relationship.

Internal resource is a natural ability or developed skill within ourselves that can be used for personal benefit, including self-regulation.

Low road survival circuit is a rapid response brain circuit that has the total focus of survival-in-the-moment once it is activated.

Mind–body connection refers to the ongoing interaction between our neurobiology and the rest of our physical body. Our physical experience affects our mind and our mind affects our body.

Mindful awareness is the experience of "neutral mind," the compassionate nonjudgmental observation of what is arising in the moment in our environment and within ourselves. With mindful awareness we press the "pause button" on our automatic and habitual responses, enabling ourselves to move toward more creative and discerning choices.

Mindsight is the ability to perceive our own subjective experience and that of others.

Miracle question refers to a solution-focused technique used to ascertain the best possible outcome hoped for by the client.

Mirror neurons are brain cells that precisely reflect and anticipate the exact neural activation pattern of another brain.

Neural integration refers to the process through which one part of the brain communicates with another.

Panoramic attention refers an experience of widened attention.

Possibility language is language that opens up the possibility for change rather than contradicting or challenging a kid's perception.

Putting on the brakes describes identifying the first small sensations of dysregulation and using mindful awareness and grounding to calm emotions before they escalate.

Reflective dialogue is interaction and conversation about thoughts, feelings, sensations, perceptions, memories, attitudes, beliefs, and intentions. It is the foundation of mindsight.

Relational attunement describes the interaction between a caregiver and a child in which the caregiver is carefully observant and responsive both physically and emotionally.

Re-regulate is the mind–body process of returning the body and emotions to a baseline state of calm.

Responsive communication is both verbal and nonverbal communication that encourages the experience of feeling seen and "felt" by another.

Scaling technique is a method for determining a client's perception of his or her progress towards his or her goal. On a scale of 1 to 10, a client indicated where he or she is in relation to achieving stated goal.

Self-regulation is the ability to manage our internal level of emotion, making it possible to make more adaptive choices about our behavior.

Self-soothe refers to both the use of the internal resources of our own physical movement and/ or body positions and the use of external resources, such as soft fabrics, gentle touching of the skin, pleasant scents, and warm baths to calm and re-regulate ourselves.

Sensations are physiological happenings inside us that are not associated with thoughts.

Sensation vocabulary refers to the words that an individual has available to describe physiological happenings.

Sense of self is the sum of the internal pictures we carry of ourselves and important others and the feelings we have about those pictures and how they guide our capacity to act in our environment.

Sensorimotor activity refers to body sensation, physiological arousal, and motor functioning.

Sensory stabilization is a state of the mind–body characterized by deep relaxation, mindful awareness, panoramic attention, and a sense of being calm and connected to our bodies.

Signals of care are communications that are primarily nonverbal and express warmth, empathy, and positive regard.

Social engagement system is the brain's innate system that enables us, beginning at birth, to express our needs and to respond to others with increasing clarity.

Somatic awareness is a term that refers to the experience of consciously noticing the body's responses in the moment.

Somatic empathy refers to experiencing in our own body what a student is feeling in his or her body.

Somatic memory is memory of how an experience felt in our body.

Tai Chi a system of slow, meditative physical exercise designed for relaxation, balance, and the health of the body and mind.

Tracking sensation refers to a range of interventions using somatic experience intended to increase our awareness of a physical feelings and use them to assist with self-regulation.

Traumatic transference occurs when the student, expecting that the counselor will be yet another abuser, is vigilant to that likelihood.

Unresolved stress is normal arousal energy that is not released following an experience of threat. It remains trapped in the body and expresses in symptoms associated with trauma.

Up-regulate is a term that refers to the brain's release of stress hormones (arousal energy) for the emergency response of fight or flight. The body is physiologically ready for action.

Window of tolerance is the range of emotional and physiological activation that can be tolerated by an individual without becoming dysregulated by too much or too little.

About the Authors

Patricia K. Tollison, PhD is a mother and a grandmother. She has taught at the preschool, middle school, high school, and university levels and has served as support staff, providing assessment and consultation for teachers and parents. She is currently a psychologist in private practice in Austin, Texas. She trains and consults at the local and national levels and wrote, with Katherine Synatschk, *SOS! A Practical Guide for Leading Solution-Focused Groups With Kids K–12.*

Katherine O. Synatschk, PhD, LPC-S has been the director of counseling for a large urban school district, a school counselor, a school social worker, and a special education teacher. She trains and consults on school counseling issues at the local, state, national, and international levels. Currently, she is a licensed professional counselor, provides supervision to LPC interns, is an assistant professor (adjunct) at Texas State University, and the Executive Editor at PRO-ED, Inc.

Gaea Logan, MA, LPC-S is a licensed professional counselor and clinical supervisor in private practice. For over 30 years, she has been active in the dialogue between Buddhist psychology, contemplative practice, and analytic group psychotherapy. Gaea has presented nationally and internationally on the topic of healing trauma. She has served as a Fellow for Psychology Beyond Borders. She is also an avid swimmer, photographer, and chef.